For Betsy —
From our hands to your
hands — with best wishes
from the other women in the
world who see their art
                    Paola Gianturco

IN HER HANDS

PAOLA GIANTURCO AND TOBY TUTTLE

IN HER

Foreword by Alice Walker

THE MONACELLI PRESS

craftswomen changing the world

HANDS

CONTENTS

First published in the United States of America by
The Monacelli Press, Inc.
10 East 92 Street, New York, New York 10128.

Library of Congress Cataloging-in-Publication Data
Gianturco, Paola.
In her hands : craftswomen changing the world /
Paola Gianturco and Toby Tuttle ;
foreword by Alice Walker.
p. cm.
Includes bibliographical references and index.
ISBN 1-58093-068-9
1. Handicraft—Developing countries. 2. Women
artisans—Developing countries—Interviews.
I. Tuttle, Toby. II. Title.
TT127.G53 2000
745'.082'091724—dc21   00-033960

Project Consultant: Joseph Publishing Services
Design: Joseph Guglietti Design, Santa Fe

Printed by Sfera International srl - Milan, Italy

Page 1: In northern Thailand, Lisu women's multistrand sashes drop from waist to hem.

Pages 2–3: In Chuinimachicaj, Guatemala, mothers sometimes rub babies' faces with sprigs of rue, an herbal plant, to protect them from evil.

Page 5: In Waterval, South Africa, Johannah Anna Mahlangu, dressed for a Ndebele celebration, creates a beaded doll that will wear clothing like hers.

Page 6: During Galungan, a Balinese festival that welcomes ancestral spirits back to earth, women carry holiday offerings from their home temples to community temples.

Opposite: Women who live in Guatemala's San Francisco Atitlan weave intricately patterned *huipiles* (blouses) whose yokes are embroidered with flowers.

Your purchase of this book
will support these nonprofit
organizations whose work helps
poor women all over the world
enhance their families' futures:

*Association for Women
in Development*

Global Fund for Women

Freedom from Hunger

The Crafts Center

Women's Edge

Aid to Artisans

The authors welcome your
comments and invite you to
visit their website,
www.herhands.com.

Preface

"My girl child must have a voice

louder and clearer than mine.

She must be able to move

with certainty—shoes on her feet,

walking with dreams at her side.

The present I have given her

is not enough.

Her arms are different;

they will reach for the sky

where freedom lives."

—NEPALESE MOTHER'S POEM

EAGERLY, I READ THE NEWS about the 1995 United Nations Fourth World Conference on Women, in Beijing, where this poem was presented. The thirty thousand women who attended from one hundred eighty-five countries and many walks of life—as well as some important news—inspired this book.

The news: throughout developing and transitional societies, poor women use the money they earn to buy food and education for their children. Most men spend on other things. But indigent women invest in their daughters and sons—motivated, like the Nepalese mother, by knowledge that the present is not good enough. They are determined to make it possible for their children to move with certainty, with shoes on their feet and with dreams at their sides, toward better lives.

Books, uniforms, shoes, notebooks and pencils, and bus fare to and from school are almost out of reach for indigent women, even if tuition is free. Many are illiterate and their access to resources is limited; yet their energy, ingenuity, and commitment make it possible for them to earn the necessary funds, often by juggling four or five income-generating projects at a time.

Education enhances social and economic conditions. If these women succeed in creating better-educated new generations, they will improve the future for their families, communities, countries, and ultimately, our world.

I wanted to meet these micro-entrepreneurial heroines. What were their dreams and disappointments, their triumphs and pleasures, their accomplishments and predicaments? How did earning money affect their lives and relationships? Did they have anything in common with the women in American corporations whom I worked with and taught?

I felt that these invisible women with their world-altering dreams deserved the spotlight. The idea for a photographic book began to grow.

My passion for folk art led me to focus on indigenous craftswomen. Like the women in the United Nations research study that was released in Beijing, many craftswomen live on less than a dollar a day in the global south and Eastern Europe. Because certain crafts are the province of women, it seemed appropriate to concentrate on crafts that mothers teach daughters, generation after generation.

I took a sabbatical from my consulting business to work on the book, but before I cashed in my frequent-flyer miles to begin traveling, I worried about whether one person could complete such an ambitious project and whether it was appropriate for a woman to travel alone in certain countries. I invited my friend and former colleague Toby Tuttle to share in the project and she agreed without hesitation.

Toby and I had photographed together in Europe and discovered that we had complementary visual perspectives. Her infectious humor and ability to pantomime converted reserved strangers into people who wanted to be photographed.

The librarians at the Museum of International Folk Art, in Santa Fe, New Mexico, helped me to identify villages where "women's crafts" are made; the Crafts Center in Washington, D.C., helped me to locate the places where they are made for sale. We selected villages that represent a range of traditional and contemporary crafts and cultures. I read the materials listed at the back of this book to help me frame our conversations with the craftswomen and inform the observations we would make.

People all over the world propelled our project. Friends offered ideas and introductions. Experts from universities, museums, retailers, collectors, and non-governmental organizations helped connect us with the craftswomen.

Toby handled trip logistics. Some of the places we visited were not even on our maps. Determined not to burden the craftswomen, we planned to carry our lunches and, in South Africa, to commute one hundred fifty miles to the nearest lodging. We carried two hundred rolls of film, not the ten that some countries allowed, causing intricate negotiations at entry and at potentially dangerous airport X-ray machines. We packed clothes and equipment in bags light enough to tote ourselves, tight enough to protect our cameras from the desert dust in India, and small enough to fit in a dugout in Panama. Toby's grandsons tested the games we bought to entertain children while we interviewed and photographed their mothers. We prepared emergency telephone lists of English-speaking physicians (whom we never needed) and authorized dealers who could repair our cameras. Toby prepared budgets in twelve different currencies.

Finally, we kissed our husbands and children—who, fortunately, shared our excitement about the project—and departed. We made six trips between August 1996 and August 1998. We interviewed ninety craftswomen in twenty-eight villages in twelve countries on four continents.

The book evolved as we traveled. For example, we discovered immediately that our plan to feature one craftswoman per chapter was unrealistic; indigenous craftswomen work in groups and were nonplussed at our plan to interview only one of them.

We spent about a week at each location, often talking with a craftswoman over several days. Most of our interpreters worked for local organizations that aid the craftswomen's income-generation efforts; they introduced us as friends. We asked all the artisans the same questions, plus some inspired by their particular cultures. Fifteen of our twenty interpreters were women, so even craftswomen in conservative cultures felt comfortable enough to volunteer personal information. We taped and transcribed the interviews, and sent each draft chapter to the local interpreter to check for accuracy.

I wrote the text, which describes our encounters with the women. Toby wrote the journal entries, which describe our other experiences, reactions, and feelings. We both took pictures with Canon EOS Elan IIE cameras and with Fujichrome Velvia and Provia film.

In Her Hands tells the craftswomen's stories as they told them to us. We have included what seemed most provocative and interesting. Scholars might have bitten off a smaller bite, learned the local languages, placed the findings in a theoretical context, and reported systematically—but ours was a subjective approach born of wondering.

The women in this book became our friends and teachers. From them, we learned about creating an artistic, social, and economic legacy. And we learned that the world is smaller—and women's spirits are larger—than we had ever imagined.

—Paola Gianturco

Foreword

WHEN I WAS A CHILD I sometimes washed my mother's feet. It was one of my favorite things to do. I don't know how this ritual came about. Perhaps I witnessed the monthly foot washing that occurred in my grandmother's Baptist church: an impressionable child, I would have been enthralled, profoundly moved, perhaps even shocked by the intense devotion such an act demonstrated. It would have seemed behavior out of time: there in the dim church made of warm, resin-scented wood; the hushed voices of the aging participants almost making one sleepy; the solemn singing of centuries-old Spirituals and the incessant fanning of the women in the congregation contributing a feeling of timeless, effortless community. These were some of the most oppressed people on the face of the earth, the literal sport of the white people who exploited their labor and stunted their lives. And yet, in this simple, sacred space, hidden far away from their tormentors (whose ancestors had bought and sold their grandparents), they reconnected to Spirit, unashamed, and humbly washed each other's feet. Each touch was filled with tenderness. Each glance an acknowledgment that "you are precious in my sight." I now realize it was this communion with each other, heart to heart and soul to soul, that kept my ancestors spiritually "safe" in the wilderness of the American "civilization" that prevailed for centuries in the Deep South.

Or maybe I washed my mother's feet, at first, because I saw how awkward it was for her to do it herself. She was a large woman; the tin basin she used, that we all used, was small. Sitting in a stiff, wooden, handmade chair she had to bend over, off balance and straining, to reach her feet. I would see her coming home from field or barn or other woman's kitchen, having been on her feet all day, while I had enjoyed the luxury, based on her labor, of going to school, and I would heat the water—or more than likely she would have heated it herself, for she was quick, and independent, and never asked for care—pour it into the basin, and after watching her enjoy a blissful ten minutes or so of soaking, I would wash her feet. Pat them dry with a towel, trim them of callus and corn, and oil them with Vaseline. I was always reluctant to let go of her feet, for the moment I did so, she seemed to bounce back into action; washing, ironing, scrubbing, quilting, cooking, gardening, taking care of her remarkably tidy and well-run household.

THE WOMEN IN THIS BOOK remind me of my mother, and they remind me of myself. Not one of them would think of herself as poor, for instance, just as my mother never would have, though she, like they, earned less than a dollar a day, when in fact money was even offered her for her work. And I would never consider myself poor either, because I had a mother who, like these mothers working for a better future for their children, gave her life for me.

That I can see this now, clearly, as I sensed it as a child, is a blessing beyond compare.

"Having tried three times to bring the Ndebele people under their control, in 1882 Afrikaners [descendants of Dutch and German settlers] dynamited their food storage caves to starve them, killed their leaders, razed their crops, confiscated their land, and assigned them to five years of indentured labor— five years that, in fact, lasted over a century. Ndebele women reacted against the Afrikaners' efforts to decimate ethnic identity by resurrecting the distinctive beaded apparel that their foremothers began creating in the sixteenth century, when the Portuguese brought Czechoslovakian and Venetian beads to southern Africa to trade for slaves and ivory."

MANY YEARS AGO Margaret Courtney-Clarke's book *Ndebele* introduced me to the stunning creativity of the Ndebele women of southern Africa. In this book I saw the colorfully painted homes of Ndebele women for the first time; and learned that the instinct to create art was so strong the women painted their houses using whatever materials were available to them, and as brush, sometimes they used their own fingers. From the moment I read this something shifted in my soul. I knew these women to be ancestors and mothers and sisters, girlfriends and aunts; I knew they had been with me forever, because I recognized a dauntlessness of spirit that I also prize, and that from now on we would never really be apart. Seeing how smitten I was with these women, how happy in my reconnection, a friend gave me a poster of a Ndebele woman standing in front of her vividly painted house in the far outback of white-dominated South Africa. Every move I've made since (and I've moved house several times) I've carried her with me. She stands at the entrance of my house, which is always, some part of it, painted, in her honor, the color of the South African sky (a sky New *countries all over the world, women's income buys food and education for children."*

World Africans lost forever because of the lure of glass beads) or, as I call it, Ndebele blue. It is these same women who today make beaded dolls and other artifacts for a tourist and export market. Their ability to work together collectively is shared by all of the women artisans in this collection, from Turkey, Panama, India, and Zimbabwe to Czechoslovakia, Indonesia, Guatemala, and Peru.

THESE WOMEN, and their less fortunate sisters, are calling to us; and we must answer. They are, the ones from the Southern hemisphere especially, with their earnings of less than a dollar a day, at the bottom of the feeding chain. Subsisting on tortillas and chilies. Porridge and millet beer. One meager meal a day. One bite of food per child per meal. Meal-less days. Every day 35,000 of their children die of starvation and malnutrition. It is a horror that has crept up on the world steadily over the last century. Too often our response has been to feel powerless, as if there is nothing we can do.

The age we are in now, however, *the Age of Knowing Who Does Not Eat, and Why*, does not permit us the luxury of inaction. Every child that starves to death should mean one less gold statue in the vaults of the church; but we cannot wait for that to happen either. What we can do is much more direct, compassionate, connected to our own Being. We can simply support Life, as these women reveal it to us.

Who are they, after all, if not us in our guise as Starving Creator?

"Husbands buy cigarettes and beer; women buy food for their families."

"It is not uncommon for children's nutrition to deteriorate while wristwatches, radios, and bicycles are acquired by the adult male household members."

WHEN YOU READ this informative book you will see how inescapable is the connection between today's misery in the so-called Third World and the overthrow of the people's way of life one, two, three, four, or five hundred years ago. I believe you will have powerful feelings in response to learning how meanly the loyalty and faithfulness of women have generally been repaid. For having endured the near absolute oppression of a greedy, brutal, racist colonialism, which often included literal enslavement

and removal from homelands, many of these women suffer just as cruelly under the domination of their own patriarchal societies. You will begin to fine tune your focus so that perhaps for the first time you will really see who these women are. The ones at the very bottom. The ones that are so low down in status, as much of the world defines it, that they seem to be part of the earth itself. It is my great privilege to say, to add my witness, that indeed they are part of it. For there they sit in their mud and straw huts, or on their bare earth patios, or on the naked ground, spinning and weaving and making pots out of the mud of the lake, and they are in relation to and in a flow of creation that is as old as the planet. I think of them as goddesses.

The children of these women do not have to starve. They have mothers, as you will see, who are giving Life everything they've got. And we must stand with them. Learning their histories, appreciating their artistry, acknowledging their worth. The world we live in, the rich, Western one, says these women owe us. That they are in our debt because we loaned their leaders (oppressors, as often as not) money to build dams or roads, or (most likely) to buy weapons. To force these women to sell their bodies, their children, and their health to pay a debt they did not themselves incur is the essence of evil. Meanwhile, the debts that they make for themselves, sometimes founding their own micro-banks because "regular" banks consider women too ignorant to transact business, are scrupulously repaid. They place themselves in debt, not to buy weapons, or even beer and cigarettes, but to buy food, clothing, health care, and education for their children. They owe us nothing. And we must refuse to take the blood money our governments squeeze out of them. It is we who owe these women. We owe them for continuing to create art that sustains our spirits as surely as good food strengthens our bodies. We owe them for holding such an incredible place of suffering in this world, and for not giving up. We owe them for reminding us of the true meaning of love and of sacrifice. Of creativity and practicality. We owe them the rich nourishment we take from their courage.

Blessed be.

ALICE WALKER
Berkeley, California

All quotes are from *In Her Hands: Craftswomen Changing the World.*

IN THESE LOCATIONS *we photographed and interviewed*

GUATEMALA

Sololá
Chimaltenango
GUATEMALA CITY

PANAMA

PANAMA CITY
Uagitupo

PERU

Pucallpa
LIMA

BOLIVIA

LA PAZ
Tarata

ZIMBABWE

HARARE

SOUTH AFRICA

Waterval
PRETORIA
Hluhluwe

ninety women living in twenty-eight villages in twelve countries.

POLAND

WARSAW ✪

Zalipie •

CZECH REPUBLIC

✪ PRAGUE

Vnorovy •

ANKARA ✪

• *Ayvacik*

Soğanli •

TURKEY

Chiang Mai •

Bang Sai • BANGKOK ✪

THAILAND

NEW DELHI ✪

• *Bhuj*

INDIA

INDONESIA

JAKARTA ✪

Surakarta
Java   *Ubud*
Bali

and the Knitters

WE ENTER THROUGH a dark store where bubbles slither to the surface of the corn beer brewing in black vats. In the main room of the house, turquoise walls bear watermarks of old storms and the roof is made of cane. We have been told that bugs drop from such ceilings at night, and that their venomous bites can damage a victim's heart thirty years later. But this is morning, we assure ourselves—the cane must be benign.

We load our cameras, unpack our tape recorders and notebooks, introduce ourselves, and wonder what a "loan generation meeting" will be like in Villa El Carmen, Bolivia. Quechua women, descendants of the Incas, gather, sitting on straight-back chairs or on the floor. They spin, knit, talk, soothe their children, and wait to begin. All are members of a Freedom from Hunger credit association, a group that has never had visitors.

At eleven o'clock sharp the musical wall clock bursts into a breathy electronic version of "Santa Lucia." Suddenly, the lilting song is engulfed by thunderous blasts. Smoke from the patio fills the entire space. The family's scrofulous watchdogs howl. We are paralyzed—but everyone else is energized. The fireworks are a signal for the women to jump up and spray each other—and us—with the contents of beer bottles as if this were a fraternity party. They throw a blizzard of white confetti. They shake hands, hug, kiss the air, and then shake hands again. Women and children share bowls of popcorn and tankards of beer, some of which they pour on the ground as an offering to Pachamama, Mother Earth.

We are witnessing a *challa*, one of the parties that begin and end the credit association's sixteen-week loan cycles. This is the way the women bless the money. Stacks of bills on the table are now buried in confetti. Loan papers are so wet that they must be spread to dry on a heap of corncobs in the patio. As the loans are distributed, the women pick up their money, look at it, count it, look again, count again.

MARINA ORTIZ IS TREASURER of this credit association, whose meetings are held at her house. We have come to the Cochabamba region to interview knitters, but when we return the next morning to talk with

Marina, we discover that she is not just a knitter but a one-woman diversified conglomerate. In addition to running a store and raising rabbits, pigeons, pigs, and cows for sale, she also spins acrylic. And knits.

With almost a high school education, Marina seems to be a born entrepreneur. "I joined the *banco* [credit association] because I wanted money to make business," she says pragmatically. "I started by buying ten pigs. Now I have twenty. I buy acrylic for three dollars a kilo and sell it for five dollars." Five hours a week of spinning nets Marina ten dollars. She earns eighty dollars for a 120-pound pig. Her dream is that in ten years she "will have two children, have visited my sister in Santa Cruz, and grown my pig business."

On a typical day, Marina tends her animals before lunch, after which she knits or spins. About five o'clock, she makes a salad and hearty soup for dinner. Throughout the day, she attends to customers who shop in her store for *chicha* (corn beer), bread, sugar, Tide, spices, and other packaged products that she stocks from the market in Cliza, the next town. Her store closes only when she goes to bed.

Her husband, Vicente, twenty-eight, is a house painter who helps Marina when there are no houses to paint. She earns more than her husband, which apparently does not cause problems. "He runs the house because he is the man," she explains.

Marina, now thirty-four, met Vicente at a party. "I liked him immediately and wanted to marry him," she says smiling. The two lived together for four years, then were married six months ago in a Catholic church.

Marina shows us her wedding album. She is wearing a white wedding dress styled with the voluminous knee-length *pollera* (skirt) that all Quechua women wear. Her wedding veil drops from a halo-like tiara to cover her faux braids and ringlets. Quechua women have worn braids since pre-Hispanic times. An unidentified problem now makes many women's hair too brittle to support the braids, and many, including Marina's, are partly synthetic fiber. She looks like an angel.

Marina explains that this is the traditional wedding headdress. "*Madrinas* and *padrinos* [godparents] pay for

Previous pages: Evangelina's daughter-in-law, Margarita Torrico de Vargas, drinks *chicha* (corn beer) from a gourd while she knits.

Opposite: In Villa El Carmen, Bolivia, Quechua women wait for a weekly micro-enterprise loan meeting to begin. Most will borrow to buy yarn so they can knit sweaters and hats to sell.

parts of weddings. For example, my fifteen-meter train was paid for by the 'train godmother.' My ring was from the 'ring godfather.' The reception went on for three days with lots of feasting and drinking. On the third day, guests threw rice and confetti for good luck and pinned *bolivianos* [Bolivian bills] on our clothes. The 'money godmother' always doubles what other people give the bride and groom."

Among the pictures of the reception, where everyone is covered with snowy confetti, we see a calf that is decked out in a garland of flowers and ribbons. "That little cow was a gift from one of the fourteen godfathers," Marina says.

The final pictures in the album show Marina and Vicente with their friends at an amusement park, sliding down the slide and cruising the pond in a pedal boat— still wearing their wedding clothes.

Marina's only disappointment about the wedding was that her mother had died six months earlier. "When I am alone, I think about my mother, a kind, good mama, and I am sad. She used to celebrate my birthday by cooking a nice meal of rabbit and pigeon and inviting the godmothers. On those days we laughed all day long."

FREEDOM FROM HUNGER has microcredit programs underway in many developing countries, and its goal is to serve over two million families around the world by the year 2005. The organization focuses on women who live on a dollar a day or less. These women are ineligible for regular bank loans since they have no collateral and no formal credit history; it is not an option to pay the one hundred to two hundred percent interest charged by independent moneylenders.

Freedom from Hunger loans can be used for any revenue-producing activity. The organization's eight thousand-member Bolivia microcredit program, Credit with Education, has been underway since 1990, and has been identified as a model for future USAID programs.

Cecilia Cossio, regional training coordinator, describes how history has set roles for the women. "Beautiful Inca women were for the king. The others were slaves who were classified by activity: childcare,

laundry, weaving. Over time, little has changed: contemporary women are typically slaves to their families; women's work is not valued and they have little self-esteem. Although Bolivian women have earned income and managed family budgets for some time, ninety percent of our new members never made money, had a job, or created anything to sell.

"For these reasons, we don't just go recruiting when we set up a credit association. We first approach community leaders (almost all are men) and explain the benefits of the program: better food, better life, better income for the whole family and the community. The men tell their wives, who organize themselves and join us. This avoids trouble. Later, these men often call us *amigas*. Men are formidable in our society. By increasing their awareness of women's worth and by helping women learn to relish their valuable role, we begin to help women increase self-esteem."

In some credit associations, for as long as two years, members are silent, afraid to speak to strangers. But Freedom from Hunger staff members return week after week. Consistent attention from educated people begins to catalyze women's feelings of self-worth, and attending weekly meetings makes women feel important.

The women's newly gained knowledge begins to pay off: nutritional education results in healthier children. Microbusiness training produces more realized income. Results build confidence. Self-respect grows. Women learn to trust what they think. The urge to express these thoughts overrides the cultural habit of keeping their heads down and mouths shut. And when they talk, they inspire new respect from their families.

WE DRIVE IN Freedom from Hunger's blue Toyota pickup through the countryside that is the breadbasket of Bolivia. Roads and houses are both made of mud, as if they were all of a piece. In town, cobblestones make the wheels clatter. Trees with bright red, pink, or yellow blossoms jolt against the azure sky.

The bridge to Tarata is temporarily impassable. Thursday is *feria* (market day), and an enterprising man has roped off the bridge so he can admit only those vehicles willing to pay admission. We pay.

Opposite, top: Women in Tarata gather to hear a candidate speak before the presidential election. They are skeptical about promises of easy solutions to their country's complex problems.

Opposite, bottom: Some members of Freedom from Hunger's microcredit associations juggle five income-generating activities. Multitasking, one spins as she walks to the meeting at Marina Ortiz's house.

I don't think they like us.

We wave to other pickup truck passengers on the road, smile and nod to people in the village, murmur "buenos dias" in the market—and get nothing back. Unless you count blank stares.

Is it resentment—or fear—or just shyness? We don't know what to make of it. Even when we go into banco *meetings, where we're properly introduced by mutual friends, we meet reticence. They're certainly a lively group when they celebrate by squirting each other with beer, but the* challa *is a brief gaiety plunked in the middle of a most reserved gathering. After the festivities, propriety reigns. Slowly we realize that what I feared was unfriendliness is simply a long-standing cultural trait: reserve.*

We sit down for some interview time with our hostess. Our questions elicit very short answers, or no answers, some vacant stares. Then we ask what we think is a simple getting-acquainted question: "How did you and your husband meet?" Our interpreter is shocked. "I would never ask her that. Much too private. Your questions are so personal! That's not done here."

We have tried so hard to be sensitive, but even so we're stepping on toes. Then we notice that Amanda, the Freedom from Hunger agent whom the women have known and trusted longest, has been sitting next to our hostess, gently stroking her arm to calm her in the face of our foreignness and our prying.

So this is shyness, and also defense of privacy. And it's something more than that. It also has to do with self-esteem, that quality in which the Freedom from Hunger people have seen a gradual but satisfying growth. As a result of that growth, even though our visit has temporarily frightened the women back into their shells, by the time we say good-bye to our quiet new friends in Tarata, we do have some conversation, some smiles, and even a few laughs.

T. TARATA, BOLIVIA

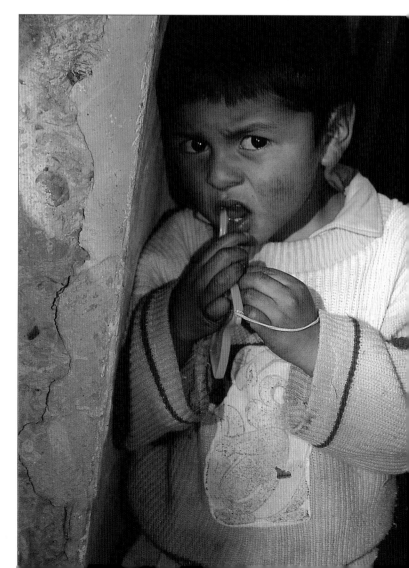

The centerpiece of the town square is a Victorian bandstand surrounded by flowers. Bougainvillea crawls up the tall trees. A sign advertises that the Grand Festival of Jokes is coming up. Ferns that require only air to survive tangle on the electric wires. In the square near the market is a statue of a nursing Indian mother. Women carry giant calla lilies and gypsophila to the San Severino church for Corpus Christi tomorrow.

Telephone poles are candy-striped with blue, red, pink, gold, and green—the colors of the political parties whose candidates are vying in the presidential election on Sunday. Most of the women we meet say they will abstain from voting, even though villagers' votes are avidly courted. They are tired of politicians' endless promises. There is an inauspicious array of politicians on the ballot: an ex-general (whom journalists identify as an "assassin" who led the country during its era of military dictatorships); a coca producer ("narco king," per the reporters); a Communist poet; a university president; the first Indian woman ever to run for President. (Women politicians are not new here. The first woman president of Bolivia served in 1980 and thirty percent of a party's candidates for the senate or congress must, by law, be women).

The new president will need to attack many problems. Bolivia is the second poorest country on the continent after Guyana. Infant mortality and female illiteracy are high. Even women die fairly young, on average at age sixty-four. A typical family has five children. There are not enough jobs, so many men seek work in Argentina and Chile, leaving their families alone for two and three years at a time. The litany of problems is long. All the candidates promise that everything will improve.

The Banco San Antonio de Tarata meets at Basilia Camacho's house, where scrawny chickens meander in and out of the doorway as the meeting gets underway. This is the eighth meeting in the current loan cycle. The group has borrowed and repaid five prior loans successfully, earning them each the right to borrow three hundred dollars instead of the lower start-up amount. Weekly, members repay twenty-six dollars, which includes the principal, three and a half percent interest each month, and the seven percent that members have voted to put into saving accounts. Loan funds came from American donors in the beginning, but interest fees ultimately will cover the cost of field agents (who provide banking and education services at the weekly meetings) and allow the credit association to become self-sustaining.

Maritza Usmayo, the Freedom from Hunger field agent, opens the meeting by calling roll ("Marcellina . . . Elena . . . Constantina . . . Sophia . . . Catalina . . . Alicia . . . Angelina . . ."). The members have decided that full attendance is crucial; colleagues who are late or absent are fined.

Freedom from Hunger's microcredit program includes education as well as loans. Maritza's lesson today is about breast-feeding. Her informal class begins with an illustrated flip-chart presentation, then expands to a discussion of the women's personal experiences and questions, and ends as the women draw their own lessons and conclusions from what they have heard.

Half the Credit with Education curriculum focuses on health for very young children. Every day, across the world, thirty-five thousand children die of hunger or malnutrition and three quarters of them are under the age of five. These courses address the causes. During a single loan cycle there will be classes on nutrition for young children, diarrhea management and prevention, immunization, and family planning.

Business topics will include inventory management, product differentiation, adding value, and accounting concepts. Education segments are not theoretical—they have been designed to improve business practices.

When class is over, women come forth one by one to put their cash on the table and sign loan repayment records, either with pens or with their thumbprints. Having approved each other's business plans and loan requests, members encourage and support one another's repayment efforts. None of the members can get another loan until everyone in the group has repaid the previous one. Loans average $128, and repayment is virtually one hundred percent.

AFTER THE MEETING Basilia tells us she uses her loan money to buy rabbits (which she raises in an old car), raw materials to make brooms, and ingredients for *chicha*, the corn beer that she makes and sells—and insists we sample. Fiendishly, she fills our gourds full again and again. We pour a lot on the ground as offerings to Pachamama and are considerably relieved when two knitters demand our attention.

Margarita Torrico de Vargas and Trifonia Balderrama de Encinas, who use their loans to buy yarn, are knitting as Bolivian women do, walking around with a ball of yarn under one arm. They loop one strand around their necks to avoid tangles, and walk and talk and drink *chicha* as they knit. As they show us their work, we spy three tiny bright knitted dresses in Margarita's knitting basket. Can the dresses possibly be for the doll-shaped purses we came here to learn about?

Last December, when we were planning our research trip to Bolivia with Claire Thomas at Freedom from Hunger's headquarters in California, she told us that Quechua women used to knit bright-colored, doll-shaped purses, which they wore dangling from their belts. Since our project focuses on the lives of women earning money from crafts, we were intrigued by the idea of craftswomen's purses and planned this visit to Cochabamba.

When we flew from Lima, Peru, at sea level, to La Paz, at thirteen thousand feet, the ascent made us feel as if we weighed a thousand pounds and as if our brains had turned to mashed potatoes. Fortunately, Freedom from Hunger sent North American liaison Robert Ridgley to welcome us, because without his rescue we would still be standing in the jetway musing about life's imponderable mysteries—such as whether or not to go through customs. Robert suggested we proceed to the airport coffee shop, where he broke the news: "Our staff has not been able to find any doll purse makers." Robbed of the ability to see logical consequences and intoxicated by oxygen depletion, I said we would go to Cochabamba as planned. Actually, all I could remember about the city was that it had a lower altitude than La Paz.

Opposite: Evangelina's family, which would love to knit and sell doll-shaped purses again, has made ten for us, each unique. Male dolls wear peaked hats; female dolls carry babies.

Above: **Brimmed hats afford protection from sun that nurtures grain in the breadbasket of Bolivia. Knitters work as they walk, carrying a ball of yarn under their arms and looping a strand around their necks to prevent tangles.**

Opposite: **Tarata, Bolivia, is the only place we visit where a major plaza has a statue of a breast-feeding mother instead of the usual famous man.**

Finally, thirty miles south of Cochabamba, it seems we might be looking at the makings of the fabled doll purses. Margarita is knitting double-faced dresses that are closed at the edges and tied with yarn bows at the neck. These little clothes-shaped pockets could certainly be used to carry money. "Come to my mother-in-law's house and you'll see more," Margarita smiles.

Her husband's mother, Evangelina Saavedra, seventy-eight, is not pleased when we explain our project. "Craftswomen?" she sniffs. "I taught everyone in my family to make the dolls! The men knit as well as the women." This is exceptional; knitting is usually a woman's activity in this area, but we assure her we will photograph the men, too. Evangelina tells us that the family has not made the dolls in over twenty years because there is no market for them, but they long to make them again. We promise that, when we get home, we will inquire about marketing opportunities in North America.

When we return to Tarata the next day, we discover that the whole household has been up since four-thirty in the morning completing ten doll purses. Evangelina sits in the courtyard, surrounded by her family: her husband, most of her five sons and daughters with their wives and husbands, and most of her seventeen grandchildren. They are all knitting—fast. Finished purses are stacked high. Lipstick red, cadet blue, kelly green, chrome yellow, and shocking pink yarns are knitted into a profusion of designs and patterns. Each doll is unique. The male dolls wear striped socks, scalloped ponchos, and peaked hats. The female dolls carry knitted babies. We are enchanted.

Evangelina asks one dollar per doll. We buy all ten as samples. When we give her the cash, she kisses the fifty *boliviano* bill, puts it in her pocket, and tells us two stories.

The day before, she confesses, the family ran out of money. They had prayed for a solution. "Today is Corpus Christi, a holiday Bolivian children celebrate by eating fruit. Now the family has enough money to buy fruit for the children."

Second, she tells us that after we left yesterday she visited an herbalist who mixed a magic plateful of herbs, seeds, candies, and charms, which the family burned as an offering to Pachamama. "The flames took the shape of a full-blown rose," she says. "The rose symbolizes good luck. It means our dolls will sell again." And some of them just had.

ONE OF THE INTENDED CONSEQUENCES of Credit with Education is women's empowerment. "Two things provide the leverage for becoming effective: a little money and a little information. Plus the freedom to do with them what they will," Claire Thomas says of the women who participate. "We give them access to resources, but it is their hope, energy, and determination that make the resources work for them."

UNITED NATIONS STATISTICS tell us that in developing countries all over the world, women's income buys food and education for children. Here in Bolivia we hear a story that literally tops them all. Two years ago, Freedom from Hunger credit association members in the Altiplano, near Lake Titicaca, saved and pooled their money until they had enough to pay for a new roof for the local school. Today their children study there.

TODAY IS DIA DE LA MADRE, Mother's Day, May 27. It is a solemn holiday. On this day in 1812, the Heroinas de la Coronilla, led by a blind woman, fought with sticks and stones to defend the city of Cochabamba from the Spanish. We see school children parading. Mothers will attend open houses in the schools this afternoon. In the historic plaza, vendors sell white-iced holiday doughnuts stacked in four-foot pyramids.

We visit the monument that honors the Heroinas, which sits high above the city where they did mortal battle. Wreaths with ribbons and messages surround the statue. The martyred Heroinas have become symbols of the courage and will of the women in Bolivia who, two hundred years later, are still intrepid and indomitable.

Opposite: **Evangelina Saavedra, who wears her high-crowned holiday hat for Corpus Christi, taught her entire family to make doll-shaped purses.**

and the Cuyuscate Weavers

"WHEN SHE WAS EIGHTY-SIX, my mother told me, 'Weaving is the only thing you will inherit. Sometime, it will make you money.' Those were her last words."

We are talking with Olivia Asij in Santo Domingo Xenacoj. Now sixty, she has earned not only money but also a reputation as the best weaver in town. She and a handful of other artisans who are considered the best in a dozen scattered highland villages have been selected to participate in the Pro-Teje project of the Ixchel Museum in Guatemala City, which provides special yarn to the weavers and markets the products they create with it.

The craftswomen weave and embroider with *cuyuscate*, natural cotton in neutral colors that has not, until now, been grown here commercially. Cool grays, sand, pale greens, rich browns—the undyed tones are as subtle and contemporary as chrome-and-glass furniture at the Museum of Modern Art in New York. These threads are woven and embroidered into Guatemala's traditional patterns, producing monochromatic tapestries. The project may just transform the paintbox-bright textiles people expect from Guatemala.

Olivia tells us of many other changes she has experienced. "For example, when I was a little girl, we didn't use *cortons* [chemises]. Since we only owned one *huipil* [blouse], when we washed it, we tied on dinner napkins for modesty. You know, these days, young girls don't want to wear traditional *huipiles*; they prefer modern, fancy ones." She interrupts herself and scurries off to find a photograph of her mother in wedding attire, to prove that old *huipiles* were fancy, too.

While she is gone we look around. A tangle of medicinal herbs grows behind her house; she drinks herb water when she gets stiff from sitting at the loom too long, and claims to have treated epilepsy with one of the most pungent plants. In a black caldron that sits over a smoldering fire, bark steams, creating a rich brown natural dye.

The centerpiece of Olivia's tan-colored, stucco home is a paved courtyard that bisects the house. Entered by the door from the street, it runs to the back garden between two pairs of small rooms. On the right are Olivia's room and the kitchen. On the left is the room where her son, Jaime, and his wife live—and soon their baby, who is due this week. The fourth room holds five table sewing machines; there, her two sons supervise the production of Levi's jeans. Anachronistically, Olivia usually sits on the cement outside this humming, modern production area, weaving at her backstrap loom.

There is no question that we are in a weaver's house; her plain, striped, and brocaded cloth is everywhere: lining baskets, covering the kitchen table, binding garden cuttings, curtaining windows. When Olivia returns with her mother's photograph she also shows us government credentials that officially identify her profession as "Artesana."

Despite Olivia's talent, her business is shrinking. The men who weave with foot looms can sell place mat sets cheaper than she can. That has forced her to compete by reducing her price from eight dollars to six. It is small solace when we tell her that all over the world, men take over women's crafts as soon as technology becomes integral to production.

Now Olivia rigs her backstrap loom, connecting the far end to a hook high on the courtyard wall. Until now, her loom has been wrapped inside her weaving-in-progress, stuffed unceremoniously into a small basket full of yarn. She kneels and begins to weave, describing more changes she has witnessed during her life. Her original language, Cakchiquel, accents her Spanish.

"I remember wearing sandals made of car tires. I remember the days before fertilizer, when we couldn't grow enough corn for tortillas, so we bought bread, which was much cheaper then: four pieces for five cents. And I remember when men used to get ten cents a day for working forty-five square yards of land. That's what my husband earned when he was doing farm work.

"Marriages were arranged back then. I didn't know my husband-to-be, so I was scared and resisted for years while my father insisted I marry this man. I actually knew other men I would have liked to marry, but if I went out with them, my father beat me. Finally my father explained that if I did not marry his choice, I would be disowned. So I got married when I was twenty-five. My husband was a good man. I learned to love him and we had two sons, but he died when I was thirty. He had been blinded in a bus accident. I nursed him. When

Previous pages: **Striped burgundy *huipiles* (blouses) are made and worn by Mayan women in Patzun. Irma Bajan wears the traditional style with abstract embroidery but** hangs to dry the new style, which has floral embroidery.

Opposite: **Traje (indigenous clothing) is everyday attire for the women and girls in this area: a *huipil* like Albertina Patunayche's, blue beads, *ikat* skirt, woven belt, and sandals.**

he fell, I would lift him. Within two years, he went insane. I believe," she says compassionately, "that he died of sadness."

At that point, Olivia, newly responsible for children she was determined to educate, established the selling strategies she still uses. "Of course, when I get orders from the Ixchel Museum, there is time for nothing else. But otherwise, Mondays and Tuesdays I sell in nearby villages that have weekly markets. On Thursdays and Saturdays, I sell at the market in Antigua. Two or three days a month I take the bus to the coast where I sell to the merchants. Today, I forgot you were coming so I was leaving to sell in Guatemala City, as I do every Wednesday and Friday."

Until Olivia opened her door for us this morning, every Mayan woman we had seen in the Guatemala highlands had been wearing the traditional apparel. Olivia, dressed in a contemporary outfit, had greeted us quickly, invited us to wait on a wooden bench, and returned wearing *traje*, an embroidered blouse and wrapped skirt. As she stood twisting yarn through her hair to create a bright coronet, she explained, "Like all the women, I wear *traje* every day—except when I sell in Guatemala City. One day when I was there, I was beaten and robbed. Now I don't wear *traje* there. It is safer not to look like a vulnerable Indian woman."

BANKS OF STEPS reminiscent of the ancient ruins at Tikal lead us to the Museo Ixchel del Traje Indigena, which is named for Ixchel, sometimes called Chac Chel, the Mayan goddess who created weaving. Her name translates to "Lady Rainbow," and she is associated with fertility and childbirth; Mayans speak of cloth as being "born" on the loom. The sacred Mayan text, the *Popol Vuh*, warns the Indians against forsaking the crafts that have been handed down through the generations: abandoning those crafts will betray the ancestors.

We tour the museum collections, which span one hundred twenty communities and two centuries. And of course, we visit the museum store, which is packed with work by the very weavers we are visiting.

AT THREE O'CLOCK, we are to meet two more superstar weavers, Albertina Patunayche and Irma Bajan, in the plaza of their village, Patzun.

Having left Guatemala City in frustratingly slow traffic, we are arriving two full hours late. We are more than just embarrassed—we are afraid we will never be able to locate Irma and Albertina. We don't have their home addresses, and we know they do not have telephones.

We squint through the dusty car windows, scanning the large plaza full of people, buses, vendors. We survey the sidewalk that hugs the tan-colored, single-story buildings surrounding the square. Every woman and girl in Patzun wears a deep-red blouse with floral embroidery at the yoke, and a skirt patterned with gray and white. Which of these identically dressed women are Albertina and Irma?

Finally, we decide to get out and ask. But as soon as our car pulls over, there is jubilant knocking on the back window, and Albertina and Irma are there laughing at us, hugging us, welcoming us.

The next morning we follow their directions through a labyrinth of one-story adobe walls, each house indistinguishable from the next for block after hilly block. Finally, we locate a trail that twines uphill and walk though plowed fields to reach Albertina's home near the top.

She is ready for us. The immaculate red surface of her porch is so glossy with wax that we ask if we should remove our dusty shoes, but she beckons us inside.

In the living room, her tabletop altar still holds an Easter display: big bouquets of gypsophila spill from vases under a framed picture of Christ. The room is decorated with children's drawings and certificates that commemorate the completion of various grades at school. A small television set sits high on a shelf in the adjacent bedroom, which is only a few inches larger than the bed.

Five smaller buildings comprise the hillside complex, each a separate room connected to the others with broken wood fencing. There is a kitchen with a large brick wood-burning oven and enamelware on the shelves. There are also a shed full of dry ears of corn for tortillas, a storage shed, a chicken coop, and an outhouse. Although there is electricity, there is no running water. Water comes from a deep well in the center of

---

Opposite, clockwise from top left: The basket under Olivia Asij's back-strap loom contains yarns and tools for weaving and brocading. At day's end, it will also hold her work-in-

progress and the collapsed loom • Olivia proves that her mother's wedding *huipil* was as fancy as the style preferred by young women today • Albertina's bright textiles

helped qualify her to work with neutral-hued *cuyuscate* for the Ixchel Museum's Pro-Teje Project • Albertina's son, Freddy Haroldo, twelve, shares his mother's artistic

talent, as evidenced by his graffiti; his dream of learning computer graphics is probably unaffordable.

the dusty yard, where there is also a metal sink for washing dishes and clothes and for other chores. A brown puppy plays nearby. Two white pet birds perch on metal garbage cans. Tall, exotic scarlet flowers blossom in a garden patch.

Many activities take place on the shady porch with the shiny floor. Albertina's fifty-eight-year-old mother, Hilaria, is already working there, warping yarn. While we talk, Albertina embroiders, then weaves.

Albertina worries that Guatemala's weaving tradition may ultimately be lost. "Some women don't know how to weave; they buy used *huipiles* from other villages instead of making their own in Patzun style. A few women even buy Western clothes. Some mothers want to teach their daughters to weave, but the girls must do homework instead. Men used to wear the woven shirts and pants their wives made, but not now.

"One reason weaving is not so popular is that few tourists come to buy. We used to have a thriving market in Patzun but the Pan-American Highway didn't come this direction, and *banditos* on the old road scare people away. So weavers must compete for business. We never work together any more; everyone wants to keep their skill to themselves."

Albertina began to weave when she was seven, learning on a child-size backstrap loom. She graduated to a grown-up loom when she was ten. "I felt very happy at that point because then I could earn some money." Her first sale netted thirty-two cents, which was enough to buy ribbons to braid into her hair.

Education is important to this family, in a country where fifty-five percent of the population is illiterate. Albertina's father joins us and describes going to night school as an adult and learning ("slightly") how to read and write. Her mother says she could never catch on. Albertina finished the second year of high school, where her favorite subjects were mathematics and language. She reports proudly that her four children are all in primary school.

"School expenses are thirteen dollars *a month*. I can barely give the children money for anything except school," she acknowledges sadly. When Albertina can't afford books, supplies, and uniforms, her parents contribute.

Opposite: Some days, Olivia weaves with *cuyuscate*, the indigenous cotton that grows in pale shades of green and brown, but today her palette is not neutral.

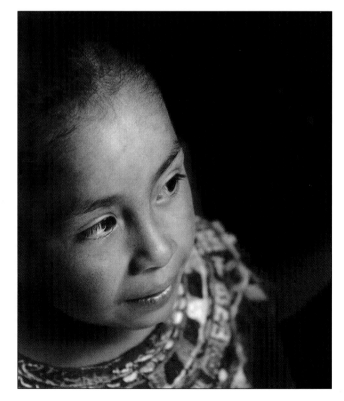

Above, clockwise from top left: Little girls in the Guatemala highlands grow up with both old and new ways. Traditional *huipiles* still worn in Santo Domingo Xenacoj differ from Patzun's style • Two of Benita's granddaughters wear *traje*, but another sports contemporary fashions • Albertina's daughter plays at weaving orders for the Ixchel Museum shop • Irma Bajan's daughters fetch water in plastic jars the Peace Corps introduced. *Opposite, top:* Irma Leticia and Gladys Maribel, Irma's little girls, walk home from school. *Opposite, bottom:* The girls and their mother wait for a bus to visit their grandmother in the village where Irma was born.

Albertina is a single mother. We assume that her husband was killed in the brutal civil war, like many women's husbands, but this is not the case. "I met my husband walking down the street, the way everyone meets. I did not finish high school because we got married. I am Catholic; my husband was Protestant. I didn't like to go to his church, so we started having problems. He started drinking. He died from it when he was thirty, seven years ago." She speaks slowly, struggling under the weight of whatever guilt she feels for this sad ending.

Her daughters, now seven and nine, can already weave. "For fun they pretend they have orders. They cut leaves into strips and weave the pieces together." Albertina wishes the girls could become teachers, but she cannot afford the required education.

Her son, Manuel Roberto, seventeen, works half days as a baker's apprentice. He will finish primary school, then work full time at the bakery, where he has worked since he was eleven. As we talk, Manuel Roberto arrives home bearing a basket of fresh warm buns for lunch.

Albertina's other son, Freddy Haroldo, is almost thirteen. He is a talented artist—we can tell from the embroidery project he did for an art class at school and the amusing cartoon figures he has painted on the shed doors. He likes computers, but there are none at his school. Albertina shakes her head. "I would like so much to see him working in an office in Guatemala City when he is older, but technical schooling would be too expensive."

Today we brought bag lunches so our hunger would not burden this family. Albertina won't hear of our sitting on the ground to have a picnic. Instead, she leads a singing, enthusiastic parade uphill, with each family member helping to carry the table and chairs that usually furnish the kitchen. It seems to be this generosity and joyful sense of family that keep Albertina from losing heart at the difficulties of her life.

IRMA LIVES HALFWAY DOWN Albertina's hill. Her daughters have names that sound like music: Irma Leticia, Gladys Maribel, and Brenda Lorena. Her fourth child is due in October. "God and my husband will decide how many I will have altogether," she admits. "I am still only twenty-five. My mother had nine babies."

The five people in her household now live in her one-room, windowless adobe house. There is no door to close, but the immaculate room contains a wooden cabinet that holds everyone's possessions, and there are two beds placed at a ninety-degree angle in the corner, covered with matching blue woven bedspreads.

Irma's husband, Remigio, does agricultural work and earns three dollars a day. Her own woven placemats contribute three dollars a month, but Irma hopes that when her girls grow up they will sell weaving and contribute, too. She is teaching them on the same child-size backstrap loom that she used when her mother taught her. Although she would like her daughters to continue school, she is pragmatic: "If the girls can't go far in school, they can weave and get along all right."

Irma rises at four in the morning, and her day is full. We accompany this energetic, sunny young woman and two of her daughters to buy eggs at the market, visit the girls' teacher, fetch water from the town spigot and carry it home on their heads in striped plastic water urns, then hang laundry.

It is almost time to cook. Irma asks with a wide smile, "Do you want to see my kitchen?" We follow her diagonally uphill and stop at the windowless kitchen building across from the corn shed. It is dim inside, but it is not difficult to see why Irma invited us—to appreciate her prized new possessions, an electric blender and a spotless white gas stove.

Opposite: **Irma's daughters go to school now but she is teaching them to weave so that, if education becomes unaffordable later on, they will be able to get along.**

Following pages: **During Easter week, people from the Guatemala highlands flood Antigua to see processions and floral carpets; while there, they wash clothes in the *pila* (community laundry pond).**

It is cold here at four-thirty in the morning. Cold and dark. And a little scary. Centuries of seismic and volcanic calamities have left a legacy of broken walls and crumbled buildings in this old colonial city, ruins that look charming in the sunshine, dressed in geraniums and bright new awnings. But now, in the eerie darkness before cockcrow, the effect is ominous—all jagged shadows and hiding places.

We are up and about at this unlikely hour because it's Good Friday, and wonderful things are going to happen. There will be no chocolate bunnies for Easter weekend here, but there will be parades. And before the Good Friday procession begins at nine, the parade route is to be decorated with "floral carpets." It's a big job, so the work begins well before the crack of dawn. We want to see it.

We wander the empty streets fruitlessly for a while, then our flashlight finds a group of people hunkered down on the pavement around a collection of baskets and plastic pails, some piled with flowers, petals, leaves, or pine needles. Other pails are full of brightly dyed sawdust in jewel colors. This little crew of neighborhood artists is doling out the "paints" with which their art will be created.

In the next block, two young couples are working together in the dark, on a long rectangular base carpet of colored sawdust. On the pavement sits a stack of stencils with flower, cross, and crown cutouts and a basket of border greenery.

Within minutes the activity level has quadrupled, and by the time the first glimmer of gray light shows in the sky, the meandering length of the procession route is fully populated with twos and fours of Antigua's citizens, industriously bent over their labors of religious love. With the growing morning light the baskets of flowers and petals bloom with color. All sorts of designs are taking shape on the six-foot to twenty-foot street paintings: birds, animals, crucifixes, blossoms and trees, and words of devotion. I am moved by one carpet that bears a stenciled plaque reflecting the recent resolution of a long and bloody political situation: "Senor, gracias por traernos la paz." Lord, thank you for bringing us peace.

Four or five rolls of film later, as sunlight streams into the street where we stand, a dramatically side-lit volcano rises in the sky beyond the end of town. It looks as if this flowery roadway of color and pattern runs right through Antigua and up the side of the mountain.

Crowds are gathering on the sidewalks, and children appear in the iron-grilled windows of the houses along the way, seated among the potted petunias on the deep windowsills to watch expectantly down the street.

Things are speeding up now; there's a sense of urgency. Finally the carpet makers put the finishing touches on their works and gather their pails and baskets to scramble out of the way, just seconds ahead of the procession. Farther up the parade route the workers have a few more minutes, but here on this block the main event has arrived.

We have a final moment to take in the beauty and color, to appreciate the creativity and effort that have transformed the cobble paving into a wonder of disposable art. And then it is gone. A thousand marching feet are trampling the floral carpets into oblivion. When the tuba players and drummers, the Roman soldiers and purple-robed Israelites, the dozens of men bearing statues of the crucified Christ and dozens of women carrying the Virgin—when finally they have all passed, continuing up the street onto fresh fields of floral design, all that is left behind is a scramble of sawdust and mangled flowers.

The carpet makers return to the street, this time with pushbrooms and dustpans.

ANTIGUA, GUATEMALA

and the Weavers

THE GATEHOUSE at the military base in Sololá is shaped like a soldier's boot: twenty feet tall, a guard window in the heel, rifle portals above the laces. Gravestones on the hillside above Chichicastenango are painted flower garden colors: buttercup yellow, lilac, rose, forget-me-not blue. In late December of 1996, only four months before our arrival, a truce was signed that ended the thirty-six years of civil war that Guatemalans call "the Violence."

We are on our way to interview weavers who live in the highlands. Like many others in the Chimaltenango region, these women lost husbands, fathers, brothers, and uncles to the Violence. For years, their weaving has been the sole support for their families.

PINE, JUNIPER, AND LAUREL line the mountain road. Rounding the next sharp turn, our Land Rover skids to a stop. Boulders block the way. Vey Smithers bounds from the car, talks with the road workers, and calls to us, "Come on, we have to move the rocks." We help her lug the huge boulders to the side, liberating the Land Rover to move forward.

Vey, now forty-seven, came to Guatemala from the United States in 1973, loved the country, and stayed. Land was affordable enough that she bought a small piece of property in Chuinimachicaj, which means "big sky." The town perches at eight thousand feet overlooking Lake Atitlán.

In 1982, fighting between government soldiers and guerrillas erupted in the village. Over the next year, as the community became more dangerous, the women and children sought safety in more peaceful places. Later, when Chuinimachicaj quieted, they returned, and Vey's neighbors asked her to buy the clothes they were wearing so they could feed their children. Their *huipiles* (woven blouses with embroidered yokes) had become old and tattered. Vey bought but warned, "This is not a good idea. Next month, your children will be out of food again, and I will be out of money."

Vey volunteered to help the women think of a way to use their weaving skills to make products people would buy, use, and repurchase, instead of the *huipiles* that tourists only buy occasionally. She now runs an elegant boutique called Colibri in Antigua, Guatemala. "I wanted the store to be their market," she tells us. "I price for fast turnover so the women will have a steady income." Backstrap weaving from four hundred fifty women in fifteen villages is available at Colibri: beautiful woven cotton domestic goods such as tablecloths, placemats, runners, small towels, and napkins.

Vey created patterns based on the women's traditional weaving skills. To standardize quality, she provides the weavers with skeins of colorfast yarn in subtle hues that appeal to Colibri's sophisticated customers.

Some of the weavers have remarried, but about three-quarters are still widows. The fact that they have a reliable stream of revenue has changed their lives. Vey is taking us to meet some of the women.

THE VILLAGE OF PACHAY LAS LOMAS peers over the hazy mountains and sprawls downhill from the Catholic church. Houses cluster below, then scatter into the woods. The only road leads to the mill where the women grind their corn every day. In the opposite direction are the school and the *pila*, the open-air pool where the women wash their laundry.

There has been a mix-up about our arrival. Ambrosia, the leader of the weavers, is at the market in San Martín Jilopepeque. Two women Vey does not know get out their backstrap looms to demonstrate for us. They worry that they cannot feed us lunch and that there are no chairs to sit on. We perch on Ambrosia's porch floor.

Slowly, members of the group gather: Lucia, Julia, Clemente, and Guadeloupe, who took a break from weaving when her baby was born. We talk, smile, listen, share our oranges and cookies. Now women venture from all directions to join us. There must be thirty grandmothers, mothers, children, and babies.

Discomfort gives way to curiosity. Many sit and nurse their infants; all seem eager to talk. "We are glad you came," they tell us. "Where do you live?" they ask. "Did you arrive by car or airplane?" "Will you take a group picture?" They ask if there are markets where women sell weaving in the United States. We describe Navajo women's rugs, and they ask whether Navajo women are

Previous pages: Benita Yaqui teaches her granddaughter to weave using the same *kema* (shuttle) her mother-in-law used long ago to teach her.

Opposite: Benita's village is Chuinimachicaj, which means "big sky" in the local Indian language. The women's burgundy *huipiles* indicate that their village is near Patzun.

more or less talented then they are. And finally, "Do you have any more cookies?"

The women tell us the stories of their first sales: what they sold, how old they were, who bought, how much they were paid, what they did with the money. Vey translates from Spanish to English; the women who speak only Cakchiquel appoint intermediary interpreters to translate to Spanish so Vey can take the next step. I worry that the multiple translations may distort what they say, as in the birthday party whisper game, but one thing is clear: these women want to talk.

EUSEVIA GUERRA IS THIRTY-THREE NOW. When her father was killed, she left school to help her mother, who taught her to weave when she was twelve. By fifteen she was good at it, and three years later she sold her first *huipil* in Chimaltenango for fifty dollars. "It took six months to make that *huipil*. Today, that much work should bring a hundred and fifty dollars."

She has been earning twenty-four dollars a month by making one set of eight napkins; she uses the money to buy sugar, salt, soap, and children's clothes. Now that she weaves only table linen, she buys the *huipiles* she and her three daughters wear. Here, only women still wear traditional clothing every day, she explains. Her husband and three sons, like most men in the Guatemala highlands, sport jeans and T-shirts. During the Violence each village's distinctive style, color, and design of traditional clothing acted as an advertisement that told enemies where the men lived, so many men stopped wearing traditional clothes.

Eusevia and her husband own four *cuerdas*, about two acres, where her husband plants corn; they contract with *coyotes*, companies that collect vegetables to sell for export. Eusevia does not know how much her weaving contributes to the household compared to the vegetables, but the amount will increase as she makes more table-cloths—she has just completed her first.

Her days begin at four in the morning. She makes cof-fee, then tortillas ("If my family doesn't have tortillas, they don't have enough strength to work with a machete or an axe . . ."). After breakfast she washes the dishes, straight-ens the house, then begins to weave. At eleven o'clock the boys come home from school for lunch before going to help their father in the fields. In the afternoon, she goes to the mill to have her corn ground, then does the laundry. After dinner and dishes, the family goes to bed as soon as it gets dark since there is no electricity here.

I ask what makes her happy. "Having weaving to do. What would we do without work? If you don't have money, you can't eat. The wind knocked the corn down last year, so we even had to buy corn. I have six children and don't want more because they would cost too much."

Asked what her dreams are for her daughters, she says, "I hope they will finish the sixth grade, then weave like I do. There is no work here except for weaving."

WE ASK THE OTHER WOMEN the same ques-tion: what makes them happy? "When we get together for a wedding or birthday, we forget our problems and are happy," one says. "When I go to church and pray, the silence and the peace make me happy," another adds. "I'm happy because I'm learning to read," a second grader offers. "I'm reading a book from the library."

A widow who still has three children at home describes her role: "I am happy when I have work. I am like the trunk of the family tree and my children are the branches. I don't know how to read or write but I want my children to go to school. If I have work, I can pay for that."

A mother volunteers, "I'm happy having work, too, so I can buy things: sugar, corn, clothing, notebooks, pen-cils, pens, books. Books cost three dollars now, but after children go beyond the first and second grade, books cost so much that people with many children cannot educate them all. Two of mine, a boy and a girl, are going to finish school," she announces. Pride, determination, and certainty are braided in her voice.

Vey later explains that often families have to choose which children to send to school, and it has usually been boys who are given the privilege. But that is changing. On highways we pass government billboards that read, "An educated girl is the mother of development."

Do the women realize that educated children often leave home to find jobs? They do, and are resigned to live

---

Opposite, clockwise from top left: Francisca Guarcax has twenty-nine nieces and nephews (two are top left and bottom right). A Mayan priestess, she performs ceremonies so her group's weavings will sell • Benita asked Vey Smithers to buy *traje* from the widows of Chuinimachicaj after civil war caused the death or disap-pearance of many men, leaving women to support families alone • Weavers in the Chimaltenango area, like this mother with her children, are among 450 women whose work is available at Colibri in Antigua. *Following pages:* Chuinimachicaj's daub-and-wattle houses are built with sticks, mud, and corrugated metal.

MARCH 28TH

What a delicious existence! To wake up in our big, comfortable beds to the busy music of a thousand birds accompanied by the gentle splashing of our courtyard fountains—while "our staff" is busy laying the patio table and preparing the world's sweetest orange juice and the world's freshest eggs with yolks the same shade as the juice. Bliss!

This is borrowed bliss. This elegant colonial-style house in Antigua was loaned to us by a generous woman who's lucky enough to have two. She advised that staying in Antigua would position us conveniently for daily forays into the mountain villages where we might not find anyplace to stay.

But what a shock when, still lying here thinking about getting up, we look back over the previous day and are confronted with the contrast between our days and our nights. We've been spending our days in the dust and the grit of lives light years removed from this serene environment.

Living in comfort in the face of others' poverty can be a guilt-maker. But it is a great satisfaction to have met some women in Guatemala who have found ways to use their advantages to make a difference. Vey Smithers is an inspiration, bouncing over the impossible mountain roads to deliver materials, payment, and encouragement to a little army of weaving war widows—while operating a most sophisticated boutique business where the weaving meets its market. And the women volunteers of the Ixchel Museum in Guatemala City are dedicated to preserving and promoting something beautiful of Mayan culture, while affording a livelihood to a hardworking contingent of Mayan mothers and grandmothers.

Such amazing women we've found around the world . . . the talented craftswomen who take family welfare into their own hands, and the caring women who support their efforts.

ANTIGUA, GUATEMALA

Above, clockwise from top left: Benita, now fifty-seven, raised her seven children alone. Uneducated herself, she is proud that all her grandchildren have finished the sixth grade • Weaver Francisca is a spiritual healer who is sought by people from Guatemala, Spain, and Mexico to help them find their destinies • This weaver in Pachay Los Lomas has no front teeth, like many here who have inadequate nutrition and suck sugarcane • Matea, Francisca's mother, continues to weave at eighty-three, even though her eyes are not as good as they used to be.

Opposite: Women in Chuinimachicaj, like indigenous women throughout Latin America, carry their babies in slings of bright weaving.

with that eventuality as long as their children have better lives. "The heartbreak," Vey comments later, "is that some educated people have to sit on sidewalks in Guatemala City selling Chiclets."

"I BOUGHT MY LAND in Chuinimachicaj from an old lady who moved to the coast," Vey remembers, "and moved in next to Doña Benita Yaqui and her husband, Bartolo. An earthquake had just hit the area, hard, but because the houses were built of sticks and mud, people weren't killed when the houses collapsed." Benita learned weaving later than most. At twenty, she married Bartolo, and his mother, the town midwife, taught her to weave. Benita still uses the fifty-year-old *kema* (shuttle) her mother-in-law left to her. When Benita is happy, she sings church songs while she weaves. But for her and for many women in this village, there have been times of heartbreaking sadness.

"The Violence began here in 1980, and lasted five years," Benita recalls. "My son Alejandro disappeared in 1982. All the women and children in the village soon fled to safety, and when we returned two years later, I found Alejandro's body. The army had camped in our woods, captured, killed, and buried him. In 1985, my husband disappeared from the streets. He was arrested for no reason that anyone knows, and was never seen again."

It was Benita who approached Vey, her neighbor and friend of seven years, asking her to buy *huipiles* when she and the other women dared to return to Chuinimachicaj in 1984. And it was Benita who helped Vey establish the first weavers' group. Fourteen widowed weavers elected Benita their leader. But being the leader was simply a necessity; the accomplishment that made Benita proudest was being able to earn money. "The weaving has been a big help in the village's recovery. It has helped me. I haven't had anything else," Benita tells us. "In the beginning, we were all sad. It helped us to know we were part of a group. We each worked in our own house, but felt we belonged to something."

Doña Benita, now fifty-five, raised her seven children alone and has many grandchildren, whom she views as blessings. Uneducated herself, she tells us that all her

Opposite: **Throughout the Guatemala highlands weavers use warping boards to prepare the vertical threads for their looms.**

grandchildren, including the girls, have finished sixth grade. "I have twenty-four grandchildren—and a good rooster," she says, satisfied. As we leave, she gives the rooster to Vey as a thank-you present.

IN XAJAXAC, a Cakchiquel word that means "new hope," we visit three generations of women in one family, all weavers: Francisca Guarcax, her mother Matea, and her niece Flora.

Francisca's husband was killed in the Violence. Matea lost her husband, a son, and three brothers—all of the men in her family. Flora was orphaned.

Matea, now eighty-three, learned to weave from her mother. When she was young, *huipiles* were brown-and-white homespun, natural cotton. "No bright colors. No decorations. Not like now," she says. Her granddaughter, Flora, wears the new fashion: there is glitter in the *randa* (connecting strip) of her *ikat* skirt.

Matea did not go to school. Her father was a healer and was well respected in the village. Matea had been married for nine years and had four young children when her husband was killed. He had sold vegetables, so it had not been necessary for her to work, but after his death she had no choice but to weave for money. Miraculously, she managed to support her family and now has thirty-five grandchildren.

Flora, twenty-two, finished the sixth grade but feels she does not speak Spanish well enough to study further. Vey points out that she is a talented weaver whose work is even and beautiful. She is an artist. Flora learned weaving when she was twelve and has been part of the weaving group for six years. She uses a small lap loom to weave cocktail napkins as she talks with us, and the striped pattern she is creating mirrors the stripes of her traditional *huipil.*

Francisca, thirty-eight, has direct, clear eyes that seem to attend to the world consciously with both energy and calm. She has long led her community's weaving group and is a spiritual healer sought by people from all over Guatemala as well as Spain and Mexico.

"I have returned to the Mayan religion. My family is both Mayan and Catholic, so they understand—we have never lost our Mayan beliefs. My grandfather had the destiny of being a Mayan healer. People who are born on my birthday in the Mayan *Imosh* [calendar] are to be healers. My fourth son—my son Albertin, who is fourteen—was also born on this day.

"My work is to tell people where they are in their life and work, to help them find the right direction. Everyone is born with a destiny—but some people have spiritual problems. They do things counter to their fate and nothing works out right for them. I feel my future is with the Mayan religion. I have dedicated myself to healing. To tell the truth, I do not weave anymore."

This is news. Vey's surprise includes worry for the leaderless weavers, joy at her friend's decision, and fascination with Francisca's path. Francisca offers Vey reassurance about business. Although she will no longer weave herself, she says her daughters, Maria and Soila, will continue, and she will lead the weavers as she always has.

When Francisca continues, she explains, "I am called *Ajqij*, which means Priestess. We have no written books. I use incense and candles in ceremonies and call on all the nature spirits: rain, sky, and wind."

Does she feel a special affinity to Ixchel, the Mayan goddess of weaving? The question brings her to a stop. She seems uncomfortable and refuses to answer. "This is very sacred. I cannot talk about it."

But she adds, "When we are ready to deliver our work, we all go out and buy incense to make a ceremony so that our weavings will sell." Vey had told us that this group's weavings fly out the door the minute they bring them into Colibri—they sell like hotcakes.

Why is weaving so important here, we ask. Francisca gives a thoughtful answer that reaches beyond facts. She does not mention that land here has been subdivided for so many generations that one plot is not large enough to feed a family, or that two percent of the population owns eighty percent of the land. What she says is, "Weaving is important because there is a sense of friendship and unity among the group."

"There is an economic component . . ." Vey suggests.

"Yes, but really, the important thing is the sense of togetherness we have from working."

Opposite: The weavers whose work is sold at Colibri adapt traditional patterns to tablecloths, napkins, placemats, runners, and hand towels. Colibri provides them with skeins of color-fast yarn in subtle hues that will appeal to contemporary consumers—but the women weave with backstrap looms and shuttles like the ones their mothers and grandmothers used.

and the Shipibo Potters

THE SETTING SUN HAS TURNED the jungle harbor an apricot hue, illuminating the water and washing the sky with a breathtaking, otherworldly orange. Fishermen, running late, collect their nets. Children take running jumps off the ubiquitous skinny long boats tied up to the floating dock.

We are trying to arrange for just such a boat to take us to San Francisco, a village on Lake Yarinacocha in the Amazon River basin a few miles north of Pucallpa, Peru. "Five hundred dollars will get you to San Francisco!" offers an entrepreneurial boatman. "San Francisco what, California?" We laugh and keep walking. The man who gets our business takes us the next morning for fifteen dollars.

Ten violent years of terrorist activity by leftist Shining Path guerrillas have kept tourists away. Although this area is peaceful now, the famous Shipibo women potters have had too few customers for a long time. The Maroti Shobo cooperative store in Puerto Callao, once haunted by savvy collectors, is dusty and almost empty. Clusters of Shipibo women hawk their pots on the city streets of Pucallpa—pots like those in museums all over the world.

Our boat trip takes us past banana and papaya plantations, past lacy pink flowering trees that stretch high above the jungle roof, past huts that hug the shore. Olga Mori and Celia Yui, Shipibo women who work for the Organización de Mujeres Indígenas de la Amazonia Peruana (OMIAP), are our guides and interpreters.

Like all Shipibo women, Olga and Celia each wear a jewel-toned satin blouse, a thick belt of many strands of white beads, and a sarong-style skirt embroidered with the linear geometric patterns that compose all Shipibo designs. This is what they always wear. OMIAP members have a soccer league, and they wear this fancy garb even when they compete!

Olga and Celia tell us that OMIAP, which is governed by a board of seven indigenous women, was founded in 1993. It has organized ninety-six Mothers Clubs with a total of four hundred members in seven Shipibo communities. A United Nations grant from Denmark in 1997 helped OMIAP market Shipibo crafts. The organization also delivers medicines to the villages and trains members to raise chickens for food and income. On Sundays, OMIAP maintains regular communications with the villages via a public-access radio network.

Our long boat veers toward a muddy shore, and we traverse a low marsh, then start uphill toward the huts of San Francisco, where about twelve hundred Shipibo live. Ahead, we hear conch-shell trumpets announcing our arrival to the residents. An official welcoming committee meets us at the crest of the hill: the mayor, his administrative assistant, and the town secretary. The mayor leads us to the Women's Pavilion, yelling through a bullhorn: "Come! Bring your things! They are here!" Women join us carrying tables, benches, chairs, and half-finished clay pots wrapped in muslin.

Collecting companions as we go, we parade past the thatch-roofed platform houses that line the wide, dusty path—a path that is lit at night with anomalous high arc lights like those used in cities. We pass a shaded communal well where children are drawing water in buckets, splashing it on each other. Fences are festooned with drying laundry: the mothers' bright blouses and embroidered wrap skirts, the children's Western-style play clothes and school uniforms.

The men, who wear jeans and T-shirts, wield machetes, slashing the high weeds around the single-story brick elementary school so snakes have nowhere to hide. We hear students inside chanting in Shipibo, perhaps memorizing multiplication tables. The Women's Pavilion is next door to the school, and several men are rethatching it, seeming to defy gravity as they balance on beams high above our heads.

About forty craftswomen convene. Some build a fire, carry in water, and start it boiling in large vats that will hold chicken-foot-and-fish-head soup. Several women have black hands, stained from dying their hair the night before in anticipation of our arrival. Shipibo women consider glossy black hair to be beautiful, and wanted to disguise the brown, brittle hair that results from inadequate nutrition.

These women, who are known for their pottery, make many other crafts as well, and although they usually work at home, today they will demonstrate all the Shipibo

Previous pages: **Shipibo women's pottery is in fine museums everywhere but tourist demand stopped when the Shining Path was active in this part of Peru's Amazon Basin.**

Opposite: **Craftswomen paint intricate geometric lines on their pots using fine brushes made, traditionally, of their own hair.**

women's arts for us at the pavilion. They unpack their bundles and get to work.

Some women and their young daughters spin cotton thread for beadwork. Others string necklaces, combining beads, seeds, piranha jaws, fish fins, and crocodile teeth. Many beaders work with their infants asleep in their laps. Other women demonstrate textile arts, weaving on backstrap looms that are lashed to the pavilion pillars. Still others are embroidering or painting cotton fabric with clay slip, the runny neutral-color paint that is made of mud from Lake Yarinacocha.

And many women are creating the pots we came to see. Mothers teach their daughters to make pottery according to a method used for many generations: knead lake mud with wood ash to make clay; mold the base and coil the pot shape on it; scrape the surface smooth with a small tool made of dried pumpkin rind; rinse the pot with oxide; glaze the pot white; paint patterns with brushes traditionally made from human hair; fire the pots in giant open bonfires; and apply enamel glaze inside and out. The final step is to burnish the glaze with lake stones.

Although each woman creates her own designs, all Shipibo patterns are a complex of lines. Shipibo embroider lines on their skirts, paint lines on their pots and clothing; they used to paint lines on their bodies, and believe that lines order the world. Some scholars theorize that the linear patterns could be a crude map of the area's waterways or of the constellations, but the true significance is unknown, at least to outsiders.

THE SHIPIBO ARE A MATRIARCHAL and matrilocal people: husbands move in with their wives' families. Ancient polygynous Shipibo chieftains used to travel from village to village to reside in rotation with the families of their four or five wives.

The men do not earn money: they fish, build huts, and clear the fields where they work with their wives to grow fruit and yucca. "It is too hot here to grow vegetables," they say, and as the day gets steamier, we accept that without question.

What do people do for fun in San Francisco? "We make yucca *chicha*," one woman says, smiling just thinking about this local brew, "and we dance from Saturday until Monday morning."

ONE FAMILY APPEARS to run everything here. Segundina Cumapa, president of OMIAP, is from San Francisco. Her brother is the mayor who greeted us. Her sister, Rosa Cumapa, is the first president of OMIAP's local Mothers Club.

Rosa, forty-four, is married to a schoolteacher and has nine children; Leah, the youngest, is eight—barely older than Rosa's first grandchild. Most of the children in San Francisco go to school, but it is expensive. Families here have four or five children, so their school costs are about two hundred dollars a year.

Rosa quit school after the eighth grade and feels that amount of schooling was not enough for her to be a success (regardless of the fact that she is president of a group in which most of the members have far less education). She is gratified to be the first mother in San Francisco to have a child in college—in fact, she has three. The first is studying to be a nurse, the second, an accountant, and the third will enter technical college this fall.

The monthly household income for most families in San Francisco is about $190. Selling crafts and, seasonally, fish is the only source of money the women have. Some weeks members of the Mothers Club have no income, although they can each make five or six small pots in a day, or one large one to fire overnight. When they have customers for their crafts, they spend their money to educate the children, help the community, and support their families.

We had been excited to read about the spiritual and ritual roles of Shipibo pottery, but Rosa says many of those traditions have vanished. "It used to be that we had special designs for special shapes, but we've lost that. We just produce."

We had read that the boa's skin is believed to carry all the linear patterns in the world, and is considered sacred. The books also said that a woman's pots are thrown in the river when she dies.

Rosa debunks the first myth. "No such beliefs. Boas are strong. They hunt animals." In the old times, pots would

Opposite, clockwise from top left: While San Francisco Mothers Club members create textiles, beadwork, and pottery, others prepare vats of chicken-foot-and-fish-head soup so the craftswomen can eat lunch together • Large pieces of Shipibo pottery are fired in the open flames of bonfires; smaller pots cook over hot coals • Patterns of geometric lines are painted on pottery, bric-a-brac, and textiles, and often embroidered on skirts. The designs may be maps of waterways or constellations • An *onaya* (practitioner of traditional medicine) suggests that the skin of the boa may have inspired the distinctive linear patterns.

be thrown in the river, she tells us, but no longer. Now, the family sells the pots or the children inherit them.

"If there were no tourist market at all, would women still make pots?" we ask. She responds, "They would have to dedicate themselves to something else they could sell."

We are disturbed by the degree to which the pottery tradition seems to have dissipated, and wonder if the loss relates to commercialization, changing times, or something else. We ask to speak to one of the Shipibo male healers, who are supposed to know a great deal about the linear patterns. Mateo Arevalo says he is not a shaman—"that word is used by North Americans"—but "an *onaya* or *meraya* [a practitioner of traditional medicine]. My Shipibo name, Isa Yoi, means 'Messenger Bird.'" Mateo integrates pragmatic beliefs like Rosa's with a spiritual understanding formed over centuries.

"Do Shipibo still put leaves on their eyes to see the geometric designs better?" we ask him.

"Every grandmother, like a baptism, puts *piri piri* plant seed drops in a girl's eyes when she is born. This transmits the designs she will make her whole life."

"What about the boa? Are the designs on a boa's skin like the designs the women draw?"

"More or less. Not exactly, but the inspiration is there. Yacaryba is the mother of the water. Water is very important to life here. The boa enters the water, connects with the water spirit, and returns to land. The energy of the water spirit is in the boa."

"Do Shipibo believe that sickness is caused by the body's internal lines becoming crooked? Do medicine men exhale smoke in lines to demonstrate the patterns of health?"

"My smoke makes the same linear patterns in the air that the women paint and embroider. Each medicine man has a pattern, just as each woman does. We are the keepers of the visions."

"Then why don't *men* render the designs on pottery?" we challenge suspiciously.

"Men leave the painting to women because they don't want to take away their inspiration," Mateo says.

We are not sure whether he is patronizing or honoring women, so we ask him.

"Men respect the women," he responds, "the women care for the medicinal plants and the children. You have to respect that. Everything else depends on that."

KEYLA ROJAS LIVES in Yarinacocha now, but her family was originally from Paullung, twelve hours north of Pucallpa; they came to the city so her mother could be treated for tuberculosis. Keyla is an expert on Shipibo design. Her first job was as head of quality control at the Shipibo cooperative store, Maroti Shobo. Now she sells handicrafts made by her mother, aunt, and two sisters, Nilda and Loriana. "I love to tell the story of how Shipibo art is made, and I love to talk with people. Not many women like to sell as much as I do."

Perhaps Keyla will reassure us after all that the traditions of the Shipibo linear designs have not been lost to the women. We ask Keyla if the designs have spiritual meaning.

"No. They are art."

"We read that Shipibo women don't make the designs when they are menstruating."

"Not true."

"A book said people here believed that there was such power in the Shipibo geometric designs that they used to hang their patterned clothes from the rafters to scare off burglars."

Keyla bursts out laughing. "No!"

We give up and ask, "What should a smart buyer look for?" She comments, "Painted fabric should have no blotches. In embroidery, the smaller the design and stitches, the better. Lines should be straight, not drunk lines. The lines should be more or less the same length. And beautiful colors in the embroidery."

We are curious about Keyla's life. She is full of energy, charm, and laughter as she tells the story of her wedding. "Mother ordered me to marry my husband. I was not in love with him. I was fourteen, and I didn't know the boy. They woke me up and said, 'Now you have to marry this guy.'" (I ask Loyda, her mother, why this marriage seemed like such a good idea. She says simply, "He was a good man and a good worker.")

"Keyla, did you know what to expect from marriage; did you know about sex?" "No and no."

Opposite: Older children attend school next door to the Women's Pavilion, but infants and toddlers accompany their mothers while their fathers fish, build huts, and clear the fields.

Above: No matter which "women's art" they practice—embroidery, spinning, jewelry making, weaving, or pottery—and no matter what else they do (including playing competitive soccer), Shipibo women wear satin blouses, embroidered sarong skirts, and thick belts of white beads.

Opposite: Olga Mori and Celia Yui, who work for the Organización de Mujeres Indígenas de la Amazonia Peruana, walk from the river to San Francisco.

"We read that a Shipibo marriage ceremony occurs when the bride's mother gets the groom's mosquito net and takes it to her house. Did your mother do that?"

"Yes."

"Then what?"

"I got used to him," Keyla smiles.

When Keyla shows us her house, we notice red lace bikini panties hanging on a hook. She grabs them and stuffs them in her pocket, giggling.

Eleven family members live together here; there were a dozen until a month ago, when Keyla's three-year-old granddaughter got a cold and did not respond to medication.

The fifteen-year-old thatch-roofed kitchen is all that remains of the original house that Keyla and her husband bought ten years ago for four dollars. Last spring, Keyla took a loan and added five small bedrooms built of brick and cement block with corrugated metal roofs. All the land that surrounds the house is hers, she says, including the mango tree and the privy with the burlap curtain in the backyard.

We talk about gender roles in a matriarchy. If Keyla's husband earns money, he gives it to her to manage. Asked if there is much physical abuse of women, she replies, "Yes. Men abuse women. Women abuse each other. And women abuse men, too."

"Are men and women equal in the Shipibo culture?"

"Yes. In the cities and the villages, equal in abilities as well as contributions."

Her sons, Orlando, Luis, and Franclin, agree; her mother, aunt, two sisters, and four nieces agree. It must be so.

THE DAY WE ARE TO LEAVE the Amazon basin, it is pouring and our plane is delayed. Itinerant vendors try to seduce us into buying dried piranhas as last-minute souvenirs.

Suddenly, Rosa Cumapa materializes. She has traveled from San Francisco by boat despite the rainstorm to ask if we know how she can get financial aid to cover a dollar and a half per day per child for college room, board, and books. Rosa's priority, her children's schooling, is of far more consequence than even the torrential rain.

Opposite: **The community duck pond lies between the river and the jungle village.**

Angela

and the Arpillera Makers

A SET OF SIX new cooking pans is stacked on the top of the refrigerator in Angela's bedroom, still wrapped in crackling-new brown paper from the store. She is paying for them on the installment plan, and will inaugurate them when a new gas stove replaces her counter-top burners. Nowhere in our travels did we meet another woman artisan who had the resources to buy anything to use later.

Angela's home is in Pamplona, one of the shantytown communities that ring Lima and house half the city's population. There, shacks like Angela's spring up from salvaged parts: old doors, used windows, panels of matting, corrugated metal, and crating. Roofs are not the first priority: it never rains in Lima. Thanks to Peruvian president Alberto Fujimori's connections, Japanese tanker trucks deliver water to the shantytown; otherwise water is unavailable.

About a million people live in Pamplona and Villa El Salvador, sections of the "Belt of Poverty." Ultimately, the squatters are given title to the land they occupy, which helps them obtain bank credit. Pueblo Jovenes, south of the city, was settled in the 1960s and demonstrates the determination with which the poor prevail: those residents now own their land; their houses have adobe walls and some, even second stories.

Crowded, dusty, indigent neighborhoods surround metropolitan areas in places as distant as Istanbul and Ahmedabad. Rural refugees flood to the cities in hope of finding jobs. The cities' infrastructures cannot support them: jobs, housing, and plumbing are inadequate. But in many cities, the shantytowns become hotbeds of artisanal activity as the struggling newcomers rely on known skills to survive.

THE WOMAN WHO IS SAVING her pots is Angela Pareona Riviera, thirty-one, president and founder of a Mothers Club that was originally funded by the government. Despite the noisy urban setting of her house in Pamplona, she and her group sew *arpilleras*, three-dimensional scenes of pastoral Peruvian country life. In a week, the sixty industrious members could easily decorate six hundred sweaters with *arpilleras*, but they can only sell two hundred in the domestic and export markets.

Angela, like many other women who live in the Pamplona and Villa El Salvador area, learned to make *arpilleras* "from a perfectionist," a Chilean woman named Rosbita who taught sewing at the German-run Humboldt School. In fact, *arpilleras* originated in Chile, where women political prisoners who were held during the Pinochet period used them to camouflage notes sent to helpers and collaborators outside. Even the most suspicious guards did not think to check the appliquéd pictures for messages, since sewing was seen as inconsequential "women's work."

Today's Peruvian *arpilleras* also carry messages in little fabric pockets, but the notes describe the scenes portrayed in the pictures. It was Rosbita's idea that the shantytown women should create fabric pictures of the village life their families had left behind.

When Angela's mother, Anna, was seven, she, her parents, and nine brothers and sisters left a village in central Peru hoping to relocate near schools and clinics in Lima. Angela, one of Anna's six daughters, is among the second generation of family members to live in the city. "The older generation here speaks either Aymara or Quechua [the pre-Inca and Inca languages], depending on where they are from," Angela tells us.

Today, Anna babysits Angela's three children while Angela supervises sewing in the workroom near the front of her house. She gives the women who belong to her Mothers Club sewing materials, acrylic or cotton cardigans to decorate, and sample sweaters on which she has basted figures. Because she knows that the export market has been saturated with *chompas* (sweaters), she changes the patterns and colors annually to rekindle demand.

Angela's education, Spanish fluency, energy, and savvy make her a natural leader. She is also a natural at business. Angela married her husband when she was sixteen, but for two years before that she managed the money he earned. She was honored that he trusted her; she learned to budget. He made enough money as a mechanic that she, whose family was very poor, believed that after the wedding the two of them would live in a big house. "I had lots of hopes and illusions; I was in love, and very emotional," she admits. But faced with reality, she became very practical.

Previous pages: **Arpilleras** are three-dimensional fabric collages. Whether wall hangings, sweaters, potholders, or cards, each typically shows life in the Peruvian countryside that is known for llamas and mountains.

Opposite: **Arpillera** makers in the "belt of poverty" that surrounds Lima create imaginative holiday nativity scenes that sometimes include Christmas trees and Peruvian mountains.

Above, clockwise from top left: Juana Huaytalla, president of an *arpillera* group, arrived in Lima with no work, skills, friends, money, or place to live • Angela Pareona Riviera's daughter attends afternoon classes (students go to school in three separate shifts) • Angela dreams of a "real" kitchen; houses in her neighborhood don't have roofs, much less real kitchens • Angela's niece (shown here) walks to school with her daughter while Angela, president of an *arpillera* group that decorates *chompas* (sweaters), works with the other women.
Opposite: In May, July, and October, craftswomen gather to sell at the Mothers Market in Lima.

Grimacing, Angela's five-year-old namesake stands in the courtyard, scrubs her face with soap, rinses with splashes of cold water from a hose, and rubs with a rough towel. The little girl squirms into her uniform, a dress of pale yellow cotton with a white collar. Threads dangle from one frayed cuff, but her uniform is starched and ironed. She is clean and ready for school, which she attends from noon to five. Her mother has always managed to provide the hundred dollars required each fall to buy school uniforms and shoes for two daughters.

Like working mothers everywhere, Angela pieces her life together like a puzzle. She gets up at six, fetches water, cleans the house, goes to the bakery a half-block away to buy bread, wakes the children, and fixes eggs for breakfast by eight. For the next three hours she works with the women, sewing. When they go home, Angela buys food and prepares lunch, the big meal of the day: meat, fish, or an egg dish. At two, the women reconvene and sew until eight or nine at night. For dinner, the children eat lunch leftovers with their grandmother. Angela and her husband eat the rest, then watch television until about eleven.

On special occasions, Angela and her husband go to a party; they love to drink and dance. Once in a while the two of them have dinner out, but not often. Sometimes on weekends the family goes to the beach south of the city or visits Angela's sister-in-law "who lives on a nice little farm where the children can run."

Angela's house is testimony to her progress. The front workroom has two solid walls, painted a peach color. In the back, woven mat walls give way to brick walls in the two bedrooms. The children's room has a bed for each child, and each bedroom has a television set. There are two electric refrigerators and a boom box. Next, there will be a "real" kitchen, and Angela will unwrap those cooking pots.

OUR DAY BEGINS with a visit to the tri-annual Mothers Market where Angela's Mothers Club sells sweaters in May, July, and October. Stalls cover the grounds of the National Art Gallery. The fair is jammed with people, musicians, fried-food vendors, baked goods,

Opposite: When this woman's *arpillera* group began in 1989, its members, displaced women who fled Shining Path violence in Ayacucho to seek refuge in Lima, were illiterate, spoke only Quechua, and had been traumatized by losing family members.

potted plants, Inca Cola stands, excited children, and an array of crafts sold by women: tapestries, chess sets, pottery, weaving, musical instruments, puppets, wood carvings, painted gourds. We meet a group of handicapped women who create greeting cards with floral designs made from feathers. We talk to many vendors, photograph craftswomen and exhibits, get separated, get completely lost in the crowds; the pandemonium of the Mothers Market swallows us.

IN NEARBY SAN JUAN DE MIRAFLORES, there are four *arpillera* workshops whose members are women who were displaced by the violence southeast of Lima near Ayacucho, the birthplace and headquarters of the Shining Path. The establishment, an alliance of landowners, the government, the military, and the church, has conducted a long, brutal civil war with the Shining Path. The peasant poor were devastated by the Shining Path's terrorist tactics, and when refugees sought sanctuary in Lima, they met discrimination because they were illiterate, spoke only Quechua, and brought their own customs, culture, and war traumas. Their obstacles went beyond economic difficulties—they had integration, socialization, and psychological problems. It was an almost insurmountable challenge for the women to concentrate enough in the *arpillera* workshops to learn how to sew, much less how to earn money or understand business. We are about to visit two of these workshops.

CIAP (Central Interregional de Artesanos del Peru) is a UN-funded non-governmental organization that markets the work of the four *arpillera* workshops for displaced women. The first CIAP group calls itself Kuyanakuy. In Quechua the word means "We love each other very much."

Of all the women we have visited in any country, these are among the poorest. A breeze could blow down the house in which they hold their weekly meetings; the straw mat walls are so broken that neighbors hand their infants through the holes. Behind this house, a dirt hill

rises steeply; except for a few huts, it is as barren as the surface of the moon. The smell of urine from the privy permeates the courtyard where the women work around a rough wood table. Almost all of them have babies bundled onto their backs. Older children do dishes in plastic tubs while their mothers sew.

The bright clothes the women wear and the intense tones of the acrylic yarn they use stand in stark contrast to the drab setting. Down the road, someone has painted cheerful, colorful pictures on the inside of the schoolyard fence: an indomitable creative spirit is surely tested here.

In 1989, this group formed with eight displaced women, *desplazadas*, all of whom had lost members of their families in the terrorism. "They were so frightened that the group began like therapy. Then a big order came in from the United States, giving them the income and encouragement to continue making *arpilleras*," says Graciela Magan, a CIAP volunteer and sociologist who is accompanying us.

Juana Huaytalla, the president of this group, fled the violence in Ayacucho with her husband in 1984, arriving in Lima with no work, skills, friends, money, or place to live. Her husband, a mason, found periodic work selling plastic products for a vendor in the market. "Little by little we started getting together with others in the same situation," she explains.

Fortunita Palomino and Juliana Quijano tell us the stories behind their *arpillera* designs: stories of planting and harvesting potatoes, tomatoes, red peppers, oranges, cabbages, grapes. Stories of spinning, and tending llamas, sheep, cows, horses, and goats. Stories of cousins, neighbors, aunts, uncles, and babies with whom they lived long ago when they were "at home."

"At first, we were inexperienced making *arpilleras*, and they were really ugly," Juana admits. "But teachers came here, and with practice our work has become a lot better." Learning is important to these women, who ask to be photographed in the room where they have sewing tutorials on Mondays. Juliana, who is the coordinator for all four of the groups, is also teaching them to read and write so they can eventually sign their own contracts.

Opposite, top: Mama Angela's five-year-old namesake pauses in the courtyard before going to school. The hose brings water to her house; the stones will replace one plywood wall.

Opposite, bottom: Angela wakes up with a splash of the cold water that flows from hose to spigot.

Although her husband finished secondary school, Juana only finished the third grade and wishes she could read and write correctly. She hopes education will help her kids avoid the kind of life she has had. We observe that she has adjusted from farm to city life and learned to make products, money, and friends, which seem to us impressive accomplishments. That may be true; but counting accomplishments does not make life better.

Before we leave, a woman takes us aside and says, "Please. You must take me home with you so I won't have to live in this horrible place."

THE AVECITAS, "Little Birds," the second group of displaced women we visit, is different from the first in every way. The president, fifty-year-old Victoria Gonzalez, lives in a brick house with flowers growing along a paved walk from the street. There are five or six books in a wall niche in the cool main room where five women have gathered to sew. Each has come from a different village with its own customs and culture, but the women are close. Three have been friends for thirty-one years. All their husbands work, though inconsistently, as a mason, a steel salesman, a civil servant, a radio technician, and a car painter.

These women are known to be the best *arpillera* makers of the four CIAP groups. They are experienced and comparatively educated. Their stitchery is fine; their *arpilleras* are complex compositions that use perspective, subtle colors, and sophisticated design ideas such as three-dimensional river grasses whose reflections are embroidered on the water's surface. But good design and workmanship do not improve revenue. Each woman will net only about a dollar and a half a day if she can sell a wall hanging to a wholesaler for fifteen dollars. We are taken aback at this information; the usual retail price in the United States for an *arpillera* wall hanging is sixty dollars.

Graciela Magan is not as worried about net profit as about the fact that the women's income is inconsistent. "We get one order now, another one in a couple of months." CIAP's goal is to get enough orders to sustain the women full-time so they can survive on their revenue if necessary.

One reason the women's cash flow is uneven is that the *arpillera* market is reaching saturation, so CIAP has initiated a new product development contest. The Avecitas are already planning to meet the first Monday in May to begin samples of their ideas. They hope to win the one-hundred-dollar prize that will be awarded in July. We are privileged to preview some of their entries: *arpillera*-decorated pot holders and note cards.

THESE WOMEN ARE NOT WELL-OFF, but they have the luxury of thinking of more than survival. For example, they know that their *arpilleras* are a historical record. Victoria shows us wall hangings they made twenty years ago, which are rougher, more political, and stylistically livelier, with naive, brighter colors. "This shows the men rioting. We were already here in Lima, remembering the political situation in our villages before we left," she explains.

Rita Serapión has gone back to high school herself, now that her daughters are through their professional schools (one is a nurse, the other an elementary school teacher), and she will graduate this year. Originally from Iquitos in the Amazon jungle, Rita recently helped document the lives of the Lima women who sew *arpilleras* in the book *Creative Women of Pamplona*, which, like the *arpilleras* themselves, chronicles the craftswomen's lives. Rita is one of the few craftswomen who speaks analytically, abstractly, and articulately about her relationship to her art. "The more we work, the more creativity we find in ourselves," she muses. "In the beginning, I never thought the *arpilleras* would help me in my life. But this is an art that has no ending. We are always trying to renew our ideas. We are very proud that our pieces are appreciated and sold. The fact that they are exported is a big compensation: it animates us. We all have a little art in our minds and in our hands; we will leave something as a legacy for society. It will stay behind us, in another place, in another time."

Opposite: Arpillera makers in groups run by Central Interregional de Artesanos del Peru meet weekly in homes to work and study sewing, as well as reading and writing, so they can sign their own contracts. The various materials used to build walls indicate a homeowner's economic progress.

Yasmina

OUR SIX-SEATER PLANE heads east from urban Panama City at four in the morning and clears the Darién jungle by dawn. We reflect on a potpourri of facts we have read about the Kuna Indians. They believe they are "Golden People" who come from the Great Mother. They are egalitarian, interested in beauty, balance, and using nature's gifts well. Columbus reported seeing them in 1502. They are supposed to be the shortest people on earth after the pygmies.

Among the few indigenous American ethnic groups who have never been conquered, they maintain an autonomous, traditional way of life on their ancestral lands, which, until twenty years ago, visitors were not allowed to enter and Kuna women were forbidden to leave. In the Kuna cosmos, everything in the world—natural, cultural, or spiritual—is allocated by gender. Virtually every Kuna woman sews *molas* and talented *mola* makers win great prestige for their families and communities. *Molas*—intricate layered and appliquéd pictures of Kuna Indian material culture, rituals, and social and political life—are sewn with skill, charm, and wit, then used as blouse panels, part of these women's gaily-colored outfits, which are unique on earth.

As we fly over the Caribbean San Blas archipelago, each island is a haven of palm trees in a sea turned peach by the rising sun. Abruptly, the plane lands on an old airstrip built on the mainland by the U.S. military. We trundle our bags and photographic equipment a hundred feet to the water's edge where a boatman with a rough deep mahogany canoe waits to take us to Uagitupo, on Dolphin Island.

THE NEXT DAY, we are put on trial on nearby Aligandi Island to determine whether we deserve permission to interview and photograph *mola* makers. The *congreso*, a sixty-by-forty-foot thatch-roofed hut, is the center of village affairs. There, citizens participate in all-day meetings for as long as they have time and interest. Benches form a theater-in-the-round, encircling the *sahilas* (deputy chiefs), who recline in suspended hammocks while governing. Usually these men smoke cigarettes during debates and wear trilby hats with dented crowns, which are the insignia of their office.

The rhythmic monologues that *sahilas* deliver during meetings are the men's art—just as *molas* are women's. We are not appropriately appreciative of the men's oratory, however; we are daunted by the fact that they are not inclined to grant us permission to do our work.

The *sahilas* are tired, they say, of foreigners who write books without crediting their Kuna informants, and who publish inaccurate information about Kuna culture. "Many people write lies. We are an independent people who govern our own territory. We are educated, and have doctors, lawyers, and people who have gone to Europe to study; Kunas place a premium on education and often travel elsewhere to obtain it. When the schooling is complete, they always return to their original island. Our history is profound. Information should come from our *sahilas*, not from superficial, lay sources."

To no apparent avail we explain through our interpreter that we are as interested in truth as the Kuna are. After about an hour, it looks as if we will be banished from the territory without seeing, interviewing, or photographing even one *mola* maker. Then, without transition or explanation, the senior *sahila*, Julio Benitez Coleman, smiles: "You have listened to us long enough." He then escorts us personally around Aligandi Island, leading us through labyrinthine footpaths between the thatched huts.

OUR FIRST STOP is a free public school, part of the National Culture Institute. A new term is just beginning and students have come to learn indigenous crafts such as pottery, hammock making, basket weaving, and of course, *mola* making.

Tirsia Fernandez, forty-nine, teaches young girls to sew *molas* the way she herself learned when she was eight. Ten little girls are working diligently on their first *molas*, which may take a month to complete. Their mothers use reverse appliqué techniques, stacking colored fabric, then cutting slashes in the top layer to outline the pattern and pulling the lower colors to the top; they add even more colors on top using traditional appliqué techniques. But the little girls are starting with just two layers of fabric. They have cut the pattern in the top piece and are sewing with big stitches that will be ripped out and redone until they are correct.

Previous pages: Kuna Indian women's outfits are unique: beaded leg and arm cuffs, patterned sarong skirts, red print headscarves, and blouses with *mola* (appliquéd picture) panels, which are sometimes offered separately for sale.

Opposite: Yasmina Eloina De La Ossa Tejada, a savvy entrepreneur and talented craftswoman, sells *molas* that she and the other women in her family create.

While they concentrate, Tirsia is creating a sophisticated *mola*, which we ask her to describe. She explains that while Kuna men are responsible for public oratory, Kuna women are responsible for lamenting death. Her *mola* shows that tradition. "The parents are in the hammock with their dead baby. The woman standing by them is showing them how to grieve. It is Kuna tradition that women weep and recite the accomplishments of the deceased. But with a baby, we must teach each other how to mourn. The right way is to express your sadness by weeping, and narrate the baby's life to date, then talk about what the baby's accomplishments might have been if he had grown up."

We ask if many babies die here. "Many babies used to die, but not now. Now nutrition is better and we have a good hospital."

IN THE AFTERNOON, we travel by canoe back past uninhabited white sand islets floating in teal water to Dolphin Island to talk with the beautiful Yasmina Eloina De La Ossa Tejada, thirty-one. Her love story reminds us of Romeo and Juliet. When Yasmina's family sent her to Nargana Island, one hour north, to attend the first two years of high school, she fell deeply in love with her teacher's son, Eric. Later, after Yasmina had finished two years of sewing school in Panama City, Yasmina and Eric were married. Since Kuna society is matrilocal—husbands move in with their wives' families—the couple returned to Yasmina's parents' home to start their lives together.

Not so fast, said fate. Yasmina's parents held traditional Kuna beliefs about what husbands should be like, and Eric didn't qualify by those standards. He was not from their island. He had neither land nor coconuts, the assets required to support a family. He was a policeman, not a farmer who could help Yasmina's father. To her parents, Eric was not an acceptable son-in-law.

Yet Yasmina and Eric adored each other and managed to live together for three years. They "never had an argument," and had two children, Eric and Erica, both named by their romantic mother.

Yasmina's parents became increasingly insistent that they separate. Her brother-in-law, Geronimo De La Ossa,

reports, "Her father has the old mentality. He criticized Yasmina for marrying this man. Finally, her husband said, 'I love you, you are my wife, but I must leave.'" Eric is now a policeman in Panama City. The couple yearns for a way to be reunited. Although Eric contributes financially to his family, Yasmina is now the single mother of their two children, ages four and seven. She sews and sells *molas*, and works part time at the Dolphin Island Lodge, which is run by Geronimo. The resort is one of very few places visitors can stay in the 138-mile-long, 378-island chain. Yasmina is the resort's hostess, and does everything from serving meals to guiding guests around the islands she knows so well.

After lunch one day, Yasmina spreads out *molas* to tempt guests to buy the work that she and the other women in her family have created. The patterns are based on daily life and show fish, boats, and lobsters; recent history, including the 1969 aqueduct opening and political campaigns; and aspects of popular culture including Ninja Turtles and package label designs. *Molas* that retail in the United States for sixty dollars are offered here for fifteen to thirty-five dollars, good prices for both buyer and seller.

Kuna women manage family money whether they earn it or not, Yasmina tells us. "The men sell coconuts, then buy cigarettes and whatever they need and give the rest of their money to their wives. In old times, the women used to put coins in a box around their neck. When they went dancing, the coins jangled."

As we talk about business with Yasmina, it becomes apparent that she is unusual among the women we have interviewed: a savvy entrepreneur whose expertise, enterprising nature, and focus have made her a financial success in her community.

When she was a nineteen-year-old sewing student in Panama City, Yasmina launched her first venture. "I had never seen *molas* on skirts; I made that idea up out of my own head. They were the first things I ever sold. I charged ten dollars for a black skirt with a round, colorful *mola* that took a week to make. My friends' mothers bought them."

Now that she is an adult, her financial skills have matured. "If I sell two or three *mola* blouses, my income

Opposite: Using both reverse and regular appliqué techniques, *mola* makers stack colored cloth, slash the pattern through the layers, pull the lower colors to the top, then stitch additional pieces on the surface. Kuna girls learn this art when they are about eight.

is ninety dollars a month," she says. She tells us that she invests what she earns in jewelry, which she can easily pawn when she needs funds. Today, Yasmina wears a beautiful necklace with dangling gold dolphins.

But jewelry is not all she owns. "I bought my grandmother's land," Yasmina tells us, "because I didn't want more arguments in our family. My father had renounced the property, and because I have five sisters and two brothers, there could easily have been fights about inheritance. Since I wanted the land, I offered my grandmother a hundred and fifty dollars and she accepted. Later, I arranged to buy ten of my grandfather's coconut trees for five dollars each. They are valuable. The traders who come here from Cartagena, Colombia, pay twelve cents for one coconut. Local people pay twenty-five cents for half a coconut leaf, and they need hundreds of leaves to make a roof that lasts fifteen years. When you buy coconut trees, you get the land under them automatically. I built a house and lived on that land for three years."

Over time, Yasmina invested four hundred dollars in five plots of land that have now been appraised at ten to fifteen thousand dollars. No other woman on the island comes close to owning this amount of property. "The others don't save, " Yasmina observes. "They purchase *molas* to wear instead of sewing them. That's squandering money." Later, she shows us a fenced plot she has loaned to the elementary school this year so the eight- and nine-year-olds can learn science by growing tomatoes, oranges, and lemons as if they had a little farm.

Yasmina sells the same *molas* she makes and wears on her own blouses, so there is a qualitative difference between her sophisticated designs and fine workmanship and those of the women who make *molas* expressly for sale to tourists. Most tourist *molas* have coarse (or worse, machine) stitching and artless motifs.

As we interview Yasmina, she sews with painstakingly small, even stitches, using many layers of colored fabric in her appliqué. We ask why we see no knots in her work. Without waiting for our English to be translated, Yasmina responds in Spanish, "We just cut the thread and fold it between the fabric layers." Noticing our sur-

prise that she understood our question, she admits, "I understand a little English."

She understands many other things too—including strategy. When we play cards after dinner, she beats the socks off us.

ROSA MARTINEZ (Geronimo's half sister on his father's side) is recycling her *winis*, the beaded cuffs that Kuna women wear on their arms and legs and change every two months. She sits by a black caldron where lobster is cooking for dinner. Her familiar, a green macaw who follows her like a puppy, keeps her company.

Rosa uses rubbery tree sap to attach the old string to a new one, then slides the beads from one string to the other. "It takes an entire ball of string to cover two legs and two arms with beads," she says, but allows that "If women don't have enough time to put on their own *winis*, they pay four dollars to have someone else apply them."

YASMINA, too, is changing her *winis* today. We sit with her all afternoon while she wraps a long bead strand around and around one leg until a Greek key–like design appears and repeats from ankle to knee. It will take her eight more hours after dinner to restring and rewrap the bead patterns on her other leg and both arms.

While Yasmina restrings beads, we confirm whether the things we have read about Kunas are right or, as the Aligandi *sahilas* implied, lies. Did Yasmina have a haircutting ceremony? "Yes, when I was eight or nine. After that ceremony, Kuna girls never wear long hair again. We believe that the head-first trip down the birth canal makes an infant's hair unclean; if you don't have a haircutting ceremony for purification before you are grown, you cannot enter God's kingdom when you die. If their parents can afford it, all girls have this ceremony sometime after the age of two, but always before puberty. It used to be that everyone in a village attended. People contributed ten fish, firewood, plantains, everything that was required to feed the village for a ceremony that lasted three days and nights. But now some villages have fifteen hundred inhabitants, so community haircutting rituals are no longer affordable."

Opposite: Molas show material culture, rituals, and political events. No two designs are identical, even when subjects are similar. Boats and fish, essential to daily life, appear often.

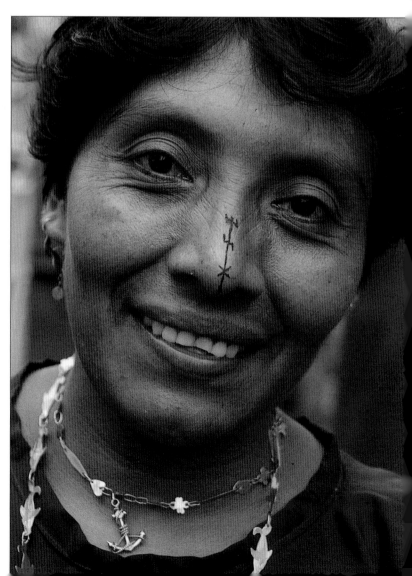

KUNA WOMEN'S FASHIONS

Before Geronimo recounts the history of Kuna women's apparel he assures us, "My father was a sahila *and taught me history, so what I will tell you is true.*

"Kicadiryay, the sister of Ibeorkun—the ancient forefather who invented our architecture and tools—invented beautiful fashions for Kuna women. She dressed a doll so she could see the whole effect. She designed a blouse with puffed sleeves, a yoke, and a flounce of printed material, and molas *as the lower panels in the front and back. Her* molas *were only geometric patterns: simple, strong designs.*

"After the blouses, she created red and yellow headscarves, wrapped skirts, beaded leggings and arm wraps, which are called winis. *But there was still something missing. She added the gold nose ring, earrings, three or four finger rings, and a gold breastplate, which women wear if there is money from coconuts to buy enough gold.*

"Kicadiryay could add nothing more. We believe the Holy Spirit touched her. Nowhere else in the world will you find women dressed like this. After puberty, Kuna women dress just as Kicadiryay planned—even today, when boys and men wear shorts and T-shirts."

Geronimo waves one hand to signal that he intends to backtrack. "Let's go back to the molas. *In 1940, the government founded schools. Molas evolved away from the original geometric designs because the children saw pictures in books. Molas began to reflect inventions like the phonograph, airplanes, and parachutes. When Kuna men worked on the Panama Canal during the war, new images found their way into* molas: *the Kool cigarettes penguin, Bugs Bunny, canned goods, and liquor labels.*

"In the 1950s, Panamanian and international tourism began. Visitors bought molas. *Today, some women earn from ten dollars to two hundred dollars selling* molas *that might take one to six weeks to complete. Our economy depends on lobsters, coconuts, and* molas, *which twenty thousand Kuna women sew. Maybe there are more, counting the young girls.*

"Some men, all under forty, are learning to make molas *from their wives, and even wear* molas *on their shirts. Older men think these guys are sissies, and don't like to see tradition change. I am one of those men," Geronimo admits. "Molas are for women."*

Yasmina is deftly wrapping the bead strand round and round her ankle. I tell her that we have read that *mola* makers sometimes soak leaves in water and put them on their eyes to help them visualize new designs.

"Yes. Sappi Karta is a sacred tree whose leaves are patterned with concentric circles by a fungal parasite. They look as if someone has drawn on them. The elders use the leaves as botanical medicine and put them on the eyes to provide inspiration for *molas*. The *puba* [soul] of the leaves helps women make beautiful *molas*. When children go to school, they sometimes receive that same medicine to help them gain knowledge. My son has had

Sappi Karta, but since he just started school, we have not yet seen an effect."

THE NEXT MORNING, we go with Yasmina to see her children at home, across the channel on Achutupo, on Dog Island. A crowd of children flies toward Yasmina as soon as our dugout canoe is made fast. She grabs her son and daughter in great hugs, and the other children on the welcoming committee spin ahead of us doing cartwheels and handstands in the sand.

Yasmina's one-room hut is part of her parent's compound, a cluster of relatives' huts and yards connected

Opposite: **Yasmina paints a cosmetic design using a fine stick to apply a mixture of charcoal powder and nut juice. She creates a similar design for her daughter (whose nose is reflected in the mirror, top left).**

Uagitupo looks like all the other gem-like islands as we approach by motorized dugout: palm trees swaying in the breezes over clustered huts of thatch are heart-stoppingly beautiful. But Geronimo's Dolphin Island Lodge, his little tropical outdoor inn, is not just any Kuna village. Its huts sit on concrete pads, nice for keeping the sand out of one's belongings; there is a shower in our hut for refreshingly frigid bathing (no hot water); there are real flushing toilets; and beds. The Kunas sleep in hammocks. We do have hammocks on our porch, where we can sneak a delicious nap in the breeze before dinner.

The lodge is tiny, with just four guest huts, an open-sided dining hall facing the beach, and a cookhouse, where the resident blue macaw lingers on the step, panhandling snacks from the camp cook. Outside in the clean-swept central yard rise a half-dozen splendid palms, and between them are stretched more hammocks. They are woven stripes of vibrant colors, each one with a different dominant hue, stretched in bright diagonals from tree to tree.

We get to know our fellow guests during a leisurely postprandial chat around the long table, then wander out for further relaxation in those palm-grove hammocks—and find that they have been rearranged into a different Hockney-esque abstract (the yellow one here and the red one there). When we get up in the morning, the composition is different yet again.

And then I catch him at it! It is that one young fellow who works here, the albino. It seems to be his job to take down all the hammocks whenever it looks like rain, then put them up again. And whether accidentally or by design, he does it differently each time, to stunning artistic effect.

An albino is very noticeable in an Indian community, and our notice of this boy has been almost painful. The sun is very, very hot and strong here, and he has no natural protection. During our stay, he ferries us from island to island, and never wears a hat, or sunglasses, or even a shirt! We yearn to leap up and smear sunblock all over him. He never touches the stuff, just accepts the fried shoulders and blistered lips.

We aren't the only ones concerned for him. One of the other Dolphin Island guests is a Frenchwoman, Dr. Pascale Jeambrun, a lovely person who is a doctor and specialist in albinism. She has been here before and has returned to continue her research on the subject, because in this unlikely little corner of the world, as in a few others—the Hopi and Zuni communities of the American Southwest, for instance—the incidence of albinism is extraordinary. One in every eighty-five Kuna babies is born albino.

This does not worry the Kunas. When a baby is born albino here, born into a brown-skinned world but glowingly white as if lit from within, the Kunas believe they have produced an angel, and they rejoice. Pascale calls those pale little babies "les enfants de la lune."

Albinos have special mythic powers and responsibilities here. For instance, when the terrible flying dog attacks the sun and attempts to take a bite out of it, producing what we would call an eclipse, only an albino has the power to shoot it down and thus save the sun. There is a favorite traditional mola design: an albino with bow and arrow taking careful aim at the mythical flying dog.

T. SAN BLAS ISLANDS, PANAMA

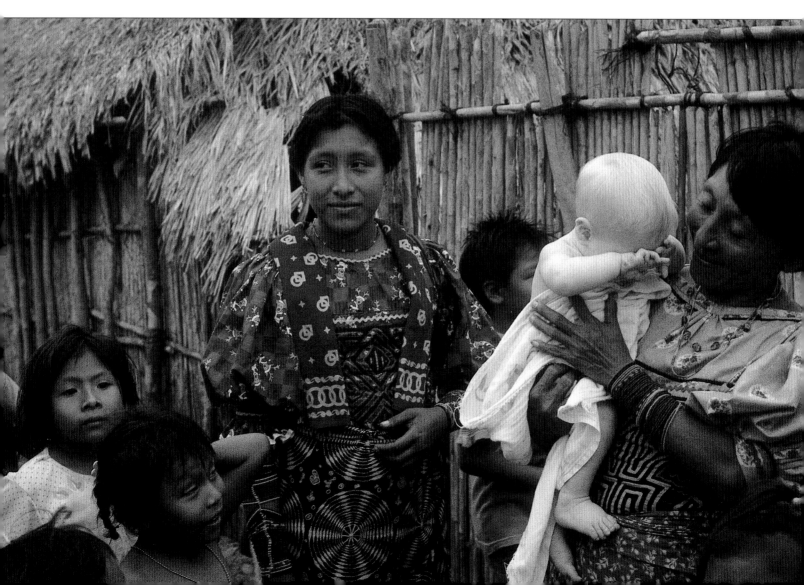

with bamboo fencing. Adjacency makes it easy for Yasmina's mother to take care of Eric and Erica while Yasmina works on the neighboring island.

Yasmina typically rises early to make meals, wash, and sew, then goes to the *congreso* in the afternoon—but today is unusual. This morning, women relatives drop in to participate in the Kuna equivalent of an Avon Party. To make a cosmetic paint, Yasmina crushes charcoal with a machete and mixes it with the juice of a nut she picks from a tree. Each woman uses a fine stick to apply the dark liquid, making a filigree pattern that runs the full length of her nose. As soon as Yasmina finishes her own design, she paints her daughter's nose—and then both of ours. Unbeknownst to us, the black lines are semi-permanent; five days later, customs officials will observe us with curiosity as we enter our country with Yasmina's designs spiraling down our noses.

BACK AT DOLPHIN ISLAND LODGE that afternoon, Yasmina's older sister, Mariela, shows us her newest *mola* designs while she tells us how she met her husband, Geronimo.

"It's different today. As you know, Yasmina followed her heart, but when it was my turn, our father looked for a husband who had a farm so he could support me. He negotiated and bargained. Geronimo's parents, seeing that my father was honest and had resources, accepted.

"At that time, I was thirteen and Geronimo was twenty-five. I was old enough to be married because I had had my puberty ceremony, but I protested that I was too young. It didn't help. My father wanted me to marry him. I was innocent; I didn't know what sex was. There was no sex education in school in those days, and it was completely forbidden—against God's law—to teach young girls about sex. My grandmother told me how to make love. My mother told me that Geronimo was an old man, and then I was even more afraid." With all those reservations, we wonder what her wedding was like.

"The ceremony is the same today. As soon as the families agree to the marriage, they pick ten men who, on the wedding day, grab the groom by the leg, the hair, whatever, and bring him to the girl's house. They put the groom in the hammock. One of the guys gets a stick of firewood and puts it under the hammock while another goes off to look for the girl, who is sitting next to the kitchen. The guy picks her up and puts her on top of the fiancé in the hammock. The ten men start swinging them and singing a song: 'She will always be in the kitchen cooking smoked fish and plantain and will always serve food for her husband.' The girl jumps out of the hammock. Then the ten men and the bride bathe themselves. The next night, the bride and her father bring the groom to the bride's house. The groom must prove himself to his new father-in-law by cutting one hundred pieces of firewood with an ax and catching enough fish for the whole family. If he can do this, there is a party for everyone who participated in the wedding. There is no honeymoon, but after that, the bride and groom get to spend time together alone."

Geronimo grins, "Now we've been married thirty-five years, have five children, and everyone realizes that I have been perfect." Mariela just smiles.

HERE, TRADITIONAL and contemporary life make a piquant counterpoint. For hundreds of years, the Kuna have participated in world commerce. They are a sophisticated, cosmopolitan people who integrate foreign influences when it serves them, who combine old and new comfortably, yet who vigilantly protect their cultural heritage.

On Mamitupo Island one of the teachers has used a twelve-volt battery to jerry-rig a television set so students can watch educational programming. The lonely, anomalous antenna reaches high over the soft roofs of the village.

On Aligandi Island the public library showcases a chess tournament prize. A modern hospital is well staffed and immaculate. Both buildings are near the *congreso* hut, where governing is done from hammocks.

On Achutupo Island Yasmina has mounted a basketball hoop on the bamboo fence that surrounds her hut so her son can practice. Old and new coexist in layers and patterns as complex as *molas*.

Previous pages: **Not only are hammocks used instead of beds, Kuna *sahilas* (deputy chiefs) sit in them to conduct town meetings and weddings occur when grooms-men swing a couple in them.**

Opposite, top: **Yasmina named Erica for Eric, her adored husband whom her parents rejected; he came from another island and was not a coconut farmer.**

Opposite, bottom: **One in eighty-five Kuna babies is albino, believed to be an angel with the power to prevent eclipses of the sun.**

and the Flower Painters

FOUR WOMEN WHO GREW UP HERE in Zalipie, a farming village on the Vistula river in south-eastern Poland, begin to sing:

Zalipie flowers! I grew up among you;
You used to be my colored world
Upon the white wall with a low roof.
I often return to you in my memories...
To painted cottages upon the Vistula.
Like mother's love through childhood years.

We are in the office at the House of Painters. While Zofia, Stasia, Renata, and Wanda sing about childhood, Renata's four-year-old, Gregorz, rolls a leaf into the manual typewriter and pretends to write a letter. He has spent most of his young life playing in this building where his mother, aunt, and grandmother paint products to sell.

Zalipie's women painters cover their houses inside and out with floral designs. They paint flowers on stoves, coffeepots, plates, aprons, tablecloths, cabinets, windows, fences, chicken coops, barns, privies, tarpaulins, and dog houses. They paint wreaths on the ceiling, garlands on the beams, floral swags under holy pictures. They have even painted blossoms on the town fire truck.

Thanks to a grant from the regional government in Tarnów, the women artists opened the House of Painters in 1977. It is the cultural center of Zalipie, with painted bouquets crowding its glass doors, its windows, and its corridors. Its theater holds dance recitals, musical competitions, and puppet shows; there is a library full of books about Polish culture; and there are classrooms where children learn floral painting.

THE TRADITION OF FLORAL PAINTING began here in the 1800s when village women brightened the walls of their two-room cottages. Originally, their brushes were birch sticks shredded at one end. They used lime to paint white dots on walls that were dark with soot because their ovens, used for cooking and heating, had no chimneys. Over time, the women began to use color to convert the white dots to daisies, peonies, cosmos, roses, lupines, and bachelor buttons like those in their fields and gardens.

By the twentieth century the advent of chimneys and whitewash gave the painters a clean palette for their creativity. They had learned to bundle cow or horse hair to make finer brushes, and flowers remained their visual vocabulary. Grandmothers taught the floral art to daughters and granddaughters. Felicja Curylo, who died at seventy in 1974, popularized the Zalipie flower art. After her death, the Ethnographic Museum in Tarnów made her home a museum. Felicja's granddaughter, Wanda Racia, herself a painter, grew up across the street and is now the museum curator. When visitors arrive, Wanda crosses the road, opens the gate, and unlocks the door.

Felicja Curylo's family, like all peasant cottage dwellers, used one room for secular and the other for sacred activities. The latter room includes a little gallery of religious pictures: Jesus and Mary, plus saints, such as Rosalie, who protects families from illness, and Florian, who protects homes from fire. The other room includes a profusion of painted flowers on walls, stairsteps, and ceilings; crocheted floral bedspreads and embroidered floral pillows; floral valences cut from paper; floral wallpapers; and flower-seed collages of the Polish national emblem, the eagle.

ALTHOUGH FLORAL PAINTING is also done in six neighboring villages, Zalipie's painting has become more innovative, individual, and nuanced because of juried springtime competitions that have encouraged experimentation and improvement for the past fifty years. Each winter the painters create new art to enter in the contest. They begin sketching in secret, eager to surprise their rivals and win one of the twenty category prizes. Although they compete enthusiastically, the painters respect and like each other. Of the eight hundred Zalipie residents, there are seventy painters—more than ever before. They are a close community of creative friends and relatives.

RECENTLY LIBERATED from Communism, the village women are beginning to sell what they create at prices they set themselves, hoping to supplement their

Previous pages: **One of seventy floral artists in Zalipie, Zofia Owca models the traditional festival costume she embroidered while she paints flowers by her front door.**

Opposite: **Maria Sierak's skill shows in her valences and curtains. Having won many painting competitions, she took first prize in the "new style" category at age seventy-five.**

families' farming incomes. During the months between harvest and planting seasons, the women gather by the stove at the House of Painters to paint flowers on vases, garlic keepers, piggy banks, door chimes, and souvenirs.

We ask how life in Zalipie has been affected by capitalism and are told, "Not much has changed. Things are more expensive. There are a few more products in the store."

We visit the store and meet Jan, a man who painted houses in Chicago for four years, then returned to Zalipie and built a modern, two-story house with a market in its garage. His wife has painted a blossom border on the walls above the shelves of liquor, canned goods, and boxed foods. Jan wears a baseball cap left over from a Lipton Tea promotion to grocers. The slogan on his hat says, in English, "Cooking Up Profits," which seems at once admirably aggressive and hopelessly anomalous.

THE HOUSE OF PAINTERS tries to help the women artists profit, too. The organization buys raw materials—pigments, brushes, items the women can decorate—then buys all the work the artists produce. Artists each receive the same money for finished products of like size. This vestige of the Communist compensation system assumes that everyone's work is equally valuable. Only privately do the painters confess that they know they are variously talented.

Wanda Chlastawa has managed the House of Painters for seventeen years. She studied culture and tourism for two years in college, and now organizes special events such as the September Harvest Festival, which will take place in a few weeks. She coordinates classes in dance, music, and art, purchases equipment and supplies, and markets the artists' products.

It is not as easy as one might think. There is a display showroom in the House of Painters where tourists could buy, "but only about five tourists come here on a good day," Wanda confides.

It is an understatement to say that Zalipie is not a tourist destination. It took us four hours to find our way from Tarnów, which is thirty miles away. Zalipie hides in a labyrinth of country roads and has no hotel, no restaurant, and in fact, no commercial district. Fields and miles

separate the painted cottages and there are no guides to help visitors find them.

Zalipie painters participated in the International Trade Fairs in Munich and Vienna in 1995 and 1996. They show their wares in the pre-Christmas exhibition in Pilzno. They also accept group commissions, as they have done for years; their mothers painted a hall in Cracow's Ethnographic Museum.

Those same women also painted the interior of the Catholic parish church in Zalipie, where each high arch is outlined with a braid of painted forget-me-nots. Felicja Curylo herself painted the flowers of the baptismal font, and talented women embroiderers in Felicja's group stitched flower designs for the priest's vestments.

Now, a shy nun invites us into the sacristy to see the holiday ecclesiastical attire. Glossy pink-and-white chrysanthemums form a stark cross on a field of black velvet. Crimson poinsettias duplicate the symbol on a field of kelly-green satin. A Madonna and Child are embroidered on midnight blue, surrounded by blossoms. The variety of embroidery patterns seems endless, each more lavish and beautiful than the one before.

ZOFIA OWCA, fifty-five, has been painting for thirty-four years and embroiders equally well. Her work is technically and artistically impressive. She worked every day for a month to complete her traditional floral waistcoat. Although costumes like this are worn for festivals and special occasions, Zofia has just worn hers to tape a Cracow television show during which she painted flowers on the studio wall to promote Zalipie. We watch the tape in a neighboring village on the only VCR around.

On the show, Zofia wears her embroidered vest laced with ribbons, a painted apron, a floral-print challis skirt, and a ruffled white blouse. She looks as if she lives in 1850. She has been scheduled on the television show as the representative of tradition, along with the Paper Bags, a shirtless, pony-tailed rock group that represents contemporary Polish culture. Every once in a while as she paints, Zofia glances surreptitiously and very skeptically over her shoulder at the gyrating youth. We can't help laughing out loud. Zofia and the Paper Bags personify the generation gap.

Opposite: **Although women in the 1800s painted blossoms on the sooty walls of their cottages to brighten the dark interiors, women today paint** bouquets on home accessories and souvenirs to sell at the House of Painters. The two vases were painted by Stasia Curylo.

My friend and collaborator, Paola, is such a scaredy-cat. She thinks I should be a lot more conscientious about all those traveler concerns—water, strangers, money belts, food, documents, dengue fever, robbery, rape, and murder. I say she's conscientious enough for any three people, and give her a hard time about it.

As darkness falls on the House of Painters, the night we've arrived in Zalipie, Paola and I, along with Barbara (our interpreter from the Peace Corps), are shown to the guestroom. The women are very proud that their community craft center can offer accommodation. We immediately dub it "the infirmary," it's so like all the summer-camp infirmaries of our childhoods: clean, white, and bare-bones simple, with four little cots all in a row.

Paola has made certain that the door to our room is locked, even though our hostesses have locked the building, leaving us with the whole place to ourselves. The building at night is very big, and dark, and empty—not to mention cold. (We've arrived a week before the scheduled date for turning on the Zalipie heating system. A schedule is a schedule, never mind the near-freezing temperature.) And the bathroom is about a quarter-mile down dark, winding hallways. But we're fine. And Paola is comfortable because our door is locked.

Suddenly I'm awake. Something's rattling. It's the door. What could make the door rattle? It's the latch! Somebody is actually rattling the latch

of our door, inside our big, dark, locked building. Can't be—must be—can't be. My insides are all aquiver, and it's fearless Toby who is whisper-shrieking, "Paola! Wake up! Somebody's trying to get in here!"

Now she's awake, too scared to bother with "I told you so!" We whisper back and forth with no useful ideas, then begin trying to rouse Barbara, who can only wake up enough to give us a muffled, "Don't be silly."

She who talks a bold story must take bold action. So I get myself, quaking, over to the door and deliver a very firm and scary, "Who's out there? Get away. Now!"

Nothing for a second—and then the door rattles again, while I'm still standing right there! What nerve. So I bang on the door.

A tiny wee furry something wiggles under the door and darts across the floor.

"Oh, good grief, it's only a teensy field mouse. He's been rattling the door trying to squeeze under it." I sigh with relief, along with Paola—and then Barbara goes ballistic. "A mouse? Oh, no! Not a mouse. Ohmygod!"

Well, well! Three scaredy-cats . . . of slightly different stripes.

T. ZALIPIE, POLAND

We meet Zofia in her kitchen to enjoy coffee and heart-shaped chocolate-dipped shortbread cookies. We are eager to see this room, which is the envy of Zalipie. When we arrived in town, we asked which painter we should interview. The artists were confounded that we might interview only one when so many were equally talented. Then they agreed unequivocally that Zofia was the best candidate because her kitchen is most photogenic. Zofia's walls and tablecloth are painted with flowers; there are flowers growing in the window boxes; there are crepe-paper flowers in vases; even the cooking pots and pans are painted with blooms.

Zofia milks the cows, gives the barn cats a saucerful, and presents the kittens to her four-year-old grandson, Tomasz, to play with. She throws a pumpkin to the ground in the yard. It splits open on impact and becomes a meal for her geese. Then she puts finishing touches on a blue floral painting near her front door.

After a lunch of soup, we join her husband and neighbors working in the potato fields across the road. Poppies, miniature daisies, and other wildflowers tangle together at the edge of the road. After a week of rain, digging the potatoes has become an urgent priority. The neighbors collaborate, working in each other's fields until the harvest is over. A neighbor woman delivers the workers' midday meal: cheese, plums, tea, and sausages to roast with fresh potatoes on a fire built on the spot.

Zofia and her husband, Franciszek, have been married thirty-five years. He lived near Felicja Curylo's house when he and Zofia were growing up. As soon as Zofia arrives, he jumps up, teasing her about being interviewed for a book, and leads her in a little jig. Like the other husbands, he appreciates that his wife is an artisan. But when there are potatoes to dig, art waits.

Zofia's thirty-one-year-old daughter, Renata Kowal, has painted for twenty years, but she is not painting now because chemicals in the paint give her terrible headaches. Zofia encourages her, "One day you will paint again. Some company will surely develop paints that will not affect you." Meanwhile, Renata's self-esteem is intact, because she does not define herself by her work but rather by her feminine roles: "I am a daughter. I am a mother. I am a grandmother. *That* is life."

ALL OVER THE WORLD, compensation comes in many forms, including spiritual income and monetary income. Zalipie's women painters mostly receive spiritual income. The most industrious artist, Stanislowa (Stasia) Curylo, contributes less than twenty percent of her household budget.

Stasia signs all her work, as do her colleagues. A small vase she made is for sale at the House of Painters for six dollars. She paints three to five hours a day and earns about sixty cents an hour, twenty percent of which goes to taxes.

Now thirty-six, she has competed in eighteen of the thirty-three Zalipie competitions and has won many of them. Stasia has long used her talent to earn money, although there are many obstacles in the path to profits. At nineteen, she painted greeting cards for Cepelia, the government-owned folk art retailer, but the chain's prices were too low to pay for the full hour required to create every card. Later, she painted skirts, but textile paints are expensive and made the skirts too pricy to sell in volume.

Stasia hopes her children will go on to university, although most Poles attend school only until they are nineteen. Her ten-year-old, Michal, might like to be a lawyer. "Or a farmer like father," the boy pipes in, "or a flower painter." A male painter? We ask Stasia how she feels about that. "Long ago, one man did painting; Michal is not the first. And he has company. He is one of three boys in the children's class at the House of Painters."

IN 1993 FOUR PAINTERS, including Zofia and Stasia, were commissioned by Cracow's old town restaurant, Kawiarnia U. Zapiianek, to re-create the floral murals their mothers had painted two decades earlier. From mothers to daughters to granddaughters—and sons—this tradition has passed not only a skill, but also a joyful spirit born of creativity. And although the women wish they made more money, they feel gratified. "We paint for affection and memories," Zofia admits. Stasia agrees: "This is an art of the heart."

Previous pages: **Stefania Lalzynska painted flowers on her house, privy and potato cellar, well and water bucket, the tarpaulin that covers cement blocks, and the shrine near the road.**

Opposite, top: **Zofia and her husband, Franciszek, are potato farmers, as are most Zalipie residents. When they work with their neighbors to harvest the crop, time for art is scarce.**

Opposite, bottom: **Zalipie artists, inspired by flowers in their fields and gardens, paint poppies, daisies, cosmos, foxgloves, roses, and marigolds, like the ones Zofia picks here.**

DURING THE COMMUNIST OCCUPATION of Czechoslovakia, fine arts were virtually snuffed out. But women's crafts like painted Easter eggs were regarded as nonthreatening, apolitical. The Communist government even sent Ludmila Kocisova on cultural exchanges to Poland and Russia to demonstrate her art. She is still one of the best egg painters in the country, and her work is on display in the permanent collections at the Ethnographic Institute in Brno.

The Communists left power in 1989. These days, a playwright is president of the Czech Republic. Jugglers, mimes, musicians, and artists vie for attention in Prague's Old Town Square, and churches open their doors for public concerts on summer nights. Tourists from all over the world flood the lively capital city. And almost everyone goes home with at least one Easter egg painted on the fragile shell with bright, intricate designs, which costs about a dollar and a half.

"Vnorovy, with its three thousand people, is the only place in the world where, in each house, at least one woman paints Easter eggs. That has been true for over a hundred years," Michal Pavlas says as we drive through rolling fields of sunflowers, poppies, wheat, and corn toward Moravia, four hours southeast of Prague. Michal, twenty-eight, is a buyer for Ceska Lidova Remesla, galleries in Prague devoted to traditional Czech crafts. Ludmila paints only for the Ethnographic Institute and these shops.

"Each village has its own style of *kraslice* [Easter eggs]," Michal explains. "The women of Vnorovy created the batik technique for coloring eggs. Theirs are always white, yellow, red, and black combined in geometric and floral patterns.

"In ancient cults, the egg was a symbol of life," he continues. "People believed that eggs ensured a successful harvest and fertility. Decorating the eggs was meant to strengthen their magical power."

Ludmila Kocisova and Josef, her husband of forty-seven years, meet us at the door of their two-story home, where window boxes spill over with nasturtiums. Across the street is a field of plum trees that we soon discover provide the fruit for plum wine.

We take off our shoes at the door, as is the custom, and climb the steps to the living room. Ludmila asks if we would like a snack. She has prepared an entire platter of open-faced sandwiches—papery slices of ham layered in ruffles on fresh bread—as well as crunchy, just-pickled cucumbers and newly made plum wine.

We have been told that this is a conservative, formal society, so we are carefully subdued. We sometimes break the ice by showing our own family pictures. Ludmila gets her box of photographs to reciprocate. She spreads snapshots of Josef, their three sons, and their six grandchildren, as well as pictures of herself with people in costume at folk festivals in Warsaw and Moscow.

"In Moscow, I was allowed to see Lenin. Everyone wanted to see him, and police guarded his tomb. I thought it was a little crazy, but I looked. It seemed to me as if the shirt he was wearing was actually made in this country. To tell the truth, I didn't think he looked very healthy," she commented, eyes twinkling.

"I didn't want to be unethical—we weren't supposed to see how people lived—but I looked through the bushes along the road. They live in very small houses in Russia; they are very, very poor."

Ludmila began painting eggs when she was five. "I sold my first egg when I was seven or eight, about when I learned to write. I wrote the name of our national anthem on that egg and painted a picture of a small house. The design was not at all traditional. My sister took my egg to the market, and it was the first one that sold. An English woman bought it and so it went all the way home with her.

"My mother taught me how to make traditional designs and how to create my own. You know, no egg design is purely traditional; every single one is different, like snowflakes."

Talking about her mother leads Ludmila to fetch her mother's tools, which she still uses. And that leads to a demonstration. She melts a mixture of beeswax and candlewax in a spoon suspended above a candle. Her special pen is made from a thin metal sheet rolled into a cylinder to hold wax for painting. She begins drawing a design on the blown white egg.

Previous pages: **Ludmila Kocisova, whose eggs are in the permanent collections of the Ethnographic Institute in Brno, has demonstrated the Czech Easter egg art in Russia and Poland.**

Opposite: **In ancient cults, the egg, a symbol of life, ensured good harvest and fertility. Decorating was believed to enhance an egg's power. Today, at least one woman in every house in Vnorovy paints eggs.**

"You begin painting in the middle of the egg, and duplicate the pattern as it progresses toward the ends. If you really want to see how beautiful painted eggs are, you must look down on them from one end.

"When you're done with the first wax designs, you dip the white egg in yellow dye; then you paint wax designs on top of the yellow and dip the egg in red; then you paint on top of the red and dip the egg in India ink. Only when you remove all these layers of wax do you see the whole design for the first time. It is a great painter's skill to imagine the whole design and create a wonderful egg. You must be very careful; every line in the whole design must be perfect."

Ludmila warms the eggshell over the flame, then rubs the now-black egg gently with a soft cloth to remove the wax and reveal a lacy, intricate pattern of circles and squares. As she had hoped, it is perfect.

Because Michal has come to pick up products for the store, it is time to do business. Ludmila approaches the wooden cabinet that runs the full length of her living room. For the first time, I notice that there are hundreds of painted eggs stored in egg cartons underneath the furniture. Michal and Ludmila sit on the floor and inspect the work. Ludmila will earn about sixty cents each for the elaborate egg designs and about fifty for the simpler ones.

Although Josef retired when he turned sixty, as most men do here, and although most women retire at fifty-five, Ludmila is still working at sixty-seven. "My work is also my hobby; I cannot imagine life without eggs. But the profit from them is not enough to live on, so I also make corn husk figures," she says. "And I teach egg painting to help keep the tradition alive. My students are old women who have retired, and young women who are pregnant. In those situations it is difficult to have enough money to live." Michal estimates that the average income for rural people is about forty-five dollars a month.

Ludmila appreciates the eggs' design history as much as their rituals. She picks up two eggs she has just finished. "This design is from the year 1895; this one, 1888. I wanted to bring forgotten traditional designs to life. It was difficult—I had to wait two years before the institute

researchers had time to help me. But now the designs are alive again and all is well."

Josef and Ludmila laughingly enact the traditional flirting that occurs at Easter time. "On the Monday after Easter, boys try to catch the girls they like by giving them a gentle tap with a willow switch decorated with ribbons. The next day, the girls do the same with the boys. The idea is that the power and health of the willow will make you strong. Each time the switch connects, another ribbon is tied to it, and the one who taps another gets a beautiful painted Easter egg."

Ludmila, who was reserved when we arrived, is now lively, relaxed, and full of stories, and clearly does not want us to leave. "I was so nervous last night that I didn't sleep at all, worrying about your visit," she volunteers. "When I was painting the eggs, I was afraid the lines would look wobbly in your pictures. But now I can't stop talking!" When we leave, I thank Ludmila and give her a good-bye hug—no longer improper, this is the affection of fast friends.

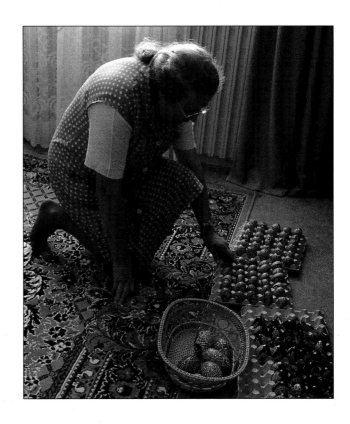

Above: Ludmila researched forgotten designs that were painted more than a hundred years ago and now she makes those in addition to the styles other contemporary painters create.

Opposite, clockwise from top left: Ludmila teaches the *kraslice* art to pregnant and retired women who would otherwise have no revenue; heating wax in a spoon over a candle,

she draws lines with wax then dips the egg in yellow dye • Czech Easter egg designs are unique to each town; these are made in Vnorovy, where Ludmila lives • She repeats the

process with red and black dyes, then heats the egg over the flame to remove the wax and see the design • Easter eggs from different towns display different patterns.

Dinah

and the Ndebele Bead Women

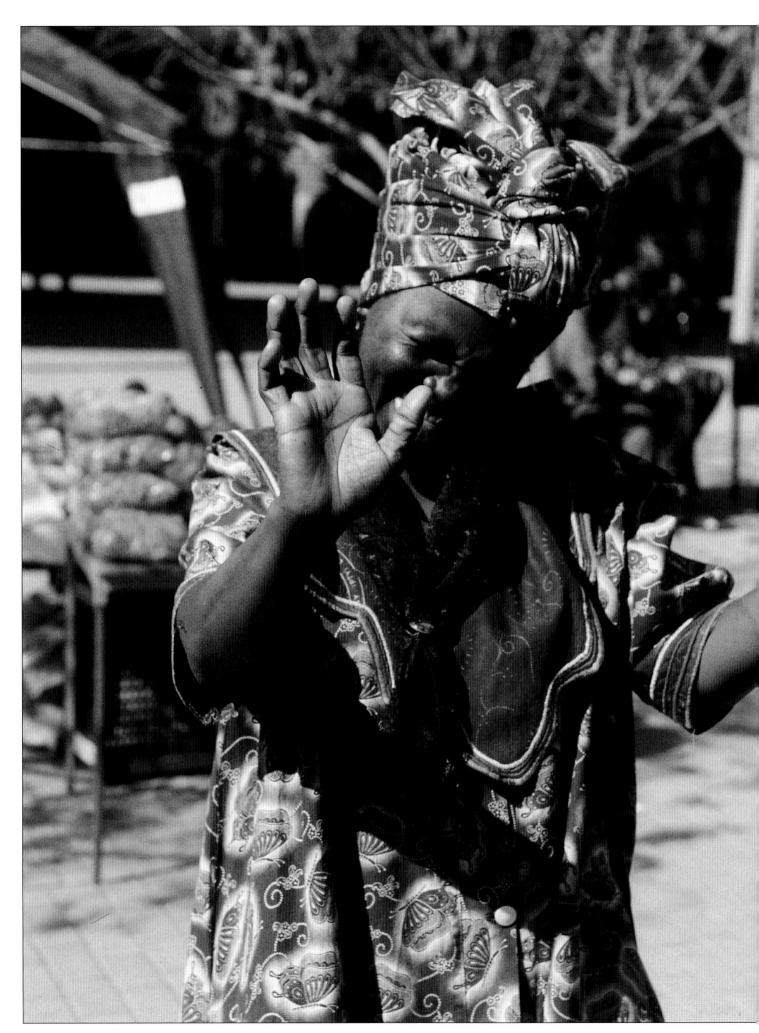

THE ROAD TO WELTEVREDE, which is three hours northeast of Johannesburg, cuts across prairies that look like Wyoming in November—bleached wheat fields, hills that open onto flat mesas, rock outcroppings—or California, with manzanita, live oaks, and rolling hills. Some towns have California names (Palm Springs, Menlo Park) and American stores (Kentucky Fried Chicken, Woolworth's). But most of this region could only be South Africa. Vendors sell bagged oranges at roadside stands and children sell roasted corn at stop signs. A funeral cortege walks through the treeless stubble to say good-bye amid the gravestones. One-room cement-block or corrugated-metal houses cluster on the flat, rust-colored earth.

Dinah Mahlangu, who leads a women's craft group in this KwaNdebele homeland, rides with us and talks about the region's history. Dutch and German settlers, whose descendants are referred to as Afrikaners, long held power here. Having tried three times to bring the Ndebele people under their control, in 1882 Afrikaners dynamited their food storage caves to starve them, killed their leaders, razed their crops, confiscated their land, and assigned them to five years of indentured labor—five years that, in fact, lasted over a century. Ndebele women reacted against the Afrikaners' efforts to decimate ethnic identity by resurrecting the distinctive beaded apparel that their foremothers began creating in the sixteenth century, when the Portuguese brought Czechoslovakian and Venetian beads to southern Africa to trade for slaves and ivory.

"I CANNOT APPROACH the King's palace without covering my shoulders with a blanket, or I will be charged one calf—and I don't have a calf," Dinah confesses as she stops to borrow a blanket near the impressive gate at Weltevrede.

We tour the royal *kraal* (compound). The king's mother and his five wives live in *rondavels* (thatched roof huts) that are covered with designs. The women of the kingdom have painted bold, colorful geometric patterns on every wall of the palace complex, designs that derive from patterns in Ndebele women's traditional beadwork.

Beadwork has influenced more than murals on palace walls; it is centrally important to Ndebele history, rituals, cultural and political identity, and commerce. A sequenced, beaded wardrobe marks the important events in a Ndebele woman's life. A single strand necklace is given at birth. An apron is worn until puberty and then a girl's mother makes a stiff front-apron for her initiation into womanhood. A back-skirt is worn after initiation to announce a woman's availability for marriage. A ceremonial apron, train, cape, and veil, or a blanket, are her bridal costume. A five-panel apron is worn after her first child is born, and two long strips that hang from a headband are worn when her sons are initiated and she has reached maturity.

Today, Ndebele people do not wear beaded clothing every day, and although traditional items are sold occasionally, the Bead Women's Club members specialize in dolls, jewelry, bead-handled brooms, mats, and trivets. Their products are marketed locally and internationally by Rural Crafts in Johannesburg, which is part of the National Crafts Association, a coalition whose low-income members are part of micro- to medium-size self-help craft businesses.

IN THE VILLAGE OF WATERVAL, wide, dusty roads are lined with two-room cement-block houses. There is a granary, a grocery, and a pool hall. The town barber, whose apron says "Black Like Me," is cutting a young woman's hair on his shop porch; three women wait, wearing wool skirts and sweaters.

Thirty women are sitting on the ground in the yard behind the Rural Crafts office, relaxing and gossiping and beading. They wear tennis shoes and cotton dresses. The married women wear their everyday blue plaid blankets and headscarves. We learn the local way to shake hands: clasp the hand, milk the thumb, and clasp the hand again, a method that reminds us of the hip handshakes of our own country. Later, we discover that Ndebele children shake differently; they reach right past our hands and grab our wrists.

Many of the women are beading doll aprons, blankets, and headdresses. Dolls play many roles in this culture. A Ndebele girl may wear a miniature doll pendant on a necklace to enhance her future fertility, or keep it hidden as a talisman to ensure that she will find a good husband. As she

Previous pages: To rekindle ethnic identity after Afrikaner efforts to decimate their group in 1882, Ndebele women resurrected the distinctive beadwork tradition their foremothers created.

Opposite: Dinah Mahlangu enjoys the "power, strength, and light" of opening a bank account for the Waterval Bead Women's Club to use to buy materials so they can make products to sell.

prepares to marry, she may take care of a new doll, whose name will become the name of her first child. If a couple is not able to conceive, sometimes initiation rites are repeated and the woman carries a doll as a surrogate child. Today, dolls also make money for Ndebele bead women.

A PLATOON OF EIGHTEEN- to twenty-one-year-old men run together down the dirt roads of Waterval, chanting, carrying staffs, and wearing loincloths and cere-monial blankets with wide stripes of crimson, green, royal blue, and yellow. They also wear tennis shoes. After three months, they have healed from their circumcisions, and their return from the bush is cause for great celebration.

"Each initiate's house is marked with a white flag," Dinah points out. "The group travels to the home of one initiate every day. His parents kill a cow and make a feast. They sleep there overnight, then go to the next house. They do not divide up until they are finished. This is the last day. The next initiation will not happen for three years."

The initiates halt in a large *kraal*, where they are joined by the elders who have been their spiritual guides and by Mr. David Mahlangu, king of the Ndebele tribe's Waterval branch.

By now, the young men have cast off their bright blankets and wear only loincloths and their mothers' beadwork. Elaborate multistrand necklaces overlap ropes of beads that cross both chest and back. Thick colored bracelets of beads cover their arms and legs, and they hold bead-covered scepters. They begin to sing, harmo-nizing and improvising with energetic, infectious chants. The older men direct the singing, brandishing shields and wearing breastplates of animal skin and fur.

July is winter here but pale pink blossoms cover the trees. The sky is sapphire, the day is exultant. The boys—now men—receive new names. They will never use their childhood names again.

Their mothers are in ritual mourning for children who have become men. Tomorrow the mothers will travel from house to house singing to the initiates' families, wearing "long tears," narrow beaded panels that cascade fifteen feet from beaded headbands, symbolizing both their sadness and their pride in their sons.

Opposite: When their grown sons return from initiation, Ndebele moth-ers wear beaded "long tears" to express both pride and sadness at their son's maturity.

We help the mothers dress for a rehearsal, watching with fascination as they sit winding ace bandages the full length of their legs, then wrapping them with cardboard, then pulling on the thick, beaded leg bracelets and stuffing foam rubber near their ankles to prevent chafing. A gymnastic maneuver is required to stand: the seated women twist to put their palms on the ground behind them, then turn over and walk stiff-legged until their legs are beneath them and they can stand.

They move like robots, but they are dignified and glorious, wrapped in traditional Ndebele ceremonial blankets and carrying beaded scepters. Their music combines chanting and singing, whistling and laughing, ululation and jubilation.

IN ADDITION TO SPEAKING NDEBELE, the bead women speak English and/or Africaans. Even their names reveal linguistic variety. Timmy, whose Ndebele name is Deliwa Ndala, is getting married in five months. Her son, fourteen, is Gavin (Phiwa in Ndebele) and her two-year-old daughter is Sharon (Lindo).

Does her fiancé, Andrew, know her children's father?

"Yes, Phiwa's father, my ex-lover, is in another Ndebele area. Andrew is Lindo's father. He likes these two children more than he likes me! He wants to do everything for them and is already keeping money for a school fund. We have to buy two uniforms plus matching shoes for each child; they must wear different colors on different days of the week. Phiwa's uniforms cost a hundred and twenty-five dollars for two outfits."

Timmy does dressmaking, but most of her money comes from beaded necklaces, bracelets, and rings. Her income ranges from twenty-two to fifty-seven dollars a month.

We ask her to describe Ndebele weddings. "Typically the husband's family will visit the bride's home, present a blanket, and agree to pay sixteen cows as *lobola* [bride price]. The first *lobola* payment is made then, and the second is paid after the first child is born, when the bride has proved her worth.

"Like all brides, I will wear two striped blankets with beads around the edges for my wedding. I will put a towel on top of my head. A big one, any color. I like red

and yellow. And I will wear tennis shoes—red ones with little bead decorations. The wedding will take place in my father's house. Afterward, we will move in with Andrew's family for maybe five years until we can afford to buy our own place."

Traditionally, *dzilla* (brass neck rings), were placed on a woman by her new husband on their wedding day to show that she was now married. The women wore them until their husbands died, then removed them for one year. We are alarmed to learn this because the rings have been known to cause bone collapse and death when they are removed. To our relief, our friends show us that contemporary plastic *dzilla* lace closed with ribbons.

BEAD WORKER MARTHA MASILELA'S initiation party was in 1991. She spent the requisite month in seclusion in a special enclosure in her house, wearing a blanket, sleeping and eating, and learning from her mother the secrets and roles of womanhood, including bead work and wall mural painting. Today, she wears the clothing she wore to her post-seclusion party. Wide bands of beaded bracelets cover her legs and waist. Her stiff, beaded apron symbolizes her ascent from childhood to womanhood. She is bare breasted.

"In 1995," she confides, "I was born again. A child of God. I heard The Word. He touched me and I took Him as my friend and king. I wear this attire to honor our tradition but inside my heart, I am always praising Him."

Martha, who wants a career in public relations, reconciles the Ndebele women's traditional and contemporary lives, saying, " We can't cast our culture away. That is why I wear these clothes. Culture is important."

TWO OF THE BEAD WOMEN, Letty Mthimunye and Anna Msiza, are *sangomas*, healers who are experts in ecstatic possession and divining. They throw bones to learn the future, diagnose sickness, and prescribe a cure. Their knowledge is gleaned through communications with ancestors while they are in dream or trance states. They describe the torment of the uncontrollable shaking that gave them privileged access to the world of the dead.

Opposite: **Brandishing scepters, whisks, and feather plumes, clapping, ululating, even making music with a drier hose, the bead women rehearse the music that will welcome their sons.**

I stop taking pictures for a minute, and just listen to the sounds of the place: insects droning, children chasing each other in the next baked-earth yard, and the low, soft burble of the women laughing and chatting, enjoying one another's company as they work. The language of the Ndebele is beautifully mellow with deep, round syllables accented by a sprinkling of the clicks and squeaks of the Zulu language from which it derives.

Then there is another sound—a chirp, a whistle; it is Betty, with a plastic referee's whistle held in her teeth, swaying and shuffling across the courtyard to the tempo of her whistle chirrups. One at a time, other women set their work aside, stand, and join her in a slow, graceful, sideways conga line of a dance. The singing starts sotto voce, with deep, sweet harmonies as a dozen of the beaders join the performance. I am told they dance only occasionally for their own amusement, but always at festive gatherings, and in this case, for us, because we are guests.

A basso note is added. Johannah is blowing into what appears to be a drier vent hose while holding the other end up over her head, creating a rhythmic tuba pulse as she takes her place in the curving line of dancers.

I can't resist. I have to start moving to the beat, doing my best to imitate their steps—and friendly hands move me right into the middle of the line. There is a brutal African sun overhead, and not a bit of breeze, but the dance is slow, the exertion minimal. And then a woman who is not dancing brings me her headdress and places it on me, with its bright loops of bead strings swinging under my chin. Another woman is inspired to put her beaded scepter in my hand, and somebody snaps a wide plastic neckpiece in place. Finally a dancer sacrifices her multicolored wool blanket to be draped around my shoulders. We sing (I contribute the occasional "yeah-yeah-yeah"). And we dance.

I am quite a picture, wearing my glorious Ndebele ceremonial regalia over my khakis and T-shirt, my blondish curls drooping, and my dripping face the color of a waning South African sunset.

WATERVAL, SOUTH AFRICA

Unlike the bare-breasted initiates, Letty and Anna wear bras for pictures. They demonstrate dancing with their elephant whisk wands. Their insect-larva ankle bracelets clank percussively. Their full skirts are dotted with red and white beads that symbolize the traditions of herbal medicine and divination. They wear "necklaces of power," made of beads; horns; magic calabashes that contain herbal and animal essences from snakes, elephants, rhinos, and crocodiles; and wood, which represents female energy.

When I admire Letty's handsome head of braids, each ending in a cowry shell, she removes her hair and, laughing at my surprise, insists that I try her wig.

DINAH MAHLANGU, thirty-seven, has three children: David, twenty; Billy, thirteen; and a ten-year-old girl named Goodness. She is a single mother—her husband was killed in a car accident in 1993.

Dinah completed Standard Ten, the equivalent of high school, and hopes her children will, too. "I especially wish them to have their will. To have the kind of job or business they want. The choice will be theirs."

More choices are now available, thanks in part to the activism of Ndebele women. For example, in 1986 President Botha tried to force the Ndebele to live with their rivals, the Pedi, on a reservation. This change was never instituted, but Ndebele women took up the fight. They demanded meetings with the white police, but instead got the riot squad with tear gas and attack dogs. Many women were injured. Still, in 1988 they took the issue of women's suffrage to the Pretoria Supreme Court—and won, just in time to elect the first Ndebele local government.

"Men and women are equal by the rules; they are paid equally, but they are not equal in action. Men believe that women are their slaves. Husbands abuse wives. They forbid them to do things. Some abuse their daughters sexually, which wives will not discuss for fear of being divorced. Most people here are not yet educated. Men feel they can do anything and women feel that without a man, they can't do anything. Most of the women in our area are resigned to suffering," Dinah says.

"In 1994's election, I worked as a voting officer, checking identification. In my area, seven hundred and fifty people voted. Everybody hoped that many things would be different after the election.

"We do have a lot of change. We can create jobs for ourselves, working at anything. There were many jobs we were not allowed to do before; it didn't matter if you had talent. To get food for the children, most people were forced to go to the town to work for somebody else. People here used to have to ride the bus four hours to work in Pretoria, leaving at three in the morning and returning at midnight.

"Now we can organize ourselves, have our own projects, and contact people from the outside like you women from America, which gives us power, light, and strength."

Dinah is a diminutive woman with gigantic ideas. When we first met, we discussed our practice of compensating the women we interview so they do not lose money by talking instead of working. I asked her what would be fair pay for a Ndebele woman. She fell silent. Finally, she asked us not to pay individuals, but to open a bank account that could be used by all the bead women to buy raw materials

We take Dinah and two other bead women to the bank to register so they can co-sign future withdrawals. We notice that, although apartheid has ended, we are the only two whites around. Our race doesn't seem to matter, though. We are introduced as friends. We listen to the local gossip. We play with the babies and admire women's hats. Hours later when the process is done, the bead women are ecstatic. Having no money for raw materials had been crippling. Dinah is already planning how to increase the bank account balance. "We will sit down with our members and discuss how the account is to be used. We will not be working to eat money like peanuts, but to push our account higher."

MONTHS LATER, Dinah writes to us that the women now have a second bank account, this one funded by the membership fees of craftspeople in twenty-two villages whom they visited and organized. The groups' accounts total $2,600, enough that many can borrow to buy the raw materials they need to create products—an opportunity that results from "power, light, and strength."

Previous pages: Dancing here, Johannah Anna Mahlangu learned doll making at fifteen. Today, she can finish three dolls a day and earns more money than her husband does as a house painter.

Opposite: Before 1994, Waterval women were domestics in Pretoria. After the watershed election, they created jobs to use their talents and enable them to feed and educate their children.

Above: Inspired by a new bank account that provides funds for raw materials, Waterval's Ndebele women bead dolls and jewelry, and decide to organize twenty-two villages into a regional handicraft group.

Opposite: Ndebele initiates return to Waterval after three months in the bush, wearing the beadwork their mothers created for them to celebrate their rites of passage.

and the Zulu Basket Weavers

AMONG THE DANCING ZULU MEN is a five-year-old wearing a loincloth and bands of fur on his arms and legs, just like the adults. He flies up from the back of the group, flourishing his shield. He jumps and stomps the earth, on fire with the excitement of performance. Tourist cameras move into position every time he speeds by, but they are never fast enough. The boy's name is Njabuho, which means "happiness."

During this mock wedding performance, his mother, Mamiza Nyawo, dances at the back of the group wearing the traditional black pleated leather skirt, flare-crowned red straw hat, and blanket that mark her as a married woman. She thinks of her own marriage ceremony and ululates in exuberant trills that signify happiness. When she is not dancing at Dumazulu Village near Hluhluwe, South Africa, Mamiza demonstrates basket making in this cultural center where tourists can eat traditional foods and sleep in traditional huts.

The huts, which many families still build, reveal something about gender roles here. Men collect saplings and frame the beehive-shaped dome. Women cover the framework with sheaves of grass, then a layer of mats, and secure the layers with braided grass rope. Today, if a family can afford it, hut walls are made of brick instead of wood, and roofs are constructed of iron or tin instead of grass. Using contemporary building supplies signals wealth, but not many huts around here are built this way.

Hluhluwe is one hundred seventy-five miles north of Durban, where the fertile earth blends from black to copper. Rounded hills are covered with spring-green sugarcane stalks tipped with lavender plumes that bend as if smoothed by an invisible hand. Later, there are miles of eucalyptus farms where uniform trees march like marines. Yesterday we saw men lead a steer to a tree near the highway, slaughter it on the spot, and hang the fresh meat from the branches so customers could cut off the parts they wanted—a roadside abattoir. Tonight in Hluhluwe, the dark sky is spangled with stars.

ON DECEMBER 25, 1497, Vasco da Gama landed here and named this region Natal, Portuguese for Christmas. In the early nineteenth century, Shaka, a

Zulu chief, developed an effective military strategy: encircle the enemy and fight at close quarters with short, sharp spears. Over the next twenty years this approach destroyed at least three hundred of Shaka's rival tribes and killed five million people during an era called *mfecane*, "the crushing." Zulus consolidated power in Natal and earned a reputation as brutal warriors.

In the 1950s, the Group Area Act enforced apartheid by dispatching all blacks, three quarters of the country's population, into ten "homelands." The Natal area was the destination for South Africa's nine million Zulus, the largest ethnic group, which comprises a third of the nation's entire population. The Zulus were relocated to geographically scattered, economically nonviable patches of land around Durban that were collectively called KwaZulu, meaning "Place of Heaven." KwaZulu/Natal is the region's official name today—Place of Heaven/Christmas, a soothing name for a place with a violent history.

Things are relatively peaceful now. The current chief, Mangosuthu Buthelezi, son of a Zulu crown princess, championed a policy of nonviolent resistance to apartheid and fostered a free market economy.

Buthelezi leads the Zulus in many ways. He is an avid collector of Zulu baskets, and fosters the art of basketry in his villages. We have come to meet the women who create baskets and mats.

FORTY-FIVE BOTANICAL SPECIES of reeds, rushes, palms, and grasses grow in this region; raw materials were always easy to collect, so baskets were made for many purposes: for agricultural use, to transport food and fuel, and to store dry foods or liquids.

Today, textured, patterned baskets are still made to carry sorghum-derived beer, which Zulus drink daily as well as for rituals and ceremonies. Traditionally, Zulus believed that rich men who went to paradise in the bowels of the earth would have many cattle, many wives, and a great deal of beer. Beer is served to unify groups of people and to symbolize hospitality. It is also used as a votive offering to the ancestral spirits.

Zulu beer baskets, *isichumo*, are made of Ilala palm leaves that swell when wet and make the vessels water-

Previous pages and opposite: Mamiza Nyawo, a Zulu basket weaver, demonstrates at Dumazulu Village near Hluhluwe. Her pleated leather skirt, flare-crowned straw hat, and shawl identify her as a married woman.

Although Zulu women did not traditionally work outside their homes, Mamiza has her husband's permission to hold a job—at least until he finds one. Her income supports seven people.

tight. *Isichumo* are considered fine art objects by galleries and museums all over the world. One arts magazine calls them "KwaZulu/Natal's answer to the Persian carpet."

MAMIZA (IRENE) NYAWO contributes to the appreciation and perpetuation of the basket weaving craft by showing visitors at Dumazulu how Zulu women do the weaving that they have passed down over the generations. She herself learned how to weave baskets from her mother when she was six.

"Specialist women cut the Ilala palm leaves. Only two of a tree's six leaves can be removed each year," Irene explains. The leaves are dyed with roots, bark, leaves, mud, berries, or cow dung, creating a spectrum of natural grays, greens, browns, and pinks.

"Basket weavers each create unique patterns, combining symbols to tell a story. Diamonds represent the feminine, and triangles, the masculine. Two stacked diamonds indicate a married woman. Two stacked triangles, joined, represent a married man." Irene shows us these patterns on a basket that is so big she can barely wrap her arms around it. She refers to the basket's foundation as "the mother" and to the basket she is starting as "the embryo," which grows strand by strand into a "fetus." We are surprised to hear how profoundly gendered the basket weaving tradition is here.

It used to be that a Zulu woman remained a minor throughout her life, always under the guardianship of a man—her father, husband, uncle, or even eldest son—and did not work outside the home. Now Irene has her husband's permission to hold a job, at least until he finds one and maybe even longer. He is a pipe fitter looking for work in Newcastle, over three hours away. Other men have left Natal to labor in South Africa's mines and industries, leaving their wives to support their families.

Money is important to Irene, who is proud that her husband paid twelve calves as her bride price—"plus one extra because my father argued that I was his favorite daughter." Our interpreter tells us that an average calf is worth one hundred thirty-five dollars, and that thirteen calves is the going rate for a fertile woman under thirty. "Sons are seen as the strength of the nation, but daughters are seen as the strength of the family," says Irene.

As the strength of the family, Irene earns a salary from Dumazulu and additional income from selling her demonstration baskets at the resort's gift shop. Her income is all the money that she, her three sons, and three daughters have to live on during her husband's absence.

CAROL SUTTON, the energetic South African white woman who runs Ilala Weavers, buys Zulu girls' first mini-baskets and sells them under the brand name Oops, an acronym for Out-of-the-Ordinary Production System.

"Little girls who can barely reach high enough stretch up to put their baskets on the counter, then shyly ask if I will buy. By the time they reach mid-teens, they can help supplement their family's income, or even put themselves through school with the proceeds of their work," Carol explains as we sort through the miniature baskets, each about two inches in diameter.

Today, Ilala Weavers provides a local and export outlet for twelve hundred Zulu women basket makers who live within a 125-mile radius of the store. Carol provides both raw materials and orders, then pays cash on delivery plus a Christmas bonus of ten percent of the value of each weaver's baskets that year. In 1996, Ilala Weavers paid over two hundred twenty-seven thousand dollars to Zulu crafters.

Carol is ebullient because an Ilala Weaver has just won a prize from the national biennial exhibition. "Sabena Mtetwa was competing against four hundred other South African artists. She is a widow, the sole breadwinner in her family, so the prize—two hundred and twenty-seven dollars—is an enormous amount of money for her. Almost no one here has a phone, so when we were notified, we sent a message with Sabena's sister. Sabena arrived dressed to kill in all her traditional finery. We met at a neighboring *kraal* [compound], with about twenty women, made the announcement, showed the catalog with all the colorful entries, and then presented a framed certificate and the cash. She burst into tears. She has decided to spend part of her money to pay off her debt at the local store. The balance will be used to fix the roof of her house."

Sabena Mtetwa's niece, Hambephi Mtetwa, fifteen, took six months to complete a giant, intricately woven basket

that sold for the same amount as Sabena's prize—two hundred twenty-seven dollars—enough to pay her school fees for the whole year.

CAROL, HER HUSBAND MIKE, and their twin sons who just graduated from university, now all work in the business. "Distances are too great for the weavers to come to us, so we go every day, deep into the rural areas, and unfold a table and chairs as an office.

"Last week an elderly woman very timidly showed us three baskets, the first she had ever made. They were beautiful and we paid her in crisp new notes. She threw the money in the air, holding out her hands to catch the bills as they fluttered. She told us this was the first money she had ever earned; tonight she could buy food instead of hoping others would have some to spare."

HAVING GROWN UP POOR, Nonhlanhla (Daphney) Zungu says, "It was a gift from God that my mother, without a cent in her pocket, taught me to make beautiful things from nothing. When I was young, I made six grass wastepaper baskets a week to sell."

Daphney teaches Zulu women how to make baskets and mats, knit, sew, and crochet, and grow food. She is a one-woman, self-funded job creation program. She lives in a simple cement-block house with her children.

Daphney's organization is called the National Multi-Skills Development Association and now numbers one thousand craftswomen in ten clubs located in Durban and the rural areas north of the city. Most members cannot read or write Zulu. Daphney, who finished Standard Eight, the equivalent of tenth grade, shares her education generously.

"Jobs recently evaporated for many black women in South Africa," Daphney explains. "Most Zulu women had been working as domestics until the minimum wage laws were passed, mandating that all employed people be paid at least one hundred dollars a month. That was far more than most employers were prepared to pay, and many women found themselves jobless. So I sat down to plan an organization that would help those women," Daphney tells us. "They need to know how to stand on

both feet and not rely on others. My aim is to train all our members to professional skill levels and teach them to market their goods by contracting with local schools, hospitals, shops, and churches."

THE FIRST MEMBER of Daphney's group we meet is Theresa Gumede, who makes grass mats, knits, and crochets. A jolly, friendly woman, she is headed for the community garden to dig root vegetables and invites us to work with her. As we scrape sticky rich black mud off turnip-like roots, she describes in mouthwatering detail the Christmas dinner she cooked for the white family she used to work for. Then she tells us how proud she is to be working for herself. She invites us to see her house up the hill.

The house is built from clots of earth wedged between logs: wattle and daub construction. In the dark rooms inside, linoleum peels off the floors. Surprisingly, Theresa owns two television sets and a stereo. The electrical system is primitive: wires wind along the ceiling connecting equipment, appliances, and bare bulbs. In the kitchen there is a gas burner and a vat for brewing beer. Outside the kitchen door is a cooking pot for use over an open fire. A traditional round hut behind the house has animal skulls drying on the roof.

Theresa is building a new house and plans to demolish her old one in November. She walks with us between the walls of cement blocks, blocks that she is making one by one from the ash of sugarcane plants. "There will be six bedrooms, each with a small window that has security bars, a bathroom, a sitting room, and a kitchen." She dreams that one day she will have a verandah that looks over a flower garden where she will relax and survey her domain.

Inspecting the construction with a critical eye, Daphney tells us that, counting Theresa, she has now taught four hundred eighty-two women to make cement blocks. "Zulu men and women do not divide labor equally," she tells us. "Traditionally, men clear the land, build the framework of the family hut, and care for the livestock. Women clean, care for the children, roof and repair the homes, collect water, carry and chop wood, make pots, weave mats and baskets, brew beer, and cook

Opposite: For hundreds of years, Africans have sat and slept on mats made expressly for each purpose. It will take this Zulu woman about two days to weave a mat and decorate it with yarn embroidery to sell at Durban's Indian market.

I love listening to South Africans speak. The Zulu language, as well as its cousin Ndebele, rumbles along in the most pleasing, melodious way. I listen to it the way one listens to music.

Besides the amazing click noises, there are combinations of consonant sounds that I have never heard in any Western language. Some words are begun with the pure consonant sound of a hummed "mmmm" or "nnnn" without an accompanying vowel sound (as in "Nnnn-de-bel-ly"). The most unlikely letters occur right next to each other: h *and* l, *for instance, as in the place name Hluhluwe ("Hloo-hloo-ee"), where the* h *and* l *are separately pronounced on the way to the* u. *When we try it we stumble over our tongues, and the locals laugh.*

Beyond the curiosities of the Zulu words, the spoken language is enhanced by the deep, soft use of the voice. And when Zulus speak English, they imbue that language with the same attributes—polishing, smoothing the words with their own linguistic style. Words slow down, draw out, become something else. Simple responses like "okay" and "yes" are softly sung, becoming "okaaaay" and "yehezz."

And the words themselves find their own usage. Just about anything we say might elicit a murmured "Izzz it?" Used like this, "Is it" might derive from "Is that a fact," but it is startling to hear it follow a statement like "I'm getting hungry." ("Izzz it?")

Even the English of white South Africans is sprinkled with pronunciations and phrases delightfully unfamiliar to our American ears. Just when we're becoming attuned, confident that we know the lingo, Carol Sutton phones from her basket shop to the busy Dumazulu Lodge to arrange for us to eat and then take some basket weaving photos: "Gordon, can't you swing a cat and make room for them at lunch? And then they need to take a hands-on picky."

food." Now, four hundred eighty-two Zulu women can add cement-block-making to their list of things to do.

HALF THE POPULATION of both Stanger and Durban is Indian. The Indian market sprawls onto the sidewalks and streets at the west end of Victoria Street in Durban. Almost two hundred stalls sell spices, basketwork, brassware, woodcarvings, meat, fish, fruit, and vegetables. Vendor permits cost a burdensome six dollars a month and there is intense competition for premium locations.

Eight Zulu women who are part of Daphney's association perch on a low concrete wall under the freeway. Some are selling mats and some are sewing yarn designs on the mats they are readying for sale. They are grousing because the Indians have the best spaces and get the most customer traffic. "Indians buy our mats in bulk and sell them for much more than we can." But this tension is not racial—the complaining seems to arise from garden-variety competition.

Ilala palm baskets are fine art, but grass mats are purely for utility. Africans have sat and slept on mats for hundreds of years. Zulu women use Ncema grass to make both *isicephu* (mats to sit on) and *icansi* (mats to sleep on). Today's mats are often decorated with scattered designs of yarn embroidery, but in essence they look the same as they always have. Mats take two days to make and sell for about nine dollars, but raw materials cost half that. If a woman makes fifteen mats she clears sixty-eight dollars a month.

DAPHNEY INTRODUCES US to two more members of her Multi-Skills group: Zenneth Thembile Shabangu, forty-seven, and her sister, Happy Bongiwe, thirty-eight.

Zenneth and Happy are talented dressmakers and wear cotton frocks they created. The long collars are like elbow-length capes; rickrack trims the skirts. Their dresses are green, red, gold, and blue—the colors of the new South African flag—and match their multicolored shoes.

The sisters live in Durban and take us through their neighborhood to show us how urban Zulu craftswomen live. They also introduce us to a group of mat makers who invite us to accompany them to cut grass for weaving. We eagerly accept, imagining the grass on a lonesome dune

above the Indian Ocean, or growing like bulrushes in a photogenic river. Instead, the women go to work with machetes, cutting grass on a nearby vacant lot.

ONE EVENING, Zenneth and Happy take us to Inhlangakazi Mountain, a hallowed place where thousands of Zulu pilgrims camp throughout July to worship the prophet Shembe. During this gathering, their beliefs require them to live as Zulus used to live, which affords us a chance to experience the traditional Zulu culture that gave birth to contemporary basket weaving and mat making.

We are the only whites here and, with Happy and Zenneth, who are Anglican, the only ones who are not Shembe followers. We are welcomed warmly and asked to remove our shoes so we won't desecrate the sacred earth. We set out through the encampment's labyrinth of wooden shacks and find our way between rows of sheds that display strips of fur and animal skins, amulets, and talismans. Older women wear white robes, columnar straw hats, and large earlobe plugs—demonstrating the Zulu belief that only ignorant people do not have their ears pierced. Many men wear loincloths plus fur bands on their arms and legs.

Young women walk toward us in droves carrying small animal-skin shields and black umbrellas, both to ward off evil. They wear nothing except beaded miniskirts, beaded anklets, and beaded "love letter" pendants with messages encoded in beads; the colors, sequence, and adjacency express affection. Their apparel and accessories display the same design motifs we noticed on Zulu baskets and mats: triangles, zigzags, rectangles, and diamonds.

There are few signs of contemporary life. We seem to be meeting the grandmothers of the craftswomen with whom we have spent this week, as if we have been propelled into the era that preceded modern Africa. Nowhere else have we had an opportunity to immerse ourselves in a traditional culture so completely.

Now the Zulus begin their worship. They dance to pray, chanting and stamping in unison. If we pretend just a little and squint, we can almost see young Njabuho, whose name means happiness, dancing with his ancestors.

Opposite: **The sun sets over KwaZulu north of Durban, where sugarcane fields give way to eucalyptus farms.**

Faina

and the Weya Artists

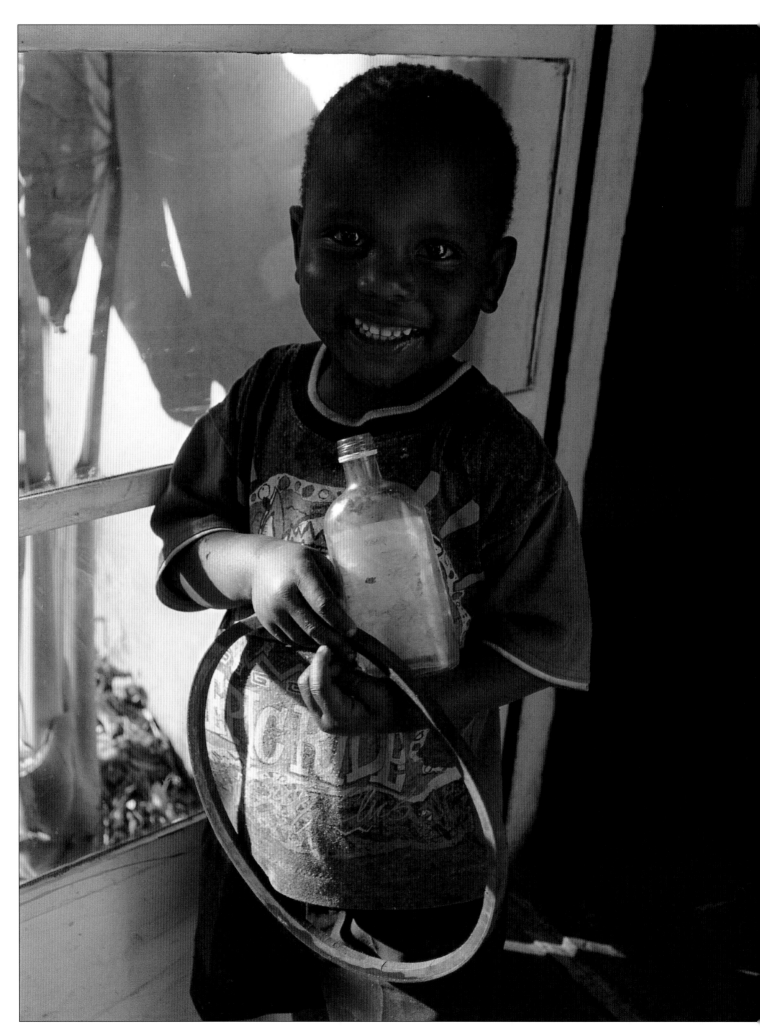

IN WEYA, A COMMUNAL AREA that the white-minority Rhodesian government established as a "native reserve" one hundred miles east of Harare, none of the women had ever painted before they met Ilse Noy in 1987. When Ilse, a German art teacher, told them painting could bring money, they thought she was fooling.

The Weya women earned more than money—they earned international acclaim with their vivid, animated, picture stories of traditional Shona life, a life based on reverence for ancestors and a belief in spirits. The women's natural artistic talent catapulted them into the contemporary world art scene.

Evangelista Mungure, one of the first five students at the Weya Community Training Centre where Ilse Noy taught, leans forward, animatedly telling us how the women began to prepare for their first exhibition in November of 1987, and early next year took the bus to Harare to attend their opening. Most of the women had never been to the monumental marble National Gallery of Zimbabwe.

"It was so exciting! Mr. Mtasa, a government minister, opened the exhibition and introduced us. There was wine. Most of us sold our work that same evening. They put red stars on paintings to show things were sold, because buyers couldn't take them until the show was over three weeks later. President Mugabe talked about the Weya women's art on the front page of the *Harare Herald* the next day; radio and television reporters covered the show."

We ask if her own work sold that first night.

"Yes, both pieces. A German named Helmut Osburn bought my first one for six dollars. The painting was titled *Whites in Zimbabwe*, and showed the story of our war for independence in 1980."

Evangelista was put in charge of sales for the Weya artists. One day when she went to Harare to make a delivery to the National Gallery, she met her mechanic husband-to-be, Lovemore. "He was fantastic. I liked him *very* much. He visited my family and paid a *lobola* [bride price] of two hundred thirty-eight dollars plus eight cows plus clothes for my mother and father. At our engagement party, we ate an ox, rice, and chicken, drank father's beer, played the drums, listened to tapes, and sang."

Six months later, they were married, and she moved from her village to Harare. Their son, Munyaradzi, whose name means "peace," was born the next year.

MARIAGORRET KAUNDO, Evangelista's sister-in-law, is thirty-five and creates appliquéd soft three-dimensional versions of the Weya paintings. One of Maria's appliqués describes in six panels the use of herbal medicine. A key to the images will be written on a note and tucked into a pouch hidden in the design:

"*Musosowafa* is used for washing after people have buried the dead. *Nhanzva* is used by pregnant women to ease delivery. *Muuyu* is used to bathe a baby. *Mumvee* is used to create swelling in women's breasts and men's penises. *Mutamba* fruits are used for softening the skin. *Mutunduru* bark is pounded and used for love medicine."

Colorful fabric dolls enact a story in the panels of another of Maria's appliqués:

"The old people are under a *murata* tree asking the spirits for rain. Here, women are packing the *rapoko* [corn] in containers. There is a hole in this rock for the *rapoko* to germinate; and they pour some water in the hole. Containers with *rapoko* must not be touched by young people, but only by the old generation. You can see these are old people only. After the *rapoko* germinates, they spread it on a rock to dry and then the old people grind it, working under a *muhacha* tree. After that, they take the ground *rapoko* and start brewing. Once the beer is brewed, they put it in molded clay pots. All this is done by old people, most of them women.

"In the last picture," Maria says, "the men have been drinking beer and they are urinating behind a tree. That is the end of the story of what is done in the forest under the *muhacha* tree. They dance and drink quite a lot, and get drunk, and sing some embarrassing types of songs, sometimes about men's and women's private parts. Afterward, it will rain. Sometimes it will rain heavily. But most of the time, it doesn't rain at all."

Married nineteen years ago ("early because of the war"), Maria has taught her daughter to do appliqué and her son to do Weya painting, a skill few men know.

Previous pages: At sixteen, Faina Shonge was selected to study at the Weya Community Training Centre. Students thought the art teacher was joking when she said they could earn money from painting.

Opposite: Enesia Nyazorwe's son lives with his mother at Cold Comfort Farm, a craft-and-horticulture cooperative. Enesia was one of the first five painters trained at Weya.

WE DRIVE TO OLD MABVUKU across the arid savannah, past rocks balanced precariously on top of each other and stacked higher than the trees, which have lilac-pink blossoms or black bark and flame-colored flowers.

The front yard of Faina Shonge's house contains one leg of an electrical tower, daisies, laundry, and curious children. She removes her canvas painting apron, turns off her soul music tapes, and invites us to have tea. She brings a basin with a towel to the living room so we can wash our hands, then offers us fat slices of fresh, crunchy wheat-nut bread with butter. Half a sandwich served with sweet, creamy tea, makes a delicious, filling lunch.

Faina Shonge was among the youngest artists accepted to study art at Weya five years ago, before she moved here to live with her father and three sisters. She paints on board, fabric, plates, cups, and drums, and has just completed a large board painting of a village teeming with the kind of activities that took place where she was born, although she claims, "*This* village only exists in my mind."

The scene is phantasmagorical: *imbas* (round huts) are decorated with stripes of green, yellow, blue, pink, and red. The background is orange, an enhanced version of Zimbabwe's rusty earth. Action occurs in five horizontal bands, but the entire surface is covered with people, chickens, birds, dogs, tables, wells, barbecues, plants, pots, baskets, cookfires, trees. "The father is beating the *ngoma* [tall drum] while the mother is playing a thumb-piano, which is used to call spirits. The next woman is kneeling, giving her husband a clay pot full of beer while he plays the rattles. Here, a woman is chuff-separating some maize, tossing it into the air from her basket."

The work seems to be allocated by gender. Faina explains the assignments: "Women fetch firewood on their heads, men fetch firewood on carts. Women fetch food, pound corn, and cook. Men drink beer, get petrol, make huts and drums."

Faina's paintings are sold at several galleries, but Martin Kwaramba, buyer for the National Handicraft Centre, has come with us hoping to purchase this one because, he says, "the color planning and the lines are fine. It is well detailed. The composition and the rela-tionship of spaces are sophisticated. That's what makes good Weya art."

Faina admits, "I became more interested in art when I sold my first painting. With the nineteen dollars I earned, I bought art materials, perfume, personal things. Today, I'd expect thirty-eight dollars for a painting like that first one."

We ask what she sees for herself in ten years.

"I am going to marry Brighton, a Mbare city council-man, next year when I'm twenty-seven. In ten years, I would like to have two children, do art part-time, and be a computer programmer. Computer programmers earn five hundred dollars a month."

FAINA'S UNCLE NOT ONLY CONCEIVED Ilse Noy's Weya Community Training Centre, but co-founded Cold Comfort Farm near Harare, a cooperative whose members do weaving, carpentry, metalwork, market gardening, and horticulture. Three of Ilse Noy's original students, Enesia Nyazorwe, Mary Chitiyo Kaundo, and Loice Nyamagoronga, now demonstrate at the Amon Shonge Gallery at Cold Comfort Farm.

"We wanted to do batik, but using wax as the resist was unaffordable," explains Loice, who joined the Weya Community Training Centre in July 1988. "We tried flour, but that was still too expensive. Ilse Noy and I figured out that *sadza* [cornmeal porridge, an affordable staple in Zimbabwe] could be applied with an applicator bottle. You draw the outline of your design with *sadza*, apply the paint, and let the piece dry. Then you wash the *sadza* out of the cloth, leaving the background color exposed.

"Whenever you see *sadza* painting in Zimbabwe, I myself was the teacher," Loice continues with satisfaction. "I had never painted before, but I was number one at draw-ing and color. From five colors—green, blue, yellow, red, and white—I can make twenty-five. Ilse did not know the colors or stories like me, so I became the *sadza* teacher."

Loice creates *sadza* paintings freehand. She shows us a wall hanging that includes lions, elephants, kudus, a monkey, a hare, a bird, and a fly. They look as if they are floating in the sky. "Yes," she says softly, with pride.

She has four daughters; the two girls old enough for school are first in their classes. We inquire about her

Opposite, top: One Weya painter, Evangelista Mungure, positions her worktable on a knoll above the family's vegetable patch.

Opposite, bottom: Faina, on the other hand, paints both inside and outside, but always with a boom box blasting soul music tapes.

We have come to Zimbabwe to meet women and see their painting, but the first art that meets our eye is stone sculpture. And it is fantastic: otherworldly faces and figures wrought from African serpentine of black, marbled green, and streaky lemon. The sculpture is everywhere: small pieces in gift shops and little galleries up and down Harare's thorough-fares, enormous works gracing the front steps of office buildings, and an entire hall of beauties in the National Gallery. We ask who does the sculpture. It is the Shona. "The Shona . . . women?" we ask hopefully. No, traditionally such sculpture is men's art, but today at least thirty women are successfully creating sculpture, many at the encouragement of their sculptor husbands and fathers. Clearly talent has overridden gender roles in this case.

We pick our way through a display and storage yard at the Canon Paterson cooperative in Harare. Hundreds of lovingly executed pieces are unceremoniously parked on the ground, where they have become speckled with muddy raindrop marks and wrapped in veils of dust. I'm looking for the one that speaks to me, but they are all speaking at once. A sculptor in coveralls, with an industrial dust mask hanging around his neck,

appears and suggests we let him show us his work. This narrows the field, and I happily settle on a graceful, serene, pregnant nude with modestly downcast eyes. And then he shows me another— and I take it, too. And then one more.

In the workyard we chat with hospitable co-op members who are happy to have us watch and photograph while they chip and shape the crude blocks. They work from no prepared sketches, there are no guide marks on the stone; it is simply freehand. They shape and then smooth the stone, then heat it in a little bonfire. While the stone is hot they rub it with coat after coat of wax, and buff it to a shining finish.

The workyard and the surrounding sheds are dusty gray, the coveralls and caps are covered in dust, as are hair, noses, and hands. It is a gray-on-gray picture, stone dust mixing with the smoke of the fires. Mounds of raw stone chunks and tall, unfinished figures loom eerily in the mono-chrome scene. But a tree hovers above the yard, full of delicate purple blooms.

HARARE, ZIMBABWE

husband. "He was a builder. He didn't know they put poison in his food. He is dead," she tells us sadly. Poisoned? We are stunned.

This is the first we have heard of witchcraft, poisonings, unexplained illnesses, and malicious spirits, but they play an important role here. Later, others tell us that there are jealousies among city and rural Weya artists, jealousies that are adjudicated by good and evil spirits.

"I was ill myself in 1990 from May to November, so I did not attend the first exhibition at the National Gallery," Loice volunteers. "I couldn't work while I was sick."

"What made you sick?"

"People wanted to kill me at Weya because I had orders and was earning too much money."

"When you say people wanted to kill you, do you mean they were so jealous that they just felt like killing you, or that they really wanted you dead?"

"They wanted me dead."

Ilse Noy's writings mention other Weya artists who experienced similar difficulties. One woman told her, "I am earning money so young; people can kill me." Another said, "If I don't give my relatives money for beer, they can bewitch me during the night and I will wake up not feeling well." And "I had a broken leg at that time, but I know who did it."

For many rural Shona, spirits are everywhere and are responsible for all things. Protective ancestral spirits—dead relatives who had children and were properly buried—are benevolent. But we are hearing now about afflicting spirits, who were not buried properly.

Something more contributes to the women artists' feeling threatened: the idea of individual accomplishment, a concept so antithetical to the Shona value system that there was no traditional word for "individual." Ilse Noy writes, "Shona people use witchcraft as protection against the rise of powerful individuals," and since Zimbabwe is a patriarchy, "the step into individuality is bigger for women than for men. As soon as a Weya woman proved to be extraordinarily talented artistically, she often fell sick, feeling too different from the rest of the people and believing she was a target for witchcraft."

For some envious women, the solution did not involve

the spirits. "When people discovered that Weya painters were earning money, they started copying. So we now have more 'Weya painters' who were *not* trained by Ilse Noy than who were," explains Florence Maposa, the twenty-six-year-old powerhouse who is marketing manager at the Zimbabwe National Handicraft Centre.

WE ASK LOICE how things are going for her now. She says, "I am renting one room for seventeen dollars a month and three of my children are with my mother in Weya. I pay everything for them because those three children are not my new husband's responsibility."

Loice earns more than her new husband—up to two hundred and twelve dollars a month, if there are many customers. "I work all the time because I want my children to go to school. I have to pay for uniforms, books. Room and board cost six hundred thirty-six dollars."

"You are about to have another child?"

"Yes. My baby will come next month. I am going to name him Bob. This is my husband's baby. He will help me pay for this one."

"WOMEN HAVE ALWAYS BEEN influential in Shona society," James Musiwacho, general manager of the National Handicraft Centre, tells us. "For example, my sister has the responsibility of counseling if my wife and I have difficulties. If I had daughters, my sister would tell them about womanhood; my daughter would tell her first if she wanted to marry, and my sister would be sure the prospective husband was from a good family.

"Many husbands seek employment in town, where their cost of living increases so they have not much, really, to send back. A large percentage of the men in town start new families. So the women are left working in the fields, building the houses, making handicrafts. Seventy-five percent of the crafts in Zimbabwe are produced by rural women," James says.

Florence Maposa joins in, "When a woman gets twenty dollars, she doesn't buy beer or cigarettes, she buys food, clothes, and education for her children. So when customers buy products made by craftswomen in Zimbabwe, they make a big difference."

and the Dollmakers

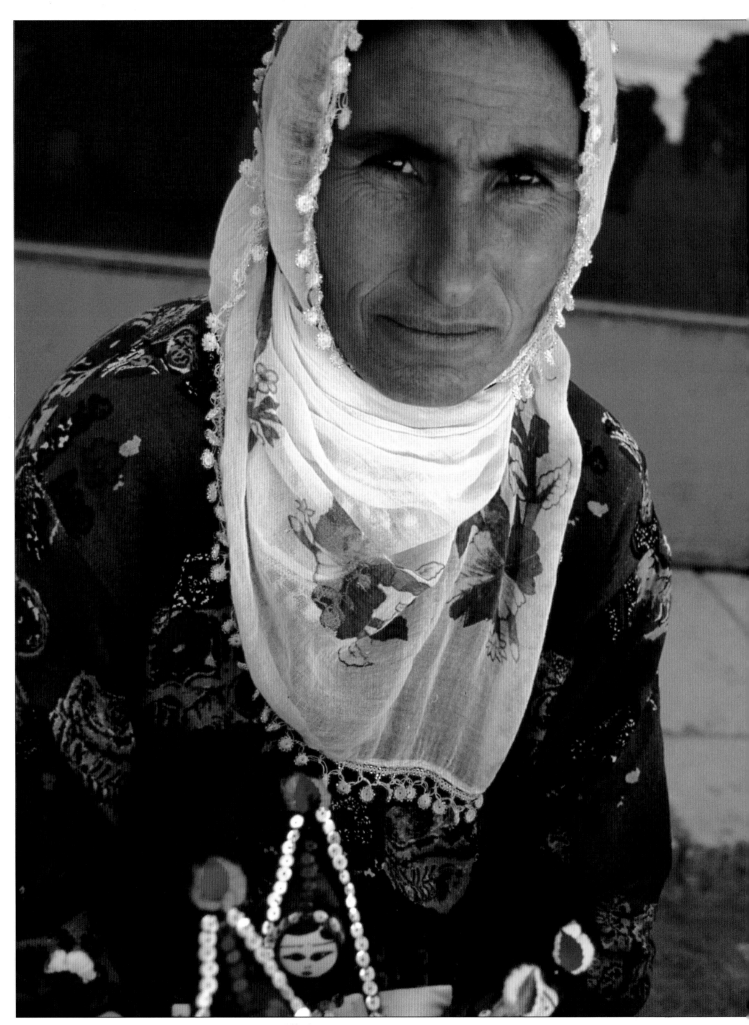

THERE IS A ROCKY LITTLE VILLAGE in central Turkey where the women make all the money. The village of Soğanli—which means "worshipers of Swaanda, the mother goddess"—is located in Cappadocia, an area full of sandstone "fairy chimney" formations and cave dwellings that draw hikers, climbers, balloonists, and sightseers. Soğanli itself is known for its four *D*s: dovecotes that riddle the cliffs; domes that top the ancient Christian cave churches; donkeys that haul firewood, goods, and people; and dolls. There are fifty stone houses in Soğanli, and fifty dollmakers.

Here, men work in the fields and gather firewood to feed and warm their families, but there are no cash crops or "men's jobs" in manufacturing or construction to provide income. So women seize the economic opportunity that tourism presents.

At nine o'clock every summer morning, tour buses begin crawling down the rubble road into the Soğanli ravine. They park near the doll market, a row of TV-tray-sized tables that hugs a sandstone cliff. Dollmakers rush from their houses at the sound of the belching, grinding coaches.

Each woman stocks her table with dolls dressed in brilliant costumes patterned after the kaleidoscopically colorful clothing all the women wear. Sequins glitter from doll scarves and skirts. Some dolls hold babies, others spin yarn. One venturesome woman has created a few boy dolls. All the dolls are similar in size and price. We get swept up in the energy of insistent salesmanship.

THE DOLLMAKERS SPEAK a sprinkling of many languages—just enough to get the attention of almost any foreigner. A spunky, handsome woman at one of the tables jumps up and demands, "You come *ma maison*." This is Ayşe Ablak.

She leads us uphill past the teahouse, a pavilion where the village men are talking and watching the world. We pass a few donkeys, tethered and waiting to take tourists on little expeditions through the town, and we pass the communal oven where the wives are baking round, flat loaves of bread for lunch.

Ayşe's house actually belongs to her seventy-six-year-old grandmother, Hanife Ablak, who started Soğanli's doll industry forty years ago.

Hanife jokes that although her fifth child was named "Enough," she had one more anyway. Her third child was a girl, Döndü, who benefited from Ataturk's policy, made in the 1920s, that every village in Turkey should have a school, and that for both sexes education should be free and compulsory through the fifth grade.

"One day, Döndü's show-and-tell assignment was to bring in something that had been made at home. Naturally she forgot about this project until it was time to leave for school that morning," her mother remembers. Thinking quickly, Hanife picked some sticks off a tree, found some scraps of cloth, and cobbled together a doll. "Mine was a very, very simple doll, not like the ones the women are making now, so beautiful." But a tourist caught sight of it as Döndü crossed the plaza after school, and bought it. "Mama! Make me another one, I can sell these!" Döndü urged when she arrived home. Her words launched a cottage industry.

Hanife has not reaped the money from doll sales that her daughters and neighbors have. "The others took the idea and started making more beautiful dolls. They learned little bits of the tourists' languages. They are bold and call out. I cannot do these aggressive things. Everyone else made the money. I can't even cry about it anymore."

It would have helped if Hanife had profited. "My husband slept outside one night, got seriously ill, and died. I became a widow with six children, and life became very difficult. I am old now. I live alone, rise before dawn and pray, return to bed, then get up again at eight to feed my donkey, my cow, and the chickens. Then I make dolls and knit socks to sell to the tourists who buy rides on my donkey."

AYŞE'S SISTER, CEMILE ABLAK, and sister-in-law, Fatma Ablak, join us for a break; a busload of tourists has just left. We wonder what would happen if for some reason tourists never came here again. Cemile responds, "The Gulf War did influence tourism in Turkey. We worried that there might not be tourists to buy the dolls, so we all learned to knit gloves, socks, and sweaters, which the local people buy."

Previous pages: The final step in creating a doll in Soğanli, Turkey, is drawing dark-rimmed eyes and a bright mouth.

Opposite: Dollmaker Hatice Güven planned her children eight years apart so she could afford to educate them; she sends meals to her son who is attending high school in another town.

We sit with them on the floor pillows that ring the larger of the two rooms in this typical home. A man's head pops up at the window every once in a while; it is one of the women's husbands wondering what we are doing in here.

We ask Ayşe if men ever make dolls. "Yes, some bend the aluminum we now use instead of twigs to make the dolls' bodies—since we all needed wood for dolls, there are no trees left in our village. Some men machine-stitch dolls' feet, hands, or clothes. One woman's husband is carving stone faces for his wife's dolls, to give her something different to sell."

Ayşe tells us that her grandmother, Hanife, with whom she lived as a girl, taught her to make dolls when she was fourteen. She was married at eighteen. Her husband, she says, "has never had a proper job. He never thought of getting one." Does he ever help her make dolls? "Yes. He sews the clothes, but cannot do the details."

Since all the women in the room are related, we ask what it is like to compete for business, particularly since product differentiation is achieved only by the dollmaker's personality, volume, energy, and sales pitch. "Not all the women in this village are related," Ayşe dodges, then admits, "Sometimes there are conflicts. Sometimes the women get cold shoulders and don't talk with each other. Yes, it can happen."

Ayşe is twenty-eight and has two daughters, ages eight and nine, who already play at making dolls, but Ayşe would rather not teach the girls. "I want them to take sewing or embroidery courses instead, so they can create dowries," she says emphatically. Ayşe hopes that by focusing on her daughters' dowries and refusing to teach her girls how to make dolls, she will save them the embarrassment she suffered before she was married, when, instead of having made her dowry, she had to buy it. This is very unusual. Most Turkish mothers start to make dowry items when their daughters are two years old, and the daughters begin to help when they are eleven or twelve, sewing, crocheting, and embroidering laces, pillow slips, towels, curtains, and dust ruffles. Before the wedding, a bride displays the treasures she and her mother have created, and neighbors

Opposite: Typically, female dolls are dressed in glittery clothing and carry babies or spinning implements, but a few dollmakers are test marketing male dolls.

"Toby, Toby! Buy my baby!" "Toby, see this baby. Toby! Here!" I guess I made a mistake when a sweet-faced young woman asked me my name—and I told her. Now the clamor is deafening; everybody up and down the line is paging me.

"Paola, buy my baby." "Paola, my baby!" Good! I'm not the only one to have divulged my name. What a powerful sales tool these vendors have now; it is hard to ignore your own name at that decibel level.

The dolls are hardly babies, with their rouged faces and sequin-bedecked costumes. But they are showy! They are all so much alike, the prices identical—how to choose? On which seller will I bestow my three dollars, and whom will I disappoint?

A pretty young girl at the beginning of the gauntlet has been calling to me, but I walk past to take a closer look at someone else's work. When I get to the end of the row, there she is again! She has picked up her little "shop" and hustled it ahead to have another crack at me. Looks like I've bought myself a doll.

T. SOĞANLI, TURKEY

admire, "So much! Such quality and artistry!" That did not happen to Ayşe, who recalls painfully, "I didn't have time to make my own dowry pieces before I got married. I was too busy making dolls. I didn't feel happy about buying; I could have made things that were more beautiful." Shame permeates her words.

NONE OF THE WOMEN in the room is idle while we talk. Before our eyes, they start and finish dolls. It takes about an hour to make one. In the winter when there are no tourists, the women sit together talking and sewing for hours, each producing nine or ten dolls a day.

A doll cooperative was formed a year ago to promote Soğanli as a craft center, broaden the market, and wholesale to vendors at other tourist sites. At the underground city of Kaymakli, a tourist attraction twenty miles away, vendors sell dolls from Soğanli that they claim to have made themselves. This is very disturbing to the Soğanli dollmakers, but their reaction is judicious: "The cooperative is new. We will see how they do."

They cannot afford to lose business to outsiders. A doll sells for three dollars, but raw materials cost a dollar and the doll cooperative gets sixty cents. The modest one dollar and forty cent net profit is barely enough to buy daily necessities, but once food is paid for, the women work toward a bigger goal: their children's education.

Every Soğanli mother we talk to hopes her children will leave this village to continue studying after completing the local primary school. "We invest in gold bracelets, which we can easily convert to tuition and book money later," the women tell us.

HATICE GÜVEN, who lives up the road, invites us to lunch. At her house, we again sit on floor pillows in a room that serves as dining room, family room, work area, and bedroom. It is furnished only with a bed for the parents; at night, Hatice's children, whose quilts are folded and stacked in the corner during the day, will sleep on the floor where we are about to have lunch.

Hatice spreads a cloth over our laps and brings serving trays of food with forks for each of us balanced on the edge. There are cucumbers, a cooked tomato-and-egg dish, just-

baked bread that can be spread with white cheese or butter, olives, and fried potatoes mixed with onions and bell peppers. Turkish hospitality always involves tea; Hatice's hot apple tea is presented in little glasses.

During lunch, we learn that in 1979 Hatice came to Soğanli, her groom's village, and learned to make dolls. We admire a giant doll Hatice made years ago. To our astonishment, she reaches over and cuts off both its knitted hands, then ties one on each of our cameras. "There," she says, "that will protect you from the evil eye."

Hatice has three children now, and volunteers that she used an IUD to space them eight years apart. "It is irresponsible to have children you cannot feed and educate," she tells us. "We are lucky that the government makes birth control available."

She dreams of sending her two daughters away to continue their schooling, "because only with education is self-sufficiency possible." She proudly tells us what she has already been able to do for her son, Bilgin (whose name means "learned"). "He is in a town down south living with his grandmother and going to secondary school. I send his food from here. Tuition and book expenses are steep, but within reach if I have good luck and plan well."

Her daughter Gülsen, fifteen, has been making dolls for three years. She shares her mother's hope that one day she will finish secondary school. Like teenage girls everywhere, she is fashion-conscious: her toenails are colored with henna, and she wears *salvar*, a silky, jewel-colored, harem-style pant-skirt. Gülsen pulls a little cardboard box from her pocket. The box, which she carries everywhere, holds yards of beautiful, cobwebby edging that she will apply to the domestic linens of a romantic, distant future. Despite her talk of selling dolls and going on to school, Gülsen is crocheting her dowry and dreaming about marrying a village boy her family will select for her.

We ask her mother what dreams she has for her own life. "My future will be good if the children are well, happy, and self-sufficient," she says. And if her dream comes true for her children, what would she like for herself? Hatice smiles, "I would like to live in a world where *everyone's* children are as well, happy, and self-sufficient as mine."

Opposite, clockwise from top left:
There are fifty stone houses in Soğanli—and fifty dollmakers; who would have imagined that Döndü Ablak's homework assignment would inspire a cottage industry • At the underground city of Kaymakli, twenty miles away, competitors sell dolls from Soğanli that they claim to have made themselves • Cemile Ablak reports that when doll-buying tourists stopped coming during the Gulf War, Soğänli women learned to knit gloves, socks, and sweaters to sell to residents • The vendors in Soğänli's doll market speak a few words of many languages—just enough to sell to tourists from virtually any country.

TWO WEAVERS SIT at the large loom singing. Their high, clear voices float above the percussive sounds of weaving. Their song is about beautiful Düriye, who wears flounced, white petticoats and flirts shamelessly; as she weaves, she thinks "God, give me patience with this job. My lover is over there with his sheep. He brings yarn . . ."

Hanks of red, yellow, and green yarn hang from nails on the walls. Yarn snakes out of boxes and baskets where the rolled balls are kept, reaching to the carpets that are rising on the looms. Four women are weaving; three gossip in the doorway; one rocks a napping infant whose face is covered with a handkerchief. There is husky chatter, laughter, a baby's gurgle. Outside on the cobblestone street a motor scooter coughs, then buzzes past. Fragile autumn sunshine penetrates the room and dust motes float lazily in the light from the only window.

The atmosphere seems peaceful, but the productivity in the room is testimony to a triumph. Fifteen years ago, the women in this weaving shed helped reverse a trend that threatened to put them—and all the weavers in the region—completely out of business.

We are in Süleymanköy, Turkey, which was named for Süleyman the Magnificent. Even so, many ghosts of past heroines inhabit this part of Turkey. Helen's Troy is thirty miles north; Athena's temple is thirty miles south. Four thousand years and four hundred miles away, the world's first known businesswoman, Lamassi, sent her weaving via donkey train to her merchant husband in the trading center, giving him instructions on a cuneiform tablet about how much tin he should get in exchange—modern money was not used for another fifteen hundred years.

Today's heroines sit in the room with us. They are respected for helping save the regional economy, are proud of their accomplishment, and are successful because of it.

Dr. Şerife Atlihan, who is on the fine arts faculty at Istanbul's University of Marmara, is the technical advisor for the DOBAG carpet cooperative. She describes the problem the women had to overcome. "Weavers in Turkey began using synthetically dyed yarn as early as 1890, when chemical dyes were first imported from Europe. By the 1970s consumers became aware that syn-

thetic colors run and fade. For the next ten years, rug sales, and the standard of living, deteriorated. By the early 1980s the women were no longer able to contribute their traditional fifty percent of their families' budgets. Few villages in western Anatolia had electricity yet, but families in those that did could not afford appliances. People became poorer and poorer."

In 1981, the University of Marmara began the DOBAG project. In Turkish, the acronym stands for the Natural Dye Research and Development Project. The project retrained women to do what their great-grandmothers did: use madder root, onionskin, oak galls, and chamomile to create harmonious colors that do not run or fade.

Natural-dyed carpets sell for three times the price of synthetically dyed ones, so Anatolian weavers converted to natural dye processes whether they were part of DOBAG or not. But many joined DOBAG because the cooperative built direct international distribution via dealers in the United States, Norway, Ireland, and Japan. That meant there were no middlemen to pocket any of the weavers' earnings. Today, the cooperative includes four hundred families in nineteen villages, and there is a waiting list.

"Applicants must have excellent weaving skill to be accepted," Şerife tells us, "and must enroll their children in school. This disallows child labor and requires the families to invest in education. It is a serious commitment."

ŞERIFE TAKES US to Süleymanköy's mosque, which blazes inside with color: turquoise walls, a kaleidoscope of patterned rugs on the floor. A little girl sits on the thick carpets, having a private lesson in how to read the Koran. Cushioning her are rugs in the best traditional patterns. No schools teach these designs— women pass them down from generation to generation. Local weavers have made them from memory for over five hundred years.

"DOBAG sells only the traditional patterns that weavers know by heart," Şerife explains, "but our rugs are not reproductions. Weavers make hundreds of design decisions. Which colors will they use? How will they crop, enlarge, or reduce the pattern to fit the size of the rug they are making? And they are free to add images

Previous pages: **After spinning, this DOBAG weaver will dye her wool with madder root, onionskin, oak galls, and chamomile to create harmonious colors that do not run or fade.**

Opposite: **Cennet Deneri, president of the DOBAG cooperative near Izmir, Turkey, demonstrates weaving at Return to Tradition, a dealer's store in San Francisco, California.**

that hold personal meaning." We notice that although the weavers honor the Muslim constraints against representing the human figure, a "traditional" DOBAG prayer rug design often includes spontaneous, contemporary additions such as hearts, houses, animals, spinning implements—the things the weavers care about most.

We have read that the Turkish word *zevk* describes the many choices a weaver makes when she is creating a rug. These choices, which express her spirit and personality, translate to "taste" or "style" in English. Turkish weavers understand that *zevk* connects artist and customer. They feel invisibly linked to the people who appreciate and purchase their work all over the world.

COUSINS SAFFET AND HAFIZE AYDIN are the weavers who sing about Düriye and her lover, the shepherd. The two women also gossip to entertain themselves while they weave. Like all the other women here, they fit weaving between household chores and coordinate their schedules so they can work as loom partners in the weaving shed. School does not start until next week, so Saffet's seven-year-old daughter sits next to her mother, blowing juicy, pink gum bubbles.

Saffet's nails are dark with henna, which prevents them from splitting from working with the wool day after day. Saffet and Hafize knot their rug in the same way their ancestresses, the Gordes, did three thousand years ago. Şerife explains, "DOBAG pays by the knot, and a seven-by-ten-foot carpet can contain over 600,000 knots, so you can understand why they need the henna."

In the Turkish countryside, only women make carpets, but men make them in the cities as well as in Iran. Nomadic women set the precedent, according to Şerife, whose Yörük family was nomadic before settling in Yuntdağ, near Izmir, 150 years ago. One of her cherished heirlooms is the carved whorl of her mother's spindle, which her grandmother and great-grandmother also used.

The weavers at the two looms are married, variously, to a carpenter, tailor, farmer, and shepherd. Some husbands in the village farm tomatoes, corn, cotton, or sunflowers, and from the roaming stock, we guess that some raise cows, sheep, and goats. When the men are not in the fields, they spend whole days sitting in the teahouse while their wives spend seven or eight hours a day weaving.

What do their husbands think of the idea that men get to relax but the women do not? "They think weaving is very nice because it brings in money," someone says. "They are proud because the weaving is beautiful," says another. "Our husbands want us to weave all the time," contributes a third, "but we do take a year off after our babies are born."

ERMINE DUDU ŞAHIN owns the weaving shed where the women are working. She is unusual because her parents arranged for her to be married at age fourteen to a boy she grew up with. Most couples marry after the man has completed compulsory military service, but Dudu lived with her parents while her husband completed his tour of duty. Now, thirty years later, she describes her husband as handsome and funny. "We love each other. We make each other laugh all the time." They seldom have time to relax, although they might roast a lamb and have a picnic during the spring festival. But on a daily basis, she is "very happy" and "wouldn't change anything."

Dudu's first child was born when she was seventeen. Like other Turkish women, who value marriage and mothering to the virtual exclusion of other lifestyles, Dudu tells us, "I live for my children and do not think about myself."

Her two sons now live in Çanakkale, thirty miles away. She visits them often, catching the bus in the nearest town. Neither is yet married, but Dudu says, "Because my husband and I are happy, I want my sons to have happy marriages, too."

Her dream daughter-in-law would, she says, "love my son, be clean, beautiful, and honest." She thinks these attributes may be difficult to find in one mortal, but hopes to find her sons "good wives, arrange engagement ceremonies, and finish all the work for them to get married." She looks forward to being a grandmother and may stop weaving to make time for her future grandchildren. Considering retirement is iconoclastic. Many DOBAG weavers work until they are sixty, and Dudu is only forty-four.

Dudu has a kitchen garden inside her walled yard, with grapevines and walnut and apple trees. At the door of her immaculate house, we remove our shoes. On the

---

Opposite, clockwise from top left: Looping the yarn around the warp threads, weavers knot their rugs the same way their ancestresses, the

Gordes, did three thousand years ago • Synthetic dyes ruined the rug market, but in 1981, DOBAG weavers' use of natural dyes reversed the

downward spiral • Cennet Deneri clips the wool, then compresses new knots against the edge of the carpet that rises on the loom as she works •

Hafize Aydin applies henna to her fingernails to prevent them from splitting in the course of handling wool yarn every day.

"Oh, please come and see my house. We'll have some tea."

That sounds just great, so Dudu leads us away—Paola and me, Şerife, Özlem (an interpreter fast becoming a friend), and one of the weavers, a beautiful young woman, wife of a schoolteacher, with a little daughter.

Dudu starts the tea while we take a look around the Şahin family home, and then settle into the divans and cushions of the main room—a simple, spotless, quiet place. The conversation is relaxed and idle, unlike the purposeful talk of interview sessions. The kettle boils, the tea appears, perfuming the room with apples and cinnamon, and we settle even more comfortably into our lazy little respite. It feels a bit as if we're cutting class, with all the other weavers still hard at it in the shed. The talk is of life and love—Dudu is so in love with her husband, Özlem has a beloved whom her parents detest, Şerife has been disappointed—the need for translation doesn't slow us down a bit.

And then the conversation does slow down, and so I offer, "Shall we dance?" I'd made all the weavers laugh when I ad-libbed a faux belly dance to their singing earlier, so now we all laugh again. And then lovely Leyla, the teacher's wife, slips a tape into the player and fills the room with Middle Eastern rhythms and minor-key melodies. She is some dancer! The sensuous, sinuous moves are punctuated by spurts of rollicking, jolly, up-tempo hip-waggling, and then like gunshots, the most amazing finger-snapping sound effects—a different sort of hand trick that I feel sure nobody in America can do. Paola is heart-broken that she can't master it.

Everybody up, we all must learn to belly dance. Well, I am no Leyla, but nonetheless, this is a hoot, bumbling my middle-aged self around the room with visions of Salome and Theda Bara undulating in my head.

Şerife, who isn't up to the exertion just now, lies back on the divan and pops another chocolate into her mouth.

T. SÜLEYMANKÖY, TURKEY

floor of her living room is an expensive machine-made rug. She owns a television set, a tape player, and a telephone. "My husband calls me five times a day," she laughs. "He likes to hear my sound." Dudu and her tailor husband seem to be proof that, as someone tells us, "although Americans marry the person they love, Turks love the person they marry."

What do Dudu and her husband do for fun? Dudu giggles. "We make love."

"THE VILLAGE BELONGS to the women during the day; its spaces are their workrooms," Şerife says. As we walk through the Süleymanköy streets, we come upon a group of women sitting in the lane. Several spin wool with their feet. Some have round trays on their laps and are separating the wheat from the chaff. Three interrupt their dowry embroidering to draw straws and determine whose wedding will occur first. Fatma Kaya, who traveled to Norway as a DOBAG demonstration weaver, leans on her garden gate, telling stories about her trip. Other women dye wool in the yard next door; it dries in the sun, still snarled with the chamomile sticks whose yellow stain turns blue wool to green.

ŞERIFE IS TAKING US to meet another Dudu, Dudu Öztoprak, who turns out to be a storyteller. "It was 1950 in Süleymanköy. Everyone agreed the baby was going to be born that night. The mother had been having labor pains all day. Finally, her husband returned from the fields, lined the cart with blankets, and urged her to lie down. He yelled at the horses to gallop faster along the country roads and prayed they would get to the doctor in time. After having four daughters, surely this baby would be the long-awaited son. The road was rough. The horses were lathered. The ride seemed endless.

"Pretty soon, with all that joggling around, I just popped out!" laughs Dudu. To this day, she believes her parents' assurances that she brought the family luck: their sixth and seventh babies were boys.

Dudu is a survivor. Little daunts her. Although she originally thought she would become a nurse, she is such

a talented weaver that she was selected by the University of Marmara to visit Ireland, Norway, and Japan to give weaving demonstrations. She describes how proud her husband and children were when she was chosen. Never having been beyond Çanakkale, she found the nine-hour trip to Istanbul a great adventure in itself. Having been born in a cart, she then found herself flying in an airplane!

She describes an elegant dinner party in Norway, and her astonishment at the fact that her male host did the cooking. "In Süleymanköy, men and women are equal in the book," she muses, "but not in reality." And she chants the only English words she knows, which she memorized as she flew into Dublin: "My name is Dudu. I am a weaver from Turkey." Then she gets out her photo album. "Someone on my trip gave me a camera as a present," she says, bubbling with delight.

She jumps up to show us the quilt she bought in Scandinavia. It is stacked with the quilts her children used to sleep on the floor when they were small—only the parents have a bed in most Anatolian households. She tells us how astonished she was to meet Iranian men who were demonstrating rug weaving in Japan. "Men weaving!" When we ask if she was tempted to move to any of the exotic places she visited, she looks as if we are out of our minds. "No. This is my village. It is my home."

Dudu married her husband when she was sixteen. He was diagnosed with cancer thirteen years ago, and one of his legs has been amputated to prevent the disease from spreading. Although in many families, weavers contribute half the household income, Dudu had to become this family's sole wage earner.

She confesses how proud she is that her family has been able to maintain its obligations to its children. When her son was born, Dudu promised herself that even though she had only been able to finish primary school, her son would have a good education. "And I managed that," she says. "He graduated from secondary school. The weaving money was very useful for that."

Her other family priority is to help her children make good marriages. Dudu's weaving income has allowed her to buy six gold bracelets to give as an engagement gift to her son's fiancée. Before the two are married, she hopes

Previous pages: **After turning in their rugs on Fridays, DOBAG weavers take their money to Ayvacik's weekly market to buy thread, beads, clothing, food, and horse harnesses like these.**

Opposite: **Süleymanköy's mosque blazes inside with colorful, traditional prayer rugs whose patterns local weavers know by heart and have made for over five hundred years.**

to buy some land and build a house for them. "In this village," she tells us, "men cannot get married if they do not have a house."

During a lunch of eggs, tomatoes, cheese, bread, watermelon, and tea, we sit on the carpet she has woven for her future daughter-in-law's dowry. Afterward, she unpacks the lace tablecloth she has made as a wedding gift. She describes the party "with dancing!" that she and her husband gave the couple one snowy night last winter to announce their engagement.

ON MONDAYS AND FRIDAYS, the weavers turn in their finished rugs at DOBAG's depot in Ayvacik. The cooperative's van picks up the women, their rugs, and their families, then drives them to town. In November and December, when there is little farming work to be done, the depot may receive thirty to fifty rugs a day. In the summer, the number diminishes to ten.

After four years, the white, two-story DOBAG headquarters is still under construction and is the subject of controversy. It is huge. The auditorium-sized showroom is intended one day to accommodate the tourists that the management hopes will detour from Troy to see the rugs and listen to speeches by the cooperative's male president. DOBAG's five-member management council is composed exclusively of weavers' husbands who supported the building referendum. "The men are not weavers!" one wife tells us angrily, mindful that her revenue will be docked to pay for the construction, and that Troy's tour operators will take thirty percent commissions.

"Eighty-five percent of the weavers present their rugs to me themselves; the others are represented by their husbands," Şerife says, as she greets the first arrivals. Weavers, husbands, and children wait as each rug is inspected for technical and artistic quality. Şerife has uncompromising standards. She teaches as she inspects, recommending ways to improve next time. The difference between an "A" and an "A+" quality is three days' pay. "Only about two percent of the rugs are rejected, but the day before you arrived," she tells us, "I sent a few rugs back to be reworked. If rugs don't lie flat or if the knots are not tight, they are not good enough."

The cooperative's contract allows the women to take any rejects to the local market. Assuming a rug passes muster, DOBAG guarantees it will purchase it. Customers are charged the same way the weavers are paid, by the knot.

All over the world, in stores like San Francisco's Return to Tradition, every DOBAG rug that is sold generates an additional bonus payment to the weaver who created the rug. That weaver's initials and village symbol are woven into the carpet, and her name and photograph appear on each hangtag. The DOBAG rugs' quality is so high that the University of Marmara guarantees them for two hundred years.

Before leaving the cooperative, each woman picks up a new carpet order and buys the materials she needs to complete her next assignment. She purchases wool sheared in the spring from live sheep reared on the surrounding hillsides—the only kind that meets DOBAG standards. "Wool sheared at the end of the summer is only good for stuffing mattresses," Şerife explains. "Even our members who are shepherds' wives buy carpet wool from DOBAG, since a single shearing from ten sheep provides barely enough wool to make a square yard of rug."

TWO CHILDREN HAVE SAT all morning on the rolled carpets in the DOBAG hall and are now cooling their heels in the wool dock. They are cousins, daughters of weavers Dudu Vural and Bahriye Arcam. It is hard to wait, especially today, which is market day in Ayvacik. Often the weavers take their rug money directly to the market to buy harnesses, thread, beads, clothing, and food. But not today. Today, Bahriye and her daughter, Nurdane, will go to the market to buy a blue primary school uniform just like the ones children wear all over Turkey. And Monday, Nurdane will go to school for the first time in her life.

We accompany mother and daughter to the weekly tented street-market. Sheep bawl from the trucks. Chickens peck at the street. Sellers compete for attention for their stalls full of toys, shoes, nuts, eggplants, chilies, and cheese.

Nurdane selects her uniform. Then, filled with excitement, she bunches up the outfit she has dreamed of and joyfully buries her face in the blue cloth.

Opposite, top: While Süleymanköy men spend time in the fields and teahouses, the women use the village streets to spin, separate wheat from chaff, and sew dowry embroideries.

Opposite, bottom: Weaver Dudu Öztoprak hopes to have earned enough to buy land and build a house for her son before he gets married. Perhaps his house will be like hers.

Opposite: Young girls all over Turkey wear royal blue cotton primary school uniforms.

Clockwise from top left: Nurdane Arcam, left, and her cousin wait on a rolled carpet for their mothers to complete their business at the DOBAG depot • Children often watch while the knots in their mothers' newly finished carpets are counted; the number of knots determines the price • Two friends dance while their mothers shop at the market in Ayvacik • Nurdane enjoys a snack before her mother buys her the uniform she will wear when she goes to school for the first time in her life.

and the Floral Offering Makers

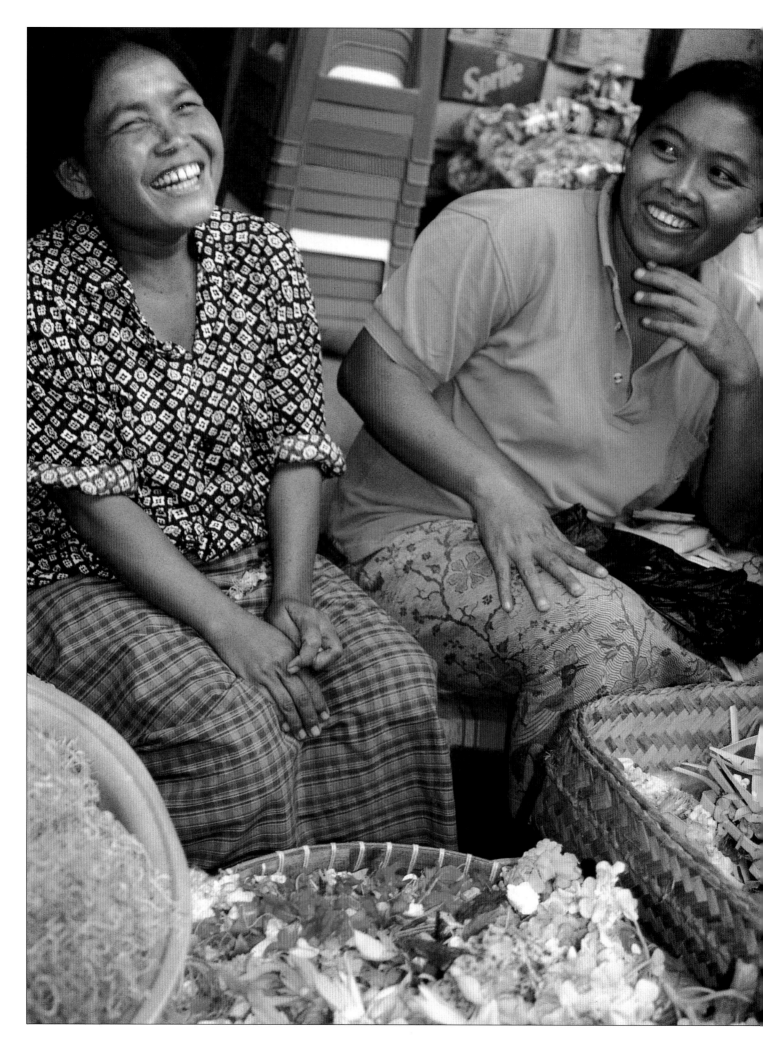

EVERY MORNING BEFORE BREAKFAST, each woman on the island of Bali conducts a series of rituals with beautiful offerings created from coconut palm fronds, flowers, rice, and betel nuts. She puts her offerings inside her home and outside around the village, in both high and low places to petition the heavenly gods above and placate the demons below. She sanctifies them with fire and water by lighting incense, wafting its smoke over each offering, then flicking drops of holy water from a fragrant white flower. This ritual requests prosperity from the gods and maintains the harmonious balance between the divine, human, and natural worlds. "If things are out of balance, it is apocalypse," a Brahmin woman tells us.

Traditionally, Balinese women spent half of every day making offerings. The act of creation suffused them with the maker's spirit and was part of their gift to the gods. But allocating so much time to the offerings is impossible for many women now: they have jobs. Yet they are still personally responsible for maintaining tradition. Their solution is to buy *canang* (daily offerings), in the market from the Brahmin women.

IDA AYU NYOMAN SAYANG, who is called Dayu, is giggling like a little girl, sitting with a friend in the Ubud market; in front of them large flat baskets are brimming with nasturtium blossoms and hydrangea petals. Both women are Brahmins, the priest caste, who make and sell the offerings to other Balinese women on this Hindu island.

Dayu tells us, "Ten women from my village now make offerings for sale. My mother was the first. I learned how to make *canang* as a child by watching and copying what she did. When I was in the sixth grade, I began to go to the market with her on Sundays. I left school and worked there full time after that year. I am now thirty-five, so that was a long time ago."

Dayu gets up at six, before anyone else in her household, dresses, skips breakfast, collects her products, and takes them to Ubud on the *bemo* (public bus). Her mother, who lives in the next village, precedes her to the market; some women arrive there as early as midnight.

While Dayu is gone her woodcarver husband, who works at home, takes care of their daughter, three, and son, six. After selling until early afternoon, Dayu returns home to create more products for the following day. Usually her husband does the cooking ("Last night, for example, he fixed eggplant for dinner, with rice. I love that"), but if dinner hasn't been prepared, Dayu cooks, and then continues making offerings until midnight.

We ask how much she earns from her eighteen-hour days. "Daily sales average four dollars," she says. "But by the time I pay for a round-trip *bemo* ticket, flowers, palm fronds, and perfumed water, I am left with a dollar sixty." A restaurant manager later tells us that forty cents will buy only a simple meal for one person.

Dayu earns more than her husband does each month: fifty dollars compared to his twenty dollars. "It's not a problem for him that I earn more," she says. "We have separate monies but a mutual understanding that we will both contribute to our expenses."

Her husband's full name is Ida Bagus Putu Sunantra, but he is called Aji, which means "father," just as Dayu means "mother." "Aji puts in money for ceremonies and food. A kilo of rice costs forty cents and then there are vegetables. We decide together how to spend our money. The amount we have is not enough—there is nothing left for extras. My son needs twenty cents for food at school. Elementary school tuition is free—tuition begins with junior high—but students need uniforms."

One day we go home with her from the market. En route, we drop off her mother who still lives in the village where Dayu grew up. When Dayu was married, she moved in with her husband's family, as wives do here.

Aji's family compound is near flooded rice fields that reflect the clouds as if there were sky, not earth, under the seedlings. Dayu disembarks from our van and carries her bundles of raw materials on her head, leading us down a dirt lane through flowering bushes.

Her husband quickly dresses their naked three-year-old daughter in a pink polka-dot sundress to welcome the visitors. Their six-year-old son camps on the deck of the house to the right to inspect Dayu's bundles. An uncle smokes, perching with us on the porch floor to chat. Aunts

Previous pages: Balinese women used to spend half of every day preparing ritual offerings from flowers, leaves, fruit, grain, and fowl. Now, women with jobs purchase daily offerings in the market.

Opposite: Ida Ayu Nyoman Sayang (who is called Dayu), right, sells daily offerings in the market in Ubud, Bali, with another Brahmin (Hindu priest caste) woman.

and nieces come to greet us. Two men carve wood sculptures, hunkered down on the porch of the house to the left. Across the courtyard is the ceremonial house. A path leads to the family temple, which has walls but is open to the sky. Unlike most temples we have passed that are already decorated for the coming holiday, it is empty.

Dayu weaves coconut palm fronds as we talk, and her daughter, who sits silently behind her, copies her every move. "If you're a good student, you can learn in ten minutes," Dayu promises. We try diligently to sew palm leaves with tiny pins of bamboo.

Dayu confesses, "I would rather have my daughter go to school than work with me in the business. I hope these children can eat, get good educations, and take care of me when I get older. I hope my daughter will marry and live nearby, just as I live close to my mother and can visit easily and often."

Having worried openly about the fact that she has nothing to offer us, Dayu has arranged with her extended family to borrow coffee and packaged cookies, which she presents on a painted tray. Each cup of coffee has a dirty pink plastic lid and, as far as we know, there is no water here to make coffee except in the muddy ditch near the road where we have seen people bathing and washing laundry. But it would be a terrible affront to refuse to partake of her proudly offered, generous hospitality.

Dayu tells us she first saw her husband passing along the road. "He just looked nice to me. There is no matchmaking here. You see each other, like each other, and just take it." Her wedding seven years ago was one of the highlights of her life. It took place in the family temple "with lots and lots of offerings that the elderly people and the young people all helped make for the ceremony. The old men made the bamboo altars and the meat sate for the wedding. I wore a *kebaya* [lace shirt] and sarong."

Other important events for her were her children's rites of passage. "First haircut rites occur in the ceremonial house after children are three months old. My husband shaved my child's head that morning, as purification. A specialist who works closely with the priest created the offerings, which were everywhere. The priest's assistant came and made blessings for my child.

"The happiest time of my life was when I was young and didn't know anything yet; my mother would come back from the market and give me money. The saddest time is now; we are having a Galungan holiday and I don't have enough money. I am angry because my husband won't share his money when I need it." Handsome Aji, who overhears Dayu share this confidence with strangers, stomps out of the courtyard.

As if to defend Aji, his uncle bounds into the conversation. "For the holiday, Aji will cook traditional ceremony food. He will slaughter a pig tonight, chop it up with vegetables, and make a feast." Compared with the daily rice diet, pork is a delicious luxury. Will the pig be slaughtered in the temple? "No, pigs are only slaughtered in the temple for village temple ceremonies. Galungan is celebrated in the family temple."

The uncle then shows us his fighting cock, which he has trained for mortal battle. Although the law prohibits cockfights, spilling cock blood in the temple on a holiday is allowed and is considered a sacrifice.

GALUNGAN, THE HOLIDAY that welcomes ancestral spirits to earth for a ten-day visit, is two days away. Festival offerings are never purchased, although individual ingredients often are. Working wives rise at four in the morning for days to prepare Galungan offerings, which are far more elaborate than *canang*.

Back in the Ubud market there are stalls and vendors selling hibiscus and frangipani blossoms. There are baskets of edible offering ingredients: hard-boiled eggs, fruit, cookies colored with neon pink and green food dye. All offering materials come from the earth (flowers, leaves, fruit, grain, fowl) and will be transformed by cooking, frying, cutting, mixing, and assembling to please the ancestors' senses of taste, smell, and beauty.

Balinese people combine ancestor worship with Hindu beliefs and animism. Here, the word "ancestors" is not reserved for ancient relatives. It includes anyone who has died and had a cremation ceremony, an event so elaborate and expensive that bodies are often buried for a few years in graves until the families can afford the cremation that will liberate the spirit. Thus, some families

will celebrate Galungan by taking food and flowers to the cemeteries. But most will fill their household temples with the lavish offerings.

IN BALI, OPPOSITES ARE BELIEVED to derive meaning from their complements. Black and white define each other; good and evil are equally necessary.

A central theme in Balinese cosmology is the combination of male and female principles in the creation of life. Black represents the feminine, red the masculine; combined with white, the two symbolize the unity of the universe.

Not surprisingly, gender roles are distinct, even in creating offerings. Men do not make daily offerings unless their wives are menstruating, in which case husbands must take over.

Men have their own Galungan assignments. Like Aji, the men slaughter the pig. Men also build the bamboo altar and *penjor* (arch) that decorate the front of every house. Women make *penjors* only if their husbands are dead. But women always create the *sampians,* which are ornamental cages of bamboo and flowers that swing from the top of the *penjors*. And each woman decorates her husband's bamboo altar with a *lamak,* a patterned banner woven of leaves or, in some districts, embellished with sequins, embroidery, and tassels.

TWO NIGHTS BEFORE GALUNGAN, the night is rent with the screams of pigs. The air is otherwise silent, humid, and close.

The next morning there is the usual natural hum: roosters crowing, crickets chirping, birds singing. Today, women will finish their work on their holiday offerings. We visit families where the women are filling tables and trays with sculptures composed of bananas, oranges, leaves, flowers, fringes of fronds, cookies, cakes. Their daughters have braided leaves into origami-like shapes. Groups of women have stacked pyramids of fruits on red pedestal plates. By evening, all the women heap the altars in their family temples with offerings of breathtaking beauty.

WE ARE TOLD THAT Balinese women have long been laborers, but until about twenty-five years ago, men did not seek jobs; they worked in the rice fields. Women typically held the purse strings, which caused some friction as men entered the work force. Recently, tourism has provided more paid employment for both sexes.

Ni Wayan Murni has been in the tourist business most of her life. As a young woman in the 1960s, Murni was the first vendor to sell sarongs on the beach when Australian and American hippies discovered Bali. She used her proceeds to open Murni's Warung in Ubud, now a popular, contemporary three-level restaurant with a boutique full of gifts, crafts, and other treasures that she buys all over the Indonesian archipelago. She also owns Murni's Houses, an enclave of cottages on the hill in the Campuan section.

On the afternoon before Galungan, while her father finishes the bamboo altar outside the wall that surrounds the family compound, Murni sits on her porch making offerings. Her life has always revolved around business and she has not, until now, made time to learn the craft that has long occupied virtually all other women on the island. "I made a choice this year that I would take two weeks off to learn this art. It is time." She and four women on her staff put finishing touches on two hundred holiday offerings, enough for all her enterprises and her home.

Murni reminisces about other Balinese celebrations. "Tooth filing is usually done between puberty and age fifteen, but my parents couldn't afford it. In our religion, it is believed that filing must be done before you die. We file the top of our teeth so they are smooth and even. If no filing takes place and your teeth remain sharp, you are assumed to be a demon after death. So here I am, a grandmother, and my tooth filing ceremony just occurred! It took three months to prepare for the celebration, which itself took four months and was attended by almost three hundred people in total. We built temporary kitchens to feed fifty guests every day."

Murni will begin her Galungan celebration at home. "In the morning, we will pray in our temple, which includes an altar for Vishnu, the sun god, plus altars to

Opposite, top: Women must wear *kebayas* (lace blouses), sarongs, and sashes to enter the village temple where a priest applies sticky rice to bless them with fertility and abundance.

Opposite, bottom: Women sanctify their offerings with fire and water: they waft incense smoke over each offering, then flick drops of holy water from white flowers.

Opposite: The afternoon of the holiday, the Balinese visit Gunung Agung, the sacred mountain, and climb to Pura Besakih, the most holy temple on the island.

Above, clockwise from top left: *Penjors* (bamboo arches) decorate the front of every house in Bali during Galungan • The market in Ubud is full of vendors whose baskets contain

hibiscus, frangipani, and marigold blossoms that are destined to become Galungan offerings • Men build the *penjors* and women create the *sampians* (end tassels) of bamboo

and flowers • After offerings are presented, they have served their ritual purpose, and the beautiful trays of food are taken home for family feasts.

our dead ancestors. My stepmother died two months ago and has not yet been cremated, so later in the morning we will take offerings and visit her in the cemetery."

At Murni's family temple, her helpers are placing tier upon tier of offerings: apples, pink jambu fruit, eggs, cakes, cookies, meats carved into filigree, layers of flowers, cones of rice, vegetables, spices. There are swags of the ubiquitous black-and-white checkered fabric. There are perfect pyramids of fruit. Surely, we think, the ancestors will be delighted.

ON GALUNGAN, friendly Balinese women arrive to help us dress properly in traditional attire. We are given *kebayas* and sarongs, complete with the sashes that must separate the upper body from the lower, less pure parts. We are asked to adhere to the Balinese rule that women who enter the temple must wear these sashes and must not be menstruating.

Hobbled by sarongs that wrap around us three times, we gratefully avail ourselves of the ramp that runs up the center of the steep hillside steps of the village. We assume the ramp is to help women walk gracefully, since only small, shuffling steps are possible. Later we discover that Balinese women do not need any help and that the ramps are built for motorcycles.

After family services, there will be visits to the village temples and perhaps to Pura Besakih, a cluster of ancient shrines that comprise the most sacred temple in Bali. Already, women parade to the moss-covered village temples wearing sarongs and pink, teal, blue, green, yellow, or red lace *kebayas*, each carrying a tower of offerings on her head. We watch the priests bless the trays and then stick a few kernels of steamed rice on each woman's forehead to bless her with fertility and abundance. Since the offerings have served their purpose, these beautiful food plates are now taken home to become family feasts. The Balinese will share this meal with their visiting ancestors.

ALL BEDS IN BALI face the sacred mountain, Gunung Agung. Pura Besakih, the holiest temple, is there. We visit Besakih on Galungan afternoon after driving through the corridor of magical *penjors* that arch across the road in front of every house. We follow the Balinese men, all dressed in pure white shirts and sarongs with gold satin sashes. The Balinese women effortlessly carry offerings on their heads. We climb up the stairs, up the mountain, to the inner temple where throngs pray under the red, black, and white umbrellas that symbolize Brahma, Vishnu, and Shiva, the trinity that creates, maintains, and destroys the universe and is responsible for the cycle of life on earth. Under each fierce dragon statue, around each muscular golden lion, are stacks of floral offerings: bouquets wrapped in leaf cornucopias; blossoms heaped in containers woven of palm.

JUST AS GALUNGAN is a "visiting holiday" for ancestors, visiting is the afternoon activity for those who live on earth. Families and friends sit by the side of the road to watch motorcycles carrying lovers (all wearing traditional holiday clothing, some balancing a bird cage containing a fighting cock) and families (always father in front, infant in the middle, mother in back). They are headed for a relative's house, or to have a picnic in the arboretum or a walk in the palace gardens. Hoards of motorcycles pass family temples decorated with umbrellas whose dangling tassels dance in the breeze, with festoons of checkerboard cloth, with streaming ice-cream-colored prayer flags, with *penjors* and *lamaks*.

The motorcyclers pass offerings placed by the streams, near the lakes, and in the rice paddies to thank the gods for the fertility of the earth and life-giving water. They pass offerings on the ground in front of buildings, on the sidewalk, and in the street to appease the demons and keep them from disturbing the harmony of the universe. Everywhere they look, offerings.

Opposite: Galungan is a "visiting holiday" for both Balinese and ancestors. After finishing rituals in their home and village temples, people ride motorcycles to call on friends and relatives.

Following pages: A lakeside temple is festooned with umbrellas and a prayer-flag-flying *penjor*.

Ubud is a delightful town—this Balinese cultural center tucked into the foothills and ravines below the island's central mountains—but we yearn to go exploring. We need to see Galungan as it is celebrated in the countryside, and to photograph holiday decorations all over the island.

Our guide for this excursion will be Wayan, who drives guests around for our hostess, also named Wayan. The name means "first-born," so every family has a Wayan, either a girl or a boy, if they follow custom. Then the next child is named Second in Balinese, and then Third and Fourth. With the fifth child the naming process starts over again with Wayan.

Our guide Wayan is dressed for the holiday. Yesterday he was in jeans and a polo shirt, like a nineteen-year-old anywhere, but today he is wearing proper Balinese attire: a white shirt/jacket with Nehru collar, a sarong of gold-colored cloth, and a white cotton square, diagonally folded and tied around his head with the corners pointing up in front.

The road out of town is a narrow, undulating, paved strip passing between walled family compounds and curving around crumbly stone temples and figures of heroes, gods, and demons. Each family home consists of a cluster of little buildings, or bales, for various functions—sleeping, cooking, washing—a family temple, and one or two freestanding shrines. The bales all have peaked roofs of thatch or tile, peeking up over the compound wall.

We drive through rice country, endless waves of terraces sculpted in graceful curves in a hundred shades of green. And then, suddenly, we have arrived at a village—a true traditional one like those of Balinese days long past, where Wayan lives with his grandparents.

The holiday decorations bestow a delicate, fairy-tale look to the village, bamboo penjors standing fifteen feet tall all along the way, then arching over and dangling fragile confections of flowers and palm leaves above the path.

There is a community pavilion, open-sided and thatch-roofed, with a performance platform at one end where a pair of gamelan instruments rests. Wayan remembers when he and other youngsters used to spend long afternoons here, trying in vain to make real music on those bamboo xylophones. Off to the side, perched on a row of sawhorses, is a Barong costume. We are delighted to imagine the little boys struggling around under the two-man shaggy lion/dog getup. Barong is an important figure in Balinese mythology. He is guardian of the people, so he is one of the recipients of abundant Galungan offerings. In the traditional play, Barong is the good guy, a mythical defender protecting the hero from evildoers.

At Wayan's grandfather's compound, one of the few we have been asked to step inside, the four or five bales are utterly simple and alike, built on raised platforms and open on one side. In one of them, Wayan's grandmother stands at a table working on her Galungan offerings. She is beautiful, and appears to be very old; she wears a sarong and sash, and is barefoot and bare breasted, in the old tradition. In another bale sacks of rice and other family necessities are stored, along with grandfather's fighting cock, who waits under his basket for the hour of his holiday duel at the temple.

UBUD, BALI

Two Batik Artists

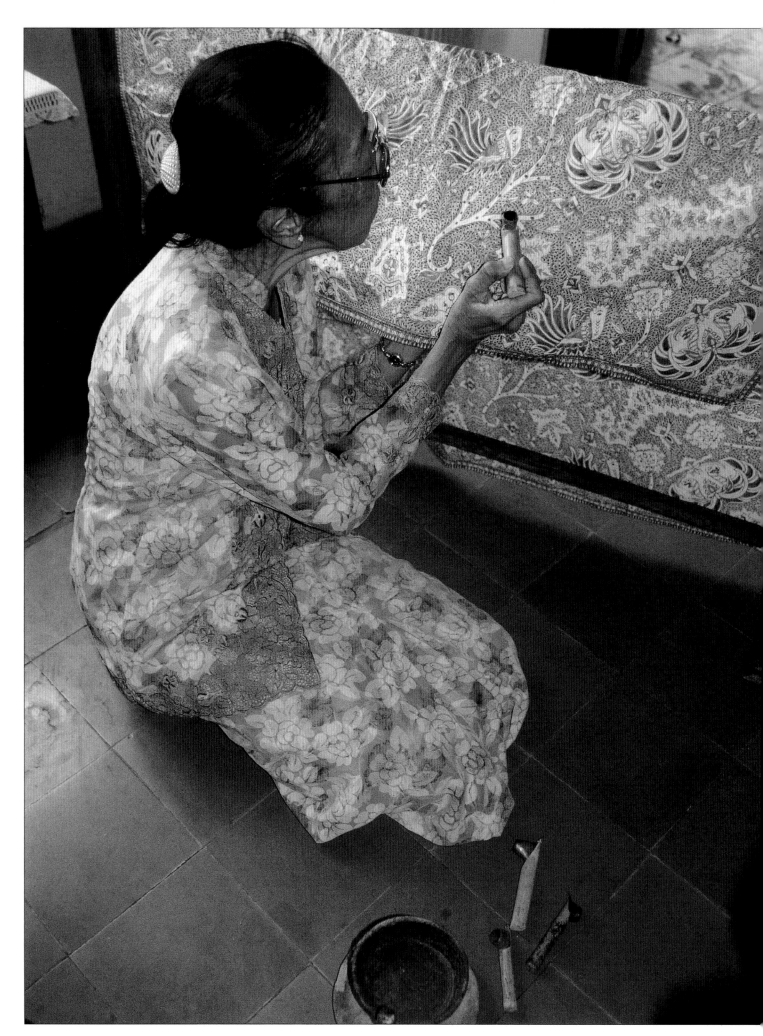

THE HISTORIES OF THESE TWO WOMEN, who live in Surakarta, central Java, contrast like colors in the batiks that are the focus of their lives. One's journey took her from nobility to indigence, the other's from poverty to wealth.

IBU PRAPTINI PARTANINGRAT lives in a house at the back of the palace compound that was built in 1860; she was born in this house in 1925. Her royal blood connects her to King Mankunegoro II who reigned over one of the seven Javanese kingdoms in the early nineteenth century. Her grandfather was a prime minister. Her father, secretary of the royal court, was later named regent.

People have told us they can see her royal heritage in her bone structure; she has the cheekbones of Javanese shadow puppets. She is dignified, but without pretense. Her first name, Praptini, means "someone is coming," which seems to acknowledge her aristocratic bearing. Like many Indonesians, she is addressed only by her given name: Mrs. Praptini.

When we meet her, she serves us an herbal rice drink with tamarind, which she says will "nourish your health and refresh you," plus sliced, fried bananas. Her generous hospitality and dignity are offset by her living room, whose windows are cracked or missing. The velvet upholstery of her elegant chairs is shabby. The walls of her little house are stained and dilapidated.

Mankunegoro IX is now only the titular king. There has not been an acting king since the Dutch rendered the monarchy powerless in 1922, but the tradition of royal life continues in its social and ceremonial functions. "Today, Javanese dynasties have no source of wealth," Mrs. Praptini explains. "They used to gain income from plantations of sugar cane, tea, coffee, and spices like white pepper and nutmeg. Today, Mankunegoro IX runs a company in Jakarta."

Mrs. Praptini reminisces about the current king's coronation, which took place five years ago. "All coronations are sacred Javanese rituals where an elder presents the *keris* [jeweled scimitar] to the prince. At Mankunegoro IX's coronation, I wore a flowered sarong and pink *kebaya* [lace blouse] and sash. Ninik, my daughter, danced in

performance. There was a gamelan, an orchestra of string, wind, and percussion instruments including gongs, bells, and xylophones—and a feast with yellow rice molded into cone shapes, like mountains."

The next day, Mrs. Praptini arranges to show us the palace, some parts of which are open to the public. With Mrs. Praptini we see much more. We remove our shoes to enter the cool central court where arches admit the breeze and allow views of caged birds in the garden. There are Chinese vases and golden chairs upholstered in red plush. She shows us the ladies' dressing rooms and describes how the women of the court used to bathe, dipping water from a pool surrounded by pink marble walls.

Only women of the court create the beautiful, ceremonial *tulis* (hand drawn) batik patterns that Mrs. Praptini learned to make when she was ten. She demonstrates what her mother taught her, drawing the intricate wax patterns freehand, making traceries so fine they remind us of ice crystals on winter windows.

For a long time, Mrs. Praptini did not sell her batik, but when her husband died, she realized she would not have enough money to send her daughter to college. It was untenable that her only child would not have an opportunity to continue learning—education is as necessary as food in Mrs. Praptini's view. She feels privileged to have been educated in fine, Dutch schools. She graduated from high school and speaks five languages. Her husband was a teacher, and so was she when she was younger.

Like millions of other mothers in a similar dilemma, she began to sell what she knew how to make. She bought white cloth and made natural dyes from roots and bark. Because it takes three months to complete a one-by-two-meter length of batik, her work did not proceed quickly. And since each color is applied separately, some of her complex designs required twenty-seven immersions in different dyes.

AFTER SOME TIME, Mrs. Sukarno, then first lady of Indonesia, saw Mrs. Praptini's work and ordered a sarong. That order catalyzed business, and Mrs. Praptini received more and more custom orders. And ultimately, her daughter graduated from Semanang University with a major in literature.

Previous pages: **A batik vendor sits on the sidewalk outside Pasar Klewer, the batik market in Surakarta, Java.**

Opposite: **Ibu Praptini Partaningrat, descended from a king, is one of few who still draw the intricate freehand batik designs that were the province of women in Javanese royal courts.**

Now semiretired at age seventy-two, Mrs. Praptini gives private lessons for the Pioneers, a foundation she co-sponsored to protect the dying art of classic batik. "Many of the old women who were experts have already died," she tells us. "All women in Java used to make batik, even if they did not create court designs. But younger women here do not want to learn batik now; they prefer to work in factories. Most of my students are foreigners from countries like Denmark and Japan."

We ask how she spends her time when she is not teaching. "I read, sew, do puzzles, and go out with five old women friends. Also, I participate in a savings club. Twenty friends chip in and once a month we buy food and give ourselves a little party."

MRS. RAHAYU'S MOTHER began to wholesale batik in Surakarta during the Japanese occupation after World War II. She was not allowed to sell from a permanent location, so she moved her inventory from place to place each day, hoping to position herself near major arteries. But there was little traffic because there was no gasoline. Business hours were short due to curfews. And there was great poverty. Sometimes she had no money to buy merchandise to sell; sometimes customers had no money to spend. Frequently, she had to barter cloth for food for her family.

In 1953, she and her husband opened a real shop. Their daughter, Rahayu, helped there after school when she was old enough. After Rahayu was married in 1969, she began to make batik at home to sell to retailers. Nine years later, when her father died, she began to work full time in her family's stall and grew the enterprise into the operation it is today.

By all standards, her business is a success. She owns a factory in Pekalongan that prints the designs she creates. Her shop, Toko Sri Djaja, is reputed to be one of the best in the city's batik market, Pasar Klewer. When Mrs. Suharto, then the first lady of Indonesia, invited ambassadors' wives to her annual coffee morning in Jakarta, where she showcased the country's finest crafts, Mrs. Rahayu's fabrics were always exhibited.

This daughter of an itinerant vendor, high school graduate, and single mother of four, has built a house worthy of a magazine feature. We interview her there at breakfast time, because she must open the shop at ten. White marble halls open onto a small private lake in the backyard. Birds sing from hanging cages. Her parrots speak reputable Indonesian. There is an aviary of peacocks. A father-mother-daughter team works for her as gardener, cook, and housekeeper. We are served sugary miniature pancakes and feel very pampered.

Later, when we visit her at the batik market, we find that Mrs. Rahayu's work environment is as clamorous as her home is calm. The batik market is surrounded by people selling sausages, whistles, prickly rambutan fruit, bananas, paintings of Javanese puppets rendered in metallic pigments on calfskin, plucked chickens in buckets. *Becaks*, bicycle taxis that look like strollers for adults, jockey in the street. As we arrive, a torrential rain floods the area without warning and sends everyone scurrying for cover.

Inside, the dim batik market is jammed with buyers, beggars, and vendors. A strolling singer carries a tin cup, microphone, and boom box. A woman struggles upstream with a tray of glasses: coconut milk and rice tea served with lemon slices. The market has two hundred fabric stalls. Goods are hung, piled, shelved. Displays reach the ceiling and sellers use hooks on sticks to get hangers down from high places. Some sell from elevated stalls surrounded by stacks of batik. Darkness is broken by hot green neon lights. Sweat pours off our noses and chins, making rivulets under our clothes.

Astonishingly, Mrs. Rahayu looks cool and elegant. She unfolds sheer silk batiks; some are *tulis* (hand drawn) and others *cap* (stamp printed), but all are drizzled with gold. Fabrics neatly wrapped in clear plastic are stacked on three sides of the counter all the way to the ceiling. "A word-of-mouth reputation for good service and fair prices has been critical to our success. Many shops here have good merchandise," Mrs. Rahayu admits, "but our shop has good customers." In total, those good customers spend two thousand dollars on an average day; Mrs. Rahayu's net profit is ten percent.

Have women always been associated with batik in Java? "Most batik stores are run by women, who are known for selling and negotiating," Mrs. Rahayu tells us.

Opposite, top left and right: Mrs. Praptini's profile echoes the bone structure and bearing of the royalty shown in the stained-glass windows at the palace.

Bottom, left: Mrs. Praptini's royal batiks are all hand-drawn on white cotton dipped in natural dyes she makes herself; some patterns require twenty-seven immersions.

Bottom, right: Mrs. Rahayu's boutique, Toko Sri Djaja, is stacked to the ceiling with batiks, each in its own glossy wrapping.

Although two of her three assistants are men ("I have supervised them for fifteen years; it does not cause resentment"), her third assistant is her mother, now seventy-two. Mrs. Rahayu hopes that her own daughter will come into the business, although Rini, sixteen, has not yet shown an interest.

We ask Mrs. Rahayu to show us her favorite batik pattern. "Sido Mukti, the most expensive batik in the shop. Enough yardage for a sarong and stole costs sixty-four dollars. It is a classic design used for weddings," she says. It is a fitting favorite, since this fabric seems to symbolize Mrs. Rahayu's life: its name means "becoming prosperous and well respected."

CRAFTS AND GENDER IN INDONESIA

In much of the archipelago, *women work only with soft materials—cloth and clay— while men work with hard materials—metal, stone, and wood.*

On Sapporo Island in Maluku, *men are not allowed in the woods where women collect the sacred clay they use for creating vessels, which are strongly associated with the feminine and fertility.*

In West Kalimantan, *weaving is known to the* iban *people as the "women's warpath" because it earned the same glory for women that headhunting did for men.*

On some islands, *color is associated with gender: black represents the feminine and red the masculine; black and red with white represent the unity of the universe that is composed of complementary opposites.*

Opposite: Mrs. Rahayu sells her own designs as well as royal batiks and hand-drawn, stamp-printed, and silk batiks, all drizzled with metallic gold.

Bia

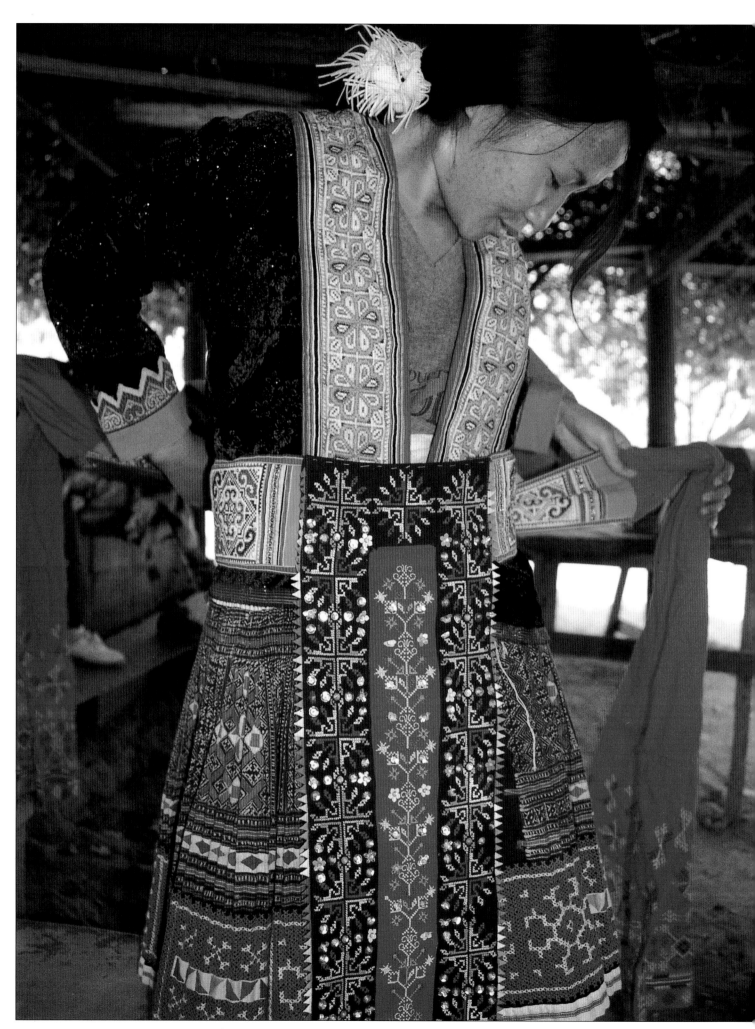

ON NEW YEAR'S DAY in Lisu communities everyone puts on brand new clothes. Women wear colors that would amaze the fashion avant-garde: shocking pink, kelly green, magenta, turquoise, lime, and lipstick red. Their tunics are adorned with appliquéd yokes, and they wear silver jewelry. Hundreds of ball tassels bounce from their bright sashes. Colorful pompons decorate their turbans. Even the men, who usually wear Western clothes and drive pickups or motorcycles, wear traditional Lisu garb today. Their black velvet jackets are embellished with silver buttons; we are told it is ideal to have a thousand. Some of the men, including the headman, are talented silversmiths and sport handsome necklaces layered with jingling conical dangles.

We are in a little village in northern Thailand. The music of Madonna is at war with the rhythms of the Macarena. People are hunkered down on the ground watching the chickens, and watching us, and waiting for the dancing to begin.

ALTHOUGH EVERYONE IN THE VILLAGE speaks Lisu, the headman's wife welcomes us in Thai. Inside her house, the floor is concrete and the walls are woven of fiber. The family uses the top of a truck cab as a table. Tea is served there, and appliqué work is spread on it to show us the fine Lisu needlework.

Orathai Saiyang, thirty-two, is seven months pregnant with her third child. "My husband also has two children by a previous marriage," she tells us. "His old wife ran away somewhere. We don't register marriages, so he just took me as his wife."

The village is named Pang Mai Dang and was founded twenty-five years ago as part of a project by the Thai king, Bhumibol Adulyadej, to replace the villagers' revenue from opium growing, which had been outlawed. The loss of that revenue for hill tribe people caused some families to sell their daughters into prostitution in distant cities. Pang Mai Dang residents accepted the king's help to pursue a better option: stable, consistent earnings from sewing and silversmithing.

"My parents grew opium, but they didn't make much money," Orathai tells us. "Traders, not farmers, get the money from opium. My family came here to participate in the king's project. Mother always sewed things for us, but this was to sell. She taught me how to sew when I was sixteen."

Now, Orathai sews on her lunch break every day. "I clean tourist bungalows. I leave the house at six in the morning and work until noon, come home to sew, then return to work again from three to eight o'clock. Meanwhile, my son, Rubal, does the cooking at my house."

She earns seventy-two dollars a month from her outside job and eighty dollars from sewing. Her husband, Alapha, serves as village headman without pay, but periodically takes special orders for silver jewelry. Orathai not only makes more than her husband but virtually supports their family of six, soon to be seven.

Orathai would like some help earning money. Although in other parts of Asia, boys are the preferred sex, she says, "I have only sons so far, so I would like my new baby to be a girl. Only girls sew here."

We talk about her pregnancy and find that it was not planned—she had been taking birth control tablets. Orathai goes to the hospital in Chiang Mai for prenatal care, and government health-care officials send doctors and nurses to the village once a month.

Except for the four-day New Year's celebration when no one works, there is little time for fun. Sewing is as close as Orathai comes to relaxation. She confides, "Sometimes I take all my stuff and go to a friend's house to visit while I'm sewing by hand."

PRETTY AMIMA SIN MEE, twenty-seven, supports a family of ten on the sixty-eight dollars a month she makes from selling her appliqué placemats, napkins, and purses.

Her husband, Ata-O, whom she married eleven years ago, farms rice for the family to eat but does not earn money. He cooks the meals and cares for their children so Amima will not have to stop working at the sewing machine she purchased with her earnings. Is Ata-O a supportive, liberated husband, or is Amima a wife enslaved? We would have to know much more.

If she lived in the United States, Amima would be considered a member of the Sandwich Generation. She

Previous pages: **Lisu children cavort on New Year's Day.**

Opposite: **Bia Sai Yak, who lives in the tribal village Hmong Chum Yen, models her New Year's outfit. It took a year to complete the appliqué, embroidery, batiking, and pleating.**

The first thing to go wrong is that she's not at the airport when we land.

After spending eons looking for a young woman with a "Gianturco and Tuttle" sign, we just take the hotel van. While we're checking in, a tiny, attractive, and breathless Thai woman runs into the lobby, looks around briefly, and makes a beeline for us.

"I'm so sorry I wasn't at the airport. There was terrible traffic. I missed you. And I also missed the driver there, but now he's here, waiting outside. I came from the airport in my car." Her name is Tui; she's to be our guide and interpreter. She does have a proper Thai name with about a hundred letters in it, but it's agreed that we'll call her Tui, as all her friends do.

So we take Tui to lunch. It is Chinese New Year, and the hotel's Chinese restaurant is offering a special lunch of a zillion courses, so we have plenty of food wrapped up for helpful bellmen to take home. And while at lunch, we discuss the agenda, which it seems Tui has not previously seen. This means, of course, that she has not located the queen's workshop (or even heard of it), nor has she arranged meetings with hill tribe women. We'll just have to improvise.

Off to meet Tony, the driver, in the parking lot. He's not there. Tui is becoming slightly crazed, realizing that she is now zero for two. Since nobody told Tony we were having lunch, he figured us for missing in action and split. So we don't have him or the nice van that the travel people arranged. A very nervous Tui offers, "No problem, we'll take my car. I'll drive."

Tui is a dear person, but she has a crunched-up little car, and she can't drive worth beans. Nor does she know where we're going. Before we left the hotel, she had checked phone books, maps, and the concierge, and found no clue to a queen's craft workshop. But she does know of a craft shop run under the auspices of the king. Close enough!

We careen around Chiang Mai, lurching, swerving, panic-stopping our way to the king's craft store. It is not at all what we're looking for, so we do a little shopping, then leave. How about heading for the hills and dropping in on the Lisu people, or the Akha or Hmong village? Well—no. It's really too far to start out at this hour. And nobody is expecting us, anyway.

So here we are, thousands of miles from home, with nothing productive to do. Our first totally wasted day.

And then Tui lifts her dejected head from the steering wheel and smiles. "Have you ever had a Thai massage?" Perfect!

CHIANG MAI, THAILAND

supports her three sons, ages five, eight, and eleven, plus her husband. Then there are her father-in-law, her mother-in-law, and three aunts. It makes her proud to be the one earning the money, and she hopes her sons will have a more comfortable life than her own because of it. Still, when asked if it is better to have girls or boys, she says, "I'd have liked girls. They make the money."

Although government health-care workers now visit this remote village, access to physicians used to be a serious problem. Three times, Amima took public transportation while she was in labor in order to get to the hospital a half-hour away and deliver her babies. Her mother died at age forty-five, even though most people here live to be seventy-five or eighty, because she couldn't get to a doctor.

The family lives in a house with paper-thin walls. We perch to talk on the platform bed in the main room where Amima and her husband sleep at night. Amima is sitting on a low wooden seat with her youngest son across her lap, flanked by a line-up of her curious women friends. Between us is a smoky fire built directly on the earthen floor. There are two small bed alcoves and a kitchen with an open fire and meat hanging on high lines to cure. Amina's sewing machine has been stored for the holiday.

A GREAT DEAL OF NEW YEAR'S FEASTING and drinking distilled liquor preceded our arrival. Now, young boys ignite firecrackers, preparing for the New Year's finale.

We are invited to join a shuffling, rhythmic circle dance inspired by music from a two-stringed gourd instrument. In the clearing, musicians and villagers gather around the New Year's tree, whose bare branches have been threaded with bougainvillea and ribbons. The Lisu, who worship spirits and ancestors, believe that the New Year's tree absorbs bad luck. At dawn the next day, they will tie pieces of pork and rice cakes to the branches, then cast the tree—and its ill fortune— into the jungle so that fortunes will be good for the next year.

THE VILLAGE OF HMONG CHUM YEN is parched. It is noon, and deep shadows cut across the earthen streets. Across the street, a heap of golden corn-cobs has been raked flat to dry. Three women bind brooms; they are clustered under a tree for relief from the scorching sun.

The word *Hmong* means "barbarian." This group, the Blue Hmong, migrated from China. They are known for their independence and their business acumen.

Deep in a porch shadow sits a family surrounded by clear plastic bags full of acrylic thread in orange, yellow, magenta, and kelly green. The father is carving a wooden gun for his son. The mother and three daughters are embroidering. We join them.

After a pleasant conversation on general topics, we ask permission to talk with nineteen-year-old Bia Sai Yak about her embroidery. The family holds counsel. Finally, her father returns: he will charge four dollars for an interview. Hmong men have virtually unlimited authority over family affairs in their patrilineal clans, so we pay. We are not surprised to discover that, although this family is hardly rich, they work hard for their assets.

"My family makes four thousand dollars a year," Bia tells us ingenuously. "We own twelve square acres, planted in lichee and longan nuts. I have five brothers and sisters; three are still in school. I finished the sixth grade, and with the others, I do farm work." Hmong women traditionally do most of the farming; agriculture is so central to Hmong existence that when the land is spent, whole villages may relocate.

"My mother taught my sister and me to embroider. Sometimes I sell to a broker in the Night Market in Chiang Mai, but there is not much money in it, so mostly I embroider for myself as a hobby.

"Only old people wear embroidery every day," says Bia, who wears jeans and a T-shirt. "But I always make a New Year's costume, which takes all year. Mother helps, but I do everything: the appliqué, the embroidery, the accordion pleats, the skirt batik." Blue Hmong women, almost all of whom have sewing machines, claim to be the only tribal people in mainland Southeast Asia who are skilled in batiking.

Previous pages: **Even the prow of a longtail boat near Bang Sai is decorated for Chinese New Year.**

Opposite: **Lisu women dress daily in shocking pink, kelly green, magenta, turquoise, lime, lipstick red, and neon orange. But for the holiday, they dress up in new, even fancier clothes.**

We invite Bia to model her newest creation. Bia's glorious holiday outfit is still missing its hat, but the colors, textures, hand-beading, complex machine embroidery, and needlework dazzle us. We cannot imagine that Bia could look more beautiful, even after she adds the silver rings, chains, and pendants that Hmong women wear to symbolize wealth and the essence of the good life.

The traditional Hmong courting period starts at the new year, and Bia is of eminently marriageable age. We are sure that, dressed like this, she has an especially happy new year ahead.

PONDS, PAVILIONS, patterned woven mats on the grass. Smells of jasmine rice and fish-in-foil cooking on coal beds in open boats below the bridge. Gardens brimming with blossoms. Lotus flowers blooming in the still river water.

At the Bang Sai Royal Folk Arts and Crafts Center near Thailand's ancient capital, Ayutthaya, the Chinese New Year opens the center's annual ten-day trade fair and exhibition of student work. Orawan Siangproh lives in a women's dorm here now, but her permanent home is in the north. "I couldn't learn there. My grandmother and grandfather used to make this difficult basketry, but they have already passed away."

The fine bamboo basket she is making will take another month to finish and will sell for $150 "if the project director examines it, pronounces it perfect, and accepts it for sale. I will give the money to my mother," Orawan says. "I am not married yet, so do not have to worry about children, but my mother has not been very healthy." Her mother did not learn this skill either, so her family and her community will both appreciate her knowledge. "I will teach others when I am good enough," she vows.

ORAWAN'S TEACHER, Viparat Wuthivake, thirty-two, was born in Ayutthaya. Now married, she has taught at the center for the thirteen years since she was a student here and was nominated by her teacher to join the staff. She receives $144 a month for teaching twenty neophyte basket makers.

She cuts a strand of Lipao vine lengthwise into three parts, then cuts each again until she has fine, fragile threads suitable for weaving. The preparation is precise and laborious. "It takes two months to make a basket purse from vines, which the palace obtains in the south," she explains.

Like the other graduates and trainees, Viparat can market her products herself or sell them at one of the queen's nine nonprofit retail stores, all named Chitralada, after the Bangkok palace. The shops take no commission; the entire price of every product goes to the artisan. The Department of Industry, Commerce, and Foreign Affairs manages export marketing and distributes all over the world.

THE QUEEN'S PROJECT began in 1976, and is called SUPPORT, which is a Thai-language acronym for Foundation for the Promotion of Supplementary Occupations and Related Techniques. Thai royalty has long worked to attack the twin problems of hunger and poverty by providing farmers with opportunities to supplement their marginal, seasonal agricultural revenue. Cultivated plots are small, and crops are sold but once a year. Hungry months stretch between harvests. "When it is not rice season, people don't work at anything," Colonel Kasem Chatsathienpong, deputy director of the Bang Sai Center, tells us.

"In the beginning, Queen Sirikit went everywhere in Thailand and saw poor Thai people growing rice in the fields. The queen thought they could also do handicrafts, at which Thais are traditionally very good. Her goals were to help the poor and give traditional crafts new life. Young people were abandoning the crafts because they didn't believe crafts could provide a living. So the queen started SUPPORT's training and marketing programs."

SUPPORT now operates four regional training centers that teach local traditional crafts. For example, north of Chiang Mai, Her Majesty's own staff has for years taught embroidery, brocade weaving, and gold- and silversmithing. Additionally, SUPPORT runs two multicraft training centers that teach both old and new crafts such as intricate machine embroidery. This is one of those centers; the other is located at the palace in Bangkok.

Opposite, top left and bottom right:
Lisu women's machine-sewn appliquéd placemats, coin purses, and hot pads incorporate surprising rainbows in new combinations of colors.

Opposite, top right and bottom left:
On New Year's Day, even the littlest Lisu children dress for the celebration.

"Each year, a thousand students are chosen from all over the country," Colonel Chatsathienpong continues. "Half are men and half are women. Each student can learn any craft. Originally only women did sewing in Thailand, but now some men choose it. If a woman wants to make furniture, fine!

"Students are selected according to need and willingness to work hard. No prior craft skill or artistic talent is required. Room, board, tuition, and living expenses are all free," the colonel tells us. "Classes take eight hours a day and courses last six to twelve months, depending on the complexity of the craft a student chooses from the eighteen that are offered. Graduates can return for four-month refresher courses at any time, and are expected to share their knowledge with others in their home villages. Twenty years after SUPPORT's launch, thousands of people in hundreds of Thai villages make and sell crafts they learned at the queen's schools."

THAILAND'S KING AND QUEEN are addressed in a separate, deferential language, a formality that underscores the social chasm between Their Royal Majesties and their Thai subjects. But in fact, royalty and subjects seem spiritually very close. The royal couple is beloved privately and publicly. Every home we visit in Thailand has a picture of Queen Sirikit and King Bhumibol Adulyadej, whose faces we also see on posters, calendars, billboards, umbrella factory walls, office building elevators, and artists' easels.

Educated in Switzerland and married in 1950, Queen Sirikit lives by the oath of accession administered that year when she and her husband were crowned at the Grand Palace: "We will reign with righteousness, for the benefit and happiness of the Siamese people."

The queen is renowned worldwide for her fundamental conviction that women deserve equal treatment. And since 1782, when Bangkok was designated the nation's capital, only one other queen has been appointed to rule, should it be necessary, in her husband's place. A manifestation of Queen Sirikit's commitment and leadership is the important role of women and traditional crafts in Thailand's contemporary culture.

Opposite: **The Bang Sai Royal Folk Arts and Crafts Center is one of the queen's training schools; farm women and men learn crafts that will generate income during the eleven nonharvest months.**

and the AIDS Project

THE PEOPLE WHO WORK in the Sa Paper Project live modern lives. The director of the project carries a cell phone. The project's grantor has urban offices with computers, videotapes, and a scientific library; everyone moves with such urgency that you would think life depended on it—and it does.

"Women represent one-third of the HIV and AIDS cases in Thailand," Dr. Usa Duongsaa tells us. "As recently as 1992, the percentage was about half that. A Thai woman who has been diagnosed HIV-positive must cope with the shock of learning about her own infection, the trauma of having a very ill husband, the knowledge of his marital infidelity, the prospect of widowhood, and if she is pregnant, the chance that her baby may be born with the disease."

Dr. Usa's organization, Thai-Australia Northern AIDS Prevention and Care Program, funds initiatives to reduce the transmission rate of the HIV virus in northern Thailand, where over half the country's cases occur. These days there are fewer new cases, but many people are already ill and mortality is expected to peak in 1999. "Typically, three generations live together," Dr. Usa explains. "So when a couple dies, both the younger and older generations are orphaned. There are no facilities to care for so many children and elderly people."

Dr. Usa has arranged for us to visit Women Against AIDS, a craft program that her organization co-sponsors, which includes both HIV-positive and uninfected women. "Both earn desperately needed money. Healthy women learn the importance of AIDS prevention, and infected women experience support instead of stigma."

WE DRIVE WITH BEN SAVASTI, the director of Women Against AIDS, down a winding dirt road along a thicket that obscures squalid villages, to an outdoor restaurant at the edge of a placid lake where we eat lunch and learn about his work. He comments, "This project began in 1985 as Thammasat University's response to a brothel fire in Phuket, where chained prostitutes burned to death. The girls' parents lived here in the village of San Pa Tong. Project founders reasoned that if there were alternative sources of income, families would not need to sell their daughters into prostitution.

"Today, our goals are broad. Twenty percent of the local population is HIV-positive, and among young adults and married couples the incidence is much higher since almost all cases are sexually transmitted."

Cacophonous music suddenly floods the silent restaurant, and Ben raises his voice. "Our life skills program began in 1992 to improve housewives' ability to earn money. Their income is not used by their husbands for drinking and gambling, so having their own money gives women the strength to fight to keep their daughters out of prostitution and to negotiate with their husbands to use condoms. It is socially acceptable here for husbands to visit brothels several times a week. It doesn't occur to the men to use condoms with their own wives, and the wives have not had the courage to insist on it."

The waitress ladles chunky vegetable soup from a crock while Ben describes the rich artistic heritage in this area. "This region used to be the center of paper making. Our organization revitalized that craft and was the first to put batik designs on paper. Members create gift boxes, cards, folders, and picture frames covered with batik-patterned, handmade *sa* [mulberry] paper.

"Today, we have three kinds of handicraft groups: AIDS patients, sex workers, and village women. Our AIDS patients are mostly widows. The work allows them to be productive and continue to earn. Sex workers in brothels make handicrafts in their slow afternoon hours to pay off the 25,000-baht [$1,000] debt they were saddled with when the brothel owner paid their parents.

"Unlike the other two groups, members of our ten village women's groups are skilled artisans whom we trained in small business practices. No one knows which of these women are HIV-positive; almost no testing is done. By now, these groups are self-run and we only do marketing. Our alternative trading organization sells in a shop in the Chiang Mai Night Bazaar and exports to the United States and the United Kingdom."

As we drive through the verdant farmland to visit the women's groups, Ben advises us, "Keep your eyes on the roofs. If they are not made of teak leaves, you know there is only one way a family could afford better roofing: they sold a daughter."

Previous pages: Craftswomen who participate in Women Against Aids create gift items covered with batik-painted *sa* (mulberry) paper, earning enough that fewer families need to sell daughters into prostitution.

Opposite: Mae Fong Nuan's grandmother comes to visit the group of local women who work every day in her shaded pavilion in San Pa Tong, which used to be a paper-making center.

WE ARE RELIEVED TO SEE that the buildings in Mae Fong Nuan's compound have teak-leaf roofs. The leaves are layered, the dry, ruffled edges overlapping capriciously as if they had been blown into place by a breeze.

Mae and the team of batik artists she captains work every day in the shade of her pavilion, which becomes a hub of activity as women draw wax patterns on the mulberry paper that will ultimately cover their products. The local lunch motorcycle buzzes up to sell midday meals. Vegetables, rice cakes, and all manner of foodstuffs hang off the handles in plastic sandwich bags—a live fish flaps languidly inside a plastic pouch of tepid water.

Umpai, Linda, Kwan, Mali . . . The women on Mae's team are neighbors and distant relatives who decided to work together three years ago. We talk to Umpai Kantabun, eighteen, who was part of the group from the beginning. She assumed that by now she would be farming longan fruit (similar to lichee nuts), working for someone else as her parents do, but she enjoys this work.

"I was an only child growing up here in a very poor family. Lots of things are changing: they are building roads; families are earning more money. But when I was young there was a drought and we couldn't grow anything. And in the winter, there were floods."

Umpai grew up a tomboy. "I was very naughty when I was little, climbing trees like a boy. I was always punished for that—my father spanked me with a stick! When I was a student—I completed fifth grade—I played volleyball. I can serve well."

She was married last year, in an unarranged marriage, to a twenty-two-year-old auto mechanic. She likes her husband, except when he is drunk. "He has a sweet mouth, talks nicely. We get along well together."

Umpai makes 3,500 baht ($140) a month, and her husband makes 5,500 baht ($220). She has never been to Bangkok, never seen a movie. For fun, she and her husband visit their families by motorcycle, and once a month they ride to Chiang Mai to shop.

When the couple were married, Umpai's husband paid a bride price of money and a gold necklace. "We had a small, traditional, Buddhist wedding with our family. I fed all the relatives. Old people came and blessed us and tied us with holy threads. We went to the temple to make an offering to the monk."

Umpai is not yet ready to have children—she takes birth control pills. "In two years I might start a family. I want only two children, ideally a boy and a girl."

Will she still work after she has children?

"I love to do this. When my children go to school I would like to continue."

AT FORTY-ONE, Mae Fong Nuan is married and has a grown daughter and a son who is thirteen. Her husband, Pau Song, sells rice and soybeans grown on their small plot of land. Mae used to earn money by making and selling decorative chandeliers fashioned from striped plastic straws, but then she learned batik art at the Sa Paper Center.

Her first Sa Paper product was a "not very good" picture frame, but she was glad to earn some money. At first, she was paid forty baht ($1.60) a day, but now she is paid by the order. She manages the money in her household and says her husband reacts positively to her economic contributions.

Mae grew up before northern Thailand had paved roads and electricity; she lived near rice paddies where water buffalo wandered. As far as she knows, her parents had no dreams for her; she did not attend school. She married the boy next door when she was seventeen and he was twenty-six, although she did not love him. Their marriage was not celebrated, just registered.

Over time, Mae came to love her husband and, unlike her parents, to have dreams. One was to send her son to school at the Buddhist temple. She uses her own earnings to pay for his food, uniforms, supplies, and the bus to get there. Her daughter, who completed sixth grade, is already working, saving to attend adult classes and hoping to finish three more years of school.

Does she ever have enough money to buy something for herself?

"Never," Mae says, but explains that as a Buddhist, she believes life is "good enough" as it is.

Opposite, top: Rural northern Thailand is the site of the Women Against AIDS project, which began after a brothel fire on the coast killed young prostitutes whose families live here.

Opposite, bottom: Since craftswomen have been trained in small business practices, the groups run themselves.

Every visitor to Chiang Mai finds the way to the Night Bazaar. We go there knowing that the handicrafts of the village women can be found there. The Lisu people, and the Hmong, Karen, and Akha, all have their wares displayed: the women's weaving, appliqué, and embroidery and the men's silver work. We see wonderful tribal headdresses that are virtual wedding cakes of silver balls and discs and chains, undoubtedly grandparents' treasures taken to market under the pressure of hard times, offered for what seem to us sadly "reasonable" prices. Back home we see one for sale in a shop in San Francisco for thousands!

There is food to buy, all kinds of toys, and clothing and shoes—we buy amazing shoes, just black rubber soles all tied up with strings and pompons of every color. There are low-end dealers in hardware and household items, and high-end traders in silk ikat, a textile that is tie-dyed before weaving.

We're looking for the White Lotus, the shop that sells the colorful batik Sa Paper Center products from Women Against AIDS. We know their retail shop is somewhere in the bazaar, but it is not easy to find anything here—it's so dark and so bright—glaring greenish neon lighting in one alleyway, and inky pools of dark just around the corner. Eventually, we find it.

Having explored the various levels and dark crannies of the permanent concrete structures, we widen our circle of exploration to include the sidewalk stalls we passed in our hurry to get into the heart of the market. The sidewalk is packed solid with people, hundreds of tourists, thousands of Thais. Not all are city denizens—standing at the curb is a Lisu girl dressed in her bright hill tribe finery, talking to a fellow on an expensive-looking motorcycle. The streets around the bazaar are jammed with motorcycles, little putt-putt scooters, cars, pickups, bicycles; and the air is stinky-thick with exhaust.

Pushing through the sidewalk crowds we find a few treasures too good to pass up, cotton pants and jackets, an antique, toys for grandkids back home . . . and make our way out of the throng to the car to call it a day—and a night.

CHIANG MAI, THAILAND

There is much to appreciate. Mae invites us to tour the house the family built a year ago. It has two stories and two bedrooms. Fenced outside the house are her sister's pig and her own chickens and ducks. There is a small fishpond near the front door, a separate laundry, and a cookhouse adjacent to a fire pit on the ground.

She narrates her day for us: "I get up at five to make sticky rice, which takes an hour. While that cooks outdoors on the fire, I prepare breakfast and lunch in the cookhouse. From eight to five I make crafts, with an hour off to eat. After work I go to the village market to shop, then cook dinner—usually pork, vegetables, or chicken with chili paste."

Mae's husband, Pau Song, is assistant headman in the village, an elected position. His salary is 2,500 baht ($100), a month and he is partially reimbursed for the family's electricity, tuition, and medical expenses. His many responsibilities include ensuring that all village children attend six years of school, and that primary-school girls are not recruited for prostitution.

Mae and her husband are unusual in that they have had AIDS tests. "The village accepts AIDS," she says, "and takes care of the people who are sick. A health-care official came to educate us, so most people understand what causes the disease."

One afternoon, a motorcycle buzzes into the yard, driven by the accountant from the Sa Paper Center who is delivering this week's pay. Mae takes her 1,000 baht ($40), a fat wad of bills, and wordlessly hands them all to her husband. Pau Song gets on his red motorcycle and rides away.

Confused, we ask Mae, "What is going on? We thought you managed the money; we thought you were paying for your son's schooling; why did you hand it all to your husband; why did he leave without a word?"

"Someone dies every day in this village," Mae Fong tells us, "and funerals are very expensive. Families must feed funeral guests three meals a day for a week, and they cannot afford it. My husband is taking our money to help such a friend."

Previous pages: Hats made near Bangkok are offered for sale—along with Sa Paper products and just about everything else—at the Night Bazaar in Chiang Mai.

Above, top: Artisans paint color into the design that will ultimately cover a picture frame. Other patterns fit tissue boxes, notebooks, and albums.

Above, bottom: An artist draws wax designs on mulberry paper, dyes the paper, and irons it between pieces of newsprint that absorb the wax, leaving swirly white designs.

Opposite: Painted strips of mulberry paper fly in the breeze. When dry, they will be cut and mounted on cardboard picture frames.

and the Mirror Embroiderers

MIRROR EMBROIDERY GLINTS like raindrops. For the women who create the sparkling designs, rain can be both a miracle and a catastrophe. For most of the year, the Little Rann of Kachchh is dry, its sandy desert bleached. But during summer monsoons, this vast salt marsh becomes impassible; floods isolate the peninsula from the rest of Gujarat, forcing families to flee to high ground.

Today, the weather is good. Truck drivers live dangerously on the road between Ahmedabad and Bhuj, passing each other, then playing "chicken" in the wrong lane at high speed. There is a roadside warning sign: "Accident Prone Zone." We slow only to see the remains of today's eight disastrous wrecks. Passersby peer curiously at the mangled trucks, then turn their heads away sadly.

We try to focus instead on what is flying past us in a blur. Teams of beige oxen pull wooden carts, their drivers squinting through the swooping horns. Six women carry brass water vessels on their heads. Motorcycles pull tiny wagons, each spilling over with at least fifteen passengers—the local transportation system. Men and women make bricks one by one in wooden molds, then fire them in trapezoidal kilns.

Soon, the terrain turns white. The landscape of salt flats is cut by canals and interrupted by high cones of salt raked into place by women in vivid, diaphanous silks.

Now, rivulets of water glide over the marsh mud. Abandoned rowboats tilt on their sides in the middle of a treeless nowhere. In July, migrating flamingos from Europe and Africa will stop over, but meanwhile, egrets keep vigil.

At last, hills. The great stone wall that has protected Bhuj since 1548 veers up the steep incline. We have arrived—alive!

Muslim prayer calls reverberate. The market is labyrinthine, bustling with animals, motor scooters, women wrapped in *bandhani* (sophisticated, tie-dyed cloth), and barefoot men who carry wood staffs and wear *dhoti* (draped pants). Cows sleep in heaps around the traffic islands and meander through dusty streets littered with trash. A citizen explains, "The pigs keep our city clean," and we watch them and their fellow itinerant street cleaners, the donkeys, snuffling through the garbage.

GUJARAT IS ONE OF THE RICHEST sources of folk embroidery in the world. The Indian textile heritage is five thousand years old and has been handed down through the generations. Here, many mothers begin at each daughter's birth to create mirror embroidery for a trousseau that will include wedding clothes for her and her as-yet-unknown husband, household linen, and camel trappings. Red is the bride's color; blue represents Lord Krishna; yellow symbolizes the sun or spring; saffron, the earth; green, fertility. In almost all Gujarat ethnic groups, women make embroidery for their own use; increasingly, they also sell it.

We must apply at the police station for permits to visit the northern villages where mirror embroiderers live and work. Files from years past, tied with string, are stacked to the ceiling. Officials hand our file from desk to desk. We watch. And watch.

Ultimately, we are denied permits to most of the villages. People have told us the Indian government may not want responsibility for Americans traveling so near the Pakistani border, but no explanation is offered for our exclusion.

We have arranged to travel with Mona Dave, the twenty-nine-year-old who heads craft operations here for SEWA, the Self Employed Women's Association. In the past two years, she has signed up twenty-five hundred Rabari, Sodha, Jat, and Ahir tribal craftswomen in eighteen Kachchh villages. SEWA trains the craftswomen both in the villages and at the Design Center in Ahmedabad, then markets their work through SEWA's Banascraft stores and on the Internet. SEWA also distributes members' products to retailers throughout India, Australia, the United States, and Europe.

We tell Mona we did not get permits. "No problem," she says calmly. How so, we wonder, already impressed with this effective, intelligent Gujarati woman who has a beautiful smile and hundred-megawatt energy. "Our jeep has black glass windows. When we drive through the military checkpoints, no one will know you are there." We climb in and, never having run a checkpoint, hope she is right.

Previous pages: **Gujarat is one of the richest sources of folk embroidery in the world. Rabari women stitch mirror embroidery while they wait to be paid for roadwork.**

Opposite: **Daily dress for many Rabari women is a bright, full skirt and a backless, embroidered bodice, but this is special—a bride's blouse.**

STORIES ABOUT THE RABARI have lured us here. As conservative Hindus, the herder Rabari understand themselves to be children of Lord Krishna, who was also of the Yadav caste of animal keepers. The Rabari, who believe camels are sacred, also believe that Momai Mata, a camel-riding goddess, protects their tribe. Grooms ride camels to their midnight group weddings, and the Rabari drink camel milk at all religious ceremonies. Originally from Rajasthan, the Rabari once provided the king with camels and camel milk. About three thousand Rabari families now live in Kachchh.

We drive past a desert corral full of camels, and suddenly, there are Rabari women and children on both sides of the road. Mona stops the jeep and jumps out.

"Traditionally Rabaris traveled through the open desert with their belongings on top of their camels, but this group owns some land in the village of Nokhania," she tells us. Because they cannot afford to irrigate the land to grow crops, the group sells milk and embroidery, which women can make even during their menstrual periods when they are not allowed to do other work. Another way both men and women earn money is by digging pits that are never used. Still, the government pays men a dollar a day to excavate, and women get sixty-six cents a day for that work. Today is payday. The women are here doing embroidery while they wait for the government paymaster to come.

Mothers and children stand so close to us that we cannot move. They stare, and we stare back. The women's clothes are splashes of brilliant magenta, orange, red, green, blue. Their tight, silken, backless bodices are dotted with flashing mirrors. The blouses serve as bras, so the bosom area is shirred and embroidered. Every gathered, voluminous skirt contains yards and yards of fabric.

We smile. Some of the women laugh; others look serious, proud, fearless. Interpreter Mona is not nearby so we mime our request to take pictures. As soon as our flashes light, young boys dance and scream to make the cameras wink and ignite again.

After they feel more comfortable with us, the women sit on the ground to embroider, unfolding little silk scarves that hold tiny, glittering spangles. Although the Rabari used to use shiny, naturally occurring mica chips, now they buy mirrored sequins in the market. Their fingers fly as they whipstitch the glitter.

In this short time, Mona has held a meeting up the road and recruited the entire group to join SEWA. "I looked at their work. They are very, very skilled. The work is A level, clean, done without an embroidery hoop, even in this wind. It will sell."

We wonder how she convinced them to join so quickly.

"I asked if they have a convenient way to get raw materials—no—if there were traders or organizations working with them—no—and if they wanted to sell—yes. I explained that if they became members, SEWA would help them market their embroidery. They said, 'Yes, you are educated. You can help us.' Next week, I will return to hold a meeting and explain the other benefits: training, health care, child care, financial services. Whatever service they need will cost five rupees [fifteen cents]. People do not want charity."

THIRTY SODHA TRIBAL WOMEN are gathering for a SEWA meeting in Kharadia, with the double agenda of forming a second craft group and selling embroidery to Mona. Late afternoon sun shining through the jewel-toned saris makes the women into butterflies. Their arms are covered with white bangle bracelets. When I raise the camera, the women hold their veils in their teeth to keep their faces covered. Mona explains that these Muslims have never seen a woman who wears pants and short hair, so they assume I am a man and cover themselves. Mona tells them that American women sometimes wear jeans and cropped hairstyles. The Sodha women relax. They offer us tea, which is carried from a hut in saucers. The invitation to drink from a saucer means we have been welcomed as family.

Age and dress distinguish Udekorba Danaji Sodha, the leader of the SEWA embroidery group that began two years ago. She is fifty, but is edentulous and looks as if she is eighty. Udekorba believes she should lead the newly forming SEWA group in addition to the old one. Mona tells her that she has not been a strong leader. "You went

Opposite, top left and bottom left: At night in downtown Ahmedabad, embroiderers set up corridors of stalls lit by kerosene lanterns; shoppers can choose from brightly colored, glittery clothing.
Opposite, top right: Rabari women have been digging pits and doing road-work all week; now they make mirror embroidery while they wait to be paid.
Opposite, bottom right: Mirror embroidery glints like raindrops. For desert people like this Rabari tribeswoman, rain can be both miracle and, if it comes with monsoon force, catastrophe.

to SEWA training sessions alone, without telling anyone else to attend. That made the sessions totally useless."

Mona explains to Udekorba and the group that Mankorba Naranji Jadeja, thirty-five, who ran SEWA's training program in the village for six months, has achieved master status as an embroiderer, has demonstrated her leadership, and has won people's respect. She will lead the second group.

Udekorba protests. She argues and yells, not about to give up easily. The crowd yells, too, taking sides. Mankorba motions the women to silence.

Mona tells them that unless all the women work together and help each other, she will not return to this village. Mona holds the trump card: not only is she a university graduate, which means she has much to teach, but she represents the only access to the market. When the Sodha women joined SEWA, they severed relationships with the usurious local traders.

The new group is formed. Women pay the five-rupee membership fee and sign the record book with thumbprints. Later, because they do not read or write, their thumbprints plus a picture will become their SEWA bank identification.

Next, the women present their embroidery to Mona, whose assistant pays in cash. Quality is consistent because SEWA has trained the less proficient embroiderers to meet a high standard. The prices, which range from one to four dollars, reflect the amount of work in each piece. The women count the bills carefully; some smile.

As the sun goes down, the women's husbands, who have been watching the proceedings from afar, climb off the fence across the road and head home.

MANKORBA SPREADS A BLANKET on the floor of her immaculate hut. There are no windows, just an open doorway. She has plastered the walls smooth with mud and dung. There is no furniture except for a *charpoy*—an aluminum bed frame with a webbed plastic surface—that is propped upright against the wall. There are a few pots on a high shelf and a curbing to contain the fire. There is no electricity. Twenty women crowd around us in the growing darkness, watching and listening

Opposite: Mankorba Naranji Jadeja, thirty-five, gestures for silence during a SEWA meeting in her Sodha tribal village, Kharadia.

silently. Someone hands a flashlight through the crowd so we can see each other.

Mankorba wears glasses that she obtained through SEWA and a red print sari that she purchased with income from her embroidery. Having completed the second grade, she is the only woman in the village who has attended school. As head of the new embroidery group, she already has a leader's bearing. We talk about the education she wants for her daughter.

"What about *you*?" Mona challenges. "Do *you* want to go back to school? Women are not well educated here; that is why all of you are in this position."

Mankorba draws herself taller and her chin goes up in warning. Her words are: "We are here talking with you. We have come out. That is a great achievement." Her unspoken caution: "Do not push us. We're changing as fast as we can."

Later, Mona explains what "coming out" means here. "Traditionally, married women in their caste cannot even go outside their houses to fetch water; if a woman wants water, she has to ask her son or husband to get it. Maybe, if they keep their faces covered and have their husband's permission and a male escort, they can visit one female friend. When strangers come, women stay inside; neither they nor their husbands talk to strangers. But recently the Sodha women decided to come out of their houses. In doing this they were afraid of the beatings they might get from their husbands, which is a problem, but actually, what they really couldn't bear was the disapproval of society. The people in their community might talk. Others might ostracize, harass, or do violence against them and their families. Women are afraid of those things, always afraid, but they are coming out. Now women convene meetings in the open air. Now they dare to talk with strangers.

"In some places, women are coming out of their villages, not just their houses. When they first go to SEWA's local, district, state, or national headquarters, many have never before had a seat on a train or a luxury bus, seen a computer, fax machine, or television. They come out because they find it useful. Even the educated men in the villages do not want women to come out, because they fear their control over the women will end. Now you see," says Mona, "that the coming out of the women means revolution."

At the end of our conversation with Mankorba, we invite the leaders of the two SEWA groups to distribute the American embroidery floss we brought as thank-you gifts. Udekorba grabs the bundles so rapaciously that we wonder if she will relinquish any. Then she asks for the plastic bag in which the floss was packed and snatches it as I remove it from my purse, as if she is terrified to lose the opportunity to acquire something so precious.

AS WE PREPARE TO LEAVE, a young woman shows us an eighteen-foot-long decorative appliqué that her mother created to decorate their hut. Its wavy, repeating design symbolizes water, the source and destroyer of life. Her asking price, forty-five dollars, is triple what most embroiderers earn in a month, but a fair price for such a large piece. When I pay, the girl takes the money to her father. "My mother is now dead; my father should have her money. What I earn from my own work, I keep," she explains.

Mona asks the father, "What will you do with the money?"

"Buy a gold ring for my son," says the man, whose habit is to convert assets to jewelry that can either be kept safe by wearing it or liquidated easily if necessary.

"You must buy something for your daughter. She is worthy. She got this money for you," Mona urges, and the man agrees. Three months later Mona writes us: "I have been back to Kharadia many times. That girl is wearing very good gold earrings. Her father did as he promised!"

HAWABAI IBRAHIM IS A MEMBER of the Jat ethnic group. Her first name means "air" or "wind." It sounds lighter and freer than her life actually is. She is illiterate, the oldest of eight children. When she was fifteen, her parents married her to a boy her own age.

"Lots of money is spent on traditional Muslim weddings. I wore a dress like the ones we wear every day, but it was new. The whole village came to the luncheon. There was a barrier to separate the men and the women guests.

Opposite, clockwise from top left: Udekorba Danaji Sodha, president of the first SEWA embroidery group in Kharadia, waves her arm angrily, fighting for leadership of a second group that's being formed • Mankorba agrees to be president of the new group; a natural leader, she has run the SEWA training program for the past six months and earned respect and power • In her new role, Mankorba presents embroidery to Mona Dave, who heads SEWA's Kutchcraft project— if the work is good quality, Mona will buy at a fair price • Mona pays, and Mankorba, the only woman who can read and write in Kharadia, signs the receipt book with a pen; illiterate women sign with thumbprints.

On our travels, the expeditions to meet women, we're meeting some fine men, too. We won't forget Rooplal of India, our driver and our companion for five days—with whom we share maybe twenty words of common language.

We meet Rooplal and the Ambassador at the little Ahmedabad airport. Rooplal is wearing his natty olive driver's uniform, looking handsome in that Indian way that is all about teeth, mustache, and black, black eyes. The Ambassador is handsome in a way, too, shiny, white, and blocky, rather like a Westinghouse deep-freeze on wheels. The Ambassador, of course, is the car. It and Rooplal take us to visit Bhuj, out on the desert, eight hours away. Because Rooplal is a bring-'em-back-alive kind of guy, we survive a round-trip in which recklessness abounds.

During our days in Bhuj and the surrounding desert, Rooplal leans patiently against the car while we tend to our lengthy business with desert women; goes shopping for fruit gifts for village children; cools his heels in town when we go off in Mona's car without him; and escorts us on a tour of countryside, temples, and a rajah's palace on a rare day off. Throughout, he has been catering to Paola's frequent whoops, "Stop! Please! Photo!" And now he's getting into it—he is spotting the photo ops, stopping along the road with a "Picture, Madame?" He's seeing shots we might like, and he's right. Good eye, Rooplal!

It's our last day, and we're negotiating the scary eight hours back to Ahmedabad. I remark, "Rooplal, at Ahmedabad, to airport. Almost bye-bye time. Too bad." He replies, proudly, "Mesdames, you come first my village."

Time crunch aside, we can't deny his sweet, completely unexpected invitation, and so, as we pull into the city's scrappy suburbs, he turns off the main road and noses the Ambassador down a muddy lane populated by children and cows.

Each house is a tiny cube on a cement slab, with an old-fashioned pump on the porch. In front of one such house stands a smiling woman in an orange sari, holding a little girl—Rooplal's family, welcoming him home. Inside is one piece of furniture, the ubiquitous cot, where parents sleep at night and guests sit during the day. Built into the wall is a ledge all around for stacking things, and on the floor, a curbed fire corner. And that's it. This is simplicity beyond even the huts in desert villages, but this "village" is a neighborhood at the edge of a major city. Surprising! Yet all is immaculate; belongings are stacked neatly on the floor or the ledge.

Paola offers to take a family photo or two, which prompts a scurry of prettying up. Wonder of wonders, Rooplal, the husband and father in this Muslim household, is changing his little daughter's dress—her "best" is silky red and fancy—and combing her hair, while simultaneously fixing tea for the guests. We become aware of a billowing orangeness in the corner, and suddenly realize that Mrs. Rooplal has magically tented herself under the sari she has been wearing, while discreetly changing into her "family photo" sari underneath, right there in the one room with husband and child, foreign visitors, and half a dozen neighbors who have crowded in.

And so we take photos, share family pictures, have tea, and give the little girl a present from our toy stash. Our host glances around the room and finds the one thing that is frivolous, not essential to daily life, and that was once pretty—a little wood-and-cloth horse dressed in faded regalia of silk, tinsel, and sequins—and he presents it to me, to take home to my little grandsons.

AHMEDABAD, STATE OF GUJARAT, INDIA

A bride says three times that, in exchange for the bride price, she agrees to marry her husband. I said that. It was the happiest day of my life."

A year later, her daughter was born at home with a midwife's help; two years after that, her son was delivered in a hospital. Then, suddenly, everything changed. Her husband died from a heart valve problem when the two of them were nineteen. Hawabai spent forty days in mourning inside the house.

Afterward, she searched for work and "did agriculture and made peanut oil to sell." But it was clear that she had to find a more reliable way to earn a living. Although Jat men can have up to four wives, widows are not considered marriageable. Hawabai knew she would be on her own for a long time.

Now thirty, Hawabai and her children live in her brother-in-law's house, but she pays her family's expenses. Although she learned embroidery when she was twelve, she has only been selling her work for seven years. Each month she earns about nineteen dollars from embroidery and eighteen more from roadwork.

Her village, Kunakhia, has electricity but is not modern. While her sister-in-law shines aluminum dishes with gritty dirt she scoops off the ground, we keep Hawabai company as she grinds chilies between two rocks. Her family used to eat only millet bread and chilies, but by selling embroidery through SEWA, Hawabai can now afford to add buttermilk to their diet and, on alternate days, *kedgeree* (rice with lentils), eggplant, potatoes, or onions.

Her days are marathons. "I get up at six and cook millet bread. Every two or three days, I take a bath. I own one cow and two bullocks and I take them to the field before I report at eight for roadwork. The children come with me, then walk back to the village for school. I work until five with an hour's recess. After work, I get the animals, feed them, and cook dinner. I embroider from eight o'clock to midnight every night. On Sundays, I clean the house, clean the children, layer mud on the floor, and wash clothes.

"There is never time for leisure," she says. "What gives us joy is to sit together, embroider and talk."

DURING OUR CONVERSATION with Hawabai, the village men try to get Mona's attention. Last week Mona asked them to sign documents agreeing to let their wives open bank accounts. Now Mona and the men surround the hood of the jeep where the papers lie flapping in the wind. The men have never had bank accounts themselves and are leery. "Is it possible to get the money out?" they ask. Mona explains, cajoles, argues, smiles, encourages, and flatters them out of their worries. Her clinching argument: "I, myself, will guarantee that you can withdraw the money. I will co-sign with you." The men are impressed. They sign.

SEWA VICE PRESIDENT Lalita Krishnaswami is also director of economic development for the organization and a director of its Mahila Bank (Women's Bank). She serves us tea in her simple basement office at SEWA headquarters in Ahmedabad.

"SEWA is the largest union in India, with over 200,000 members—all women, all self-employed. They make handicrafts such as quilts, weaving, embroidery; they are handcart pullers, used-garment dealers, vegetable vendors, junksmiths, waste pickers, firewood collectors, salt rakers, and toymakers.

"The biggest difficulty for self-employed women was lack of access to credit. So we had a meeting. Four thousand women came. We asked for ideas. One woman got up and said, 'Though we are poor, we are many. Why can't we have a bank of our own?' Right there, each woman gave ten rupees, so there were over a thousand dollars immediately; over six months that became almost three thousand dollars.

"As usual, we had a problem with the government, which said we could not have a bank for illiterates. 'It's suicidal,' said the bureaucrats, 'they can't even write their names to register the charter.' Our bank directors included tradeswomen: block printers, agricultural workers, incense stick rollers. It was true, they could not write. They had never held pencils. That night, no one slept. The fifteen directors sat up all through the night, practicing, and they learned to write their names. The next morning, they walked in and signed the registration papers. The Mahila Bank, the women's bank, became official.

Previous pages: Local women wear—and walk under flags of—*bandhani* as they shop in the labyrinthine Bhuj market.

Opposite, clockwise from top left: Thirty Sodha embroiderers participate in the outdoors SEWA meeting; until recently, many women in this Muslim village and others did not leave their houses • A Rabari woman from

Nokhania has decorated her hands with patterns of henna • While we photograph Rabari girls and boys, Mona assesses their mother's embroidery talent and invites them to join SEWA's Kutchcraft project • Jat children are

better nourished now: Hawabai Ibrahim sells enough embroidery that she can add buttermilk and vegetables to her children's diet of bread and chilies.

"The bank is a cooperative—owned, managed, and used by sixty thousand women. The bank will accept a woman's jewelry as collateral for a loan and give her sixty percent of the value in cash immediately. A woman can pay five rupees and get insurance against accidents, riots, debt. The bank will give her a home loan because this is considered a capital investment in her workplace. The women know that, through the bank, they are loaning their own money to other women, so they are not about to write off bad debts. If a payment is late, a neighbor woman goes to the debtor to see if she can help. Maybe the woman has sick family members, or just can't get to the bank, or maybe she is in trouble with money."

We ask Lalita how SEWA women have been affected by greater financial independence.

"Confidence is one thing. You know, in India, a woman never says her husband's name."

"What does she call him?" "Nothing. Maybe 'my children's father.'"

"Why?" "How can you say your husband's name? He is so much somebody. I am an educated person with two master's degrees but when I got married at twenty, I did not call my husband by his name, either. When women first come to SEWA and we ask them to say their husbands' names, they laugh and giggle. They are so shy they don't even say their own names.

"But after a while, very gradually, the women start feeling confident. They get a little respect from their family. The children begin to view their mothers differently. Domestic violence can be reduced. Everywhere, economic stability is the major factor that lowers birth rates: if extreme poverty is alleviated, families do not need so many children to earn money. Each change creates new possibilities for change."

Lalita tells about a woman describing the Mahila Bank. "One sister talks about money as grains of wheat: if the grains are scattered, you do not know how much you have; if they are in a bag, you can lift it and feel the weight."

Each year, thousands of SEWA members attend the bank's annual meeting. Collectively, these women now hold $404,000 in working capital. And when that is all in one bag, you can feel the weight.

Opposite: Mona, standing behind two Rabari women, has organized over two thousand indigent tribal craftswomen in Kachchh; Kutchcraft markets their products all over the world.

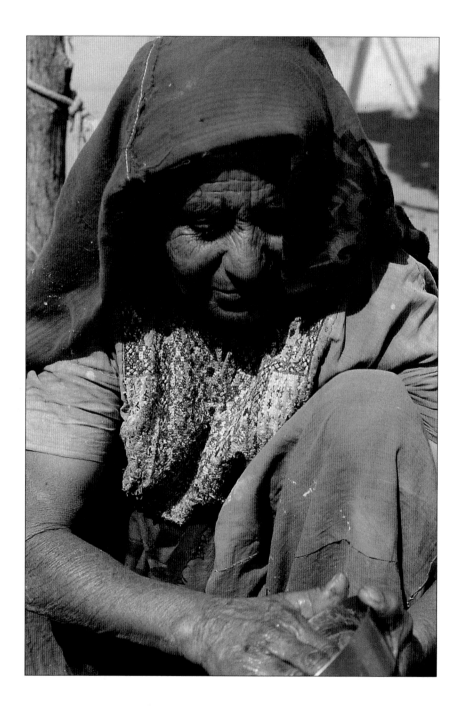

Above: Jat women wash their aluminum dishes with gritty dirt they scoop from the ground; it polishes bowls to a shine.

Opposite: Mankorba dreams that her daughter will attend school. Mona urges Mankorba, who finished second grade, to finish school herself.
Following pages: Gujarati women fetch water in the early morning.

"We are poor women in a hostile land
With no food in our bowls.
Droughts come often and unemployment is rife.

We have neither land nor work.
Our houses are as small as our hands
And our needs are many.

We are women, illiterate women,
Coming together to make a union . . .
We are illiterate, but what of that?

We challenge everyone with our strength."
SEWA ORGANIZING SONG

(translated from the Gujarati)

Conclusion: Craftswomen Changing the World

"We will leave something as a legacy for society.
It will stay behind us, in another place, in another time."

RITA SERAPIÓN, arpillera *maker, Lima*

POVERTY IS DAILY REALITY for most of the craftswomen we visited. They do not see themselves as poor; they simply believe that life is hard. Many make less—and few make more—than one dollar a day, which is the amount the United Nations defines as international income-poverty. A dollar a day does not support a family in any cash economy.

POOR AS THEY ARE, the craftswomen in this book are virtually unanimous in their determination to improve the future for their children. Many work twelve to eighteen hours a day earning money, cooking, and taking care of their homes and children. Some juggle as many as five income-generating projects, at least one of which is a craft.

Many of them get surprisingly little financial help from their husbands. Women, according to the United Nations Development Program, provide the primary support for a quarter of the world's families—and the sole support for another quarter.

In Zimbabwe, women head a third of the households. In Poland, women head a quarter of them, although husbands support the particular families we visited. In Soğanli, Turkey, husbands do not earn any cash but provide food for their families by doing sub-

sistence farming. In fact, in every country we visited, although marriage was the only acceptable lifestyle, and it might be expected that husbands would contribute, often wives were the breadwinners.

Many wives support their families because their husbands are sick or old, or because they died of natural causes. In India, Guatemala, Bolivia, Zimbabwe, and Thailand, we saw ample evidence for the medical research that shows that women everywhere live healthier, longer lives than men.

In Guatemala, most of the craftswomen head their households because their husbands were killed or disappeared during three decades of civil war. Other women in Guatemala are "seasonal widows" whose husbands travel to the coast to seek agricultural work during planting and harvest months. In South Africa, Zimbabwe, and Thailand, husbands leave their villages to seek employment in cities, and in Bolivia, husbands seek work in adjacent countries whose economies are more robust. Many of these men do not get jobs at all; if they do, they earn so little that they have nothing left to send home after paying their living expenses. Some send stipends to their families or return to help out periodically. Others start new families and never come back.

Some women find themselves supporting their families because their cultures allow men to spend their own money on personal pleasures. Florence Maposa, marketing manager of Zimbabwe's National Handicraft

WOMEN AND POVERTY

A third of the world's population, *1.3 billion people, survives on less than $1 a day; seventy percent of those people are female.*

No society treats women *as well as it treats men. Women work longer hours than men in almost every country. Women earn less than men earn and have less access to land, credit, and employment opportunities.*

In developing countries, *illiterate women outnumber illiterate men by sixty percent.*

While more than 300 million *low-income women run micro-businesses, only about 5 million have access to credit from sources other than money lenders.*

Worldwide, *the invisible contribution of women is $11 trillion a year (unpaid and underpaid work valued at prevailing wages).*

The number of rural women *living in absolute poverty rose by nearly fifty percent from 1977 to 1997.*

SOURCE:
United Nations Development Program, Human Development Report,
1995, 1998, 1999

Opposite: **A weaver in Zimbabwe carries fresh cabbage home for supper. Women like her are a centerpiece for the United Nations'** **ten-year campaign to reduce poverty worldwide, because the money they earn is invested in their children.**

Centre, told us, "Husbands buy cigarettes and beer; women buy food for their families." Observing the situation in most developing countries, the World Bank states: "It is not uncommon for children's nutrition to deteriorate while wristwatches, radios, and bicycles are acquired by the adult male household members."

Where polygyny is still practiced, men often find it impossible to support their multiple families. This is common among certain Muslim, Shipibo, Ndebele, and Zulu families—and in Zimbabwe, where one wife in six is married to a man with at least one other spouse.

For all of these reasons, many craftswomen have no choice but to be the engines that will propel their families from poverty—or at least, to try.

THE FIRST THING most craftswomen buy with their income is food for their children. Often, they can only afford to make incremental nutritional changes. In India, women told us that they served millet bread and ground chilies every day until they earned enough to buy buttermilk, eggplant, potatoes, and onions to serve once a week, and then, as their income grew, on alternate days.

Perhaps the most important social legacy craftswomen will leave is a better educated next generation. As more girls attend school, the chances increase of subsequent generations attending school. A mother's education determines her children's—education begets education.

EDUCATION'S IMPACT

Between 1990 and 1997, *the percent of secondary-school-aged girls enrolled in school increased from thirty-six to sixty-one percent globally; yet in developing countries, there are still sixty percent more illiterate women than illiterate men.*

In Pakistan, *a year of schooling has been shown to raise women's wages by twenty percent.*

A study of India, *Thailand, Indonesia, and the Ivory Coast reveals that one year of school can increase a women's future earnings by about fifteen percent.*

Cross-country econometric studies *have indicated that an extra year of schooling for girls reduces birth rates by about five to ten percent.*

In India, *providing a thousand girls with an extra year of primary schooling is estimated to cost $32,000 and to avert two maternal deaths, 43 infant deaths, and 300 births.*

The infant mortality rate *of Indian children whose mothers have a primary education is half that of children whose mothers are illiterate.*

SOURCE:
United Nations Development Program, Human Development Report, 1995, 1999

WE WERE CURIOUS ABOUT how craftswomen who had no formal education became so committed to schooling. We discovered that craft group leaders, often the only women in their villages who have had even a few years of schooling, serve as models for what education can do. In India, an embroidery group president had finished the second grade; in Peru, a pottery group president had an eighth-grade education. Their leadership allowed craftswomen to see that education makes people more effective, and that even a little education can increase the ability to see beyond the way things are.

Although primary education is free in the countries we visited, books, school supplies, uniforms, and transportation are onerous expenses that escalate as children reach higher grades. In South Africa, a woman who makes beaded jewelry invests two months' income to buy two pairs of school shoes and two uniforms for her fourteen-year-old son. In Peru, the first Shipibo woman in her village to send children to college was frantic about the school and living expenses for four years of school for her three children in the city; at a frugal dollar and a half a day, the tab will be more than six thousand dollars.

Although these craftswomen carry the optimistic hope that more schooling promises a better future for their children, there are no guarantees. In Harare, Zimbabwe, we saw unemployed college-educated people sitting on park benches writing poetry; in Guatemala City, we saw them sitting on the sidewalk selling Chiclets. Yet, when education does lead to employment, it can change everything.

WHEN THE UNITED NATIONS Development Program identified $11 trillion as the worldwide annual value of women's unpaid and underpaid work (valued at prevailing wages), the organization concluded: "The goal of development must be justice, not charity. Women must be regarded as agents and beneficiaries of change. Investing in women's capabilities and empowering them

to exercise their choices is the surest way to contribute to economic development."

Women's substantial economic and social role convinced the United Nations to designate women as a focus for its campaign to eradicate poverty worldwide. This decade-long program, which will end in the year 2006, includes such innovations as traveling classes for nomadic women in Mongolia's Gobi Desert and political rights seminars for India's untouchable-caste women.

The craftswomen of this book—and other women like them—have already begun to improve the destiny of their families, communities, countries, and our world.

SEQUENCE OF RESULTS WHEN WOMEN EARN MONEY AND EDUCATE CHILDREN

SELF-CONFIDENCE IMPROVES. *Dr. Muhammad Yunus, the economist who founded the Grameen Bank in Bangladesh, which serves women, describes the typical experience of a woman paying off her first micro-enterprise loan: "Everybody said, 'She's nobody.' Today, she feels she is somebody. She can do things. She can take care of herself and her family."*

DOMESTIC VIOLENCE MAY DECREASE. *Lalita Krishnaswami, vice president of India's Self Employed Women's Association, reports that "as women earn money and become more confident, they get more respect. Domestic violence can be reduced."*

FAMILY PLANNING INCREASES. *Women who have bank accounts are twice as likely as the national average to use family planning practices. "When people start making their own decisions about life, they also start making decisions about the size of their families," Dr. Yunus comments.*

BIRTH RATES DROP. *Lalita Krishnaswami observes that "everywhere, economic stability is the major factor that lowers birth rates. If extreme poverty is alleviated, families don't need so many children to earn money."*

INFANT AND MATERNAL MORTALITY ARE REDUCED. *According to United Nations research, these rates decrease as education increases.*

NUTRITION, HEALTH, LIFE EXPECTANCY ARE ENHANCED. *United Nations data show significant correlations between increased education and advances in nutrition, health, and life span.*

HOUSING AND SANITATION GET BETTER. *"Housing and sanitation also improve," Dr. Yunus reports, as women's incomes allow families to upgrade their living environments.*

GROSS DOMESTIC PRODUCT GROWS. *The United Nations reports that in developing countries, when women start businesses, their countries' prospects are enhanced immediately.*

SOURCE:
United Nations Development Program, Human Development Report, 1995, 1999

Following pages: The sun sets over Peru's Lake Yarinacocha harbor near the villages where Shipibo women create pottery, jewelry, and textiles.

When I think about the lives of the village women we've met, I wonder how it must feel to live in primitive surroundings within today's high-tech world. Such a jumble of contrasts these people must face! Much about life in their villages hasn't changed in a century. But then, there are startling changes, too.

As we travel, we constantly notice and compare the differences in rate and degree of change among indigenous communities. All have had some exposure to "the modern world" and all have been affected by it, but differently. The Rabari people we met, out in the western Indian desert, have had so little contact with the likes of us that they crowded around us to stare and touch; any prior contact with Westerners has rubbed off very little. There are carpet weavers

in Süleymanköy, Turkey, who sometimes get all the way to Oslo, Osaka, and San Francisco to demonstrate their art. Then they return to rustic, dusty little Süleymanköy, where daily life continues as always. The people of Bali have had their world drastically upended by the twin booms of tourism and commercialism, and yet they hold fast to their religious and cultural traditions. The Kuna Indians sometimes leave their San Blas Islands; some have gone all the way to Europe for education, then have returned. Most of them make their way from time to time, by boat, plane, bus, and pickup, to busy, noisy Panama City.

World travel and commercial trade will eventually make us a homogenous people, I think. But for now, the various corners of the world change and

update themselves, sometimes eagerly and sometimes unwillingly or inadvertently, in odd little spurts. How is it determined what modern methods, conveniences, and attitudes will be adopted, and what will be left just as it has always been— at least for a while longer?

In a world of accelerating cultural rub-off, how long will these handicrafts survive? How long will the fragile indigenous cultures that spawned them produce people willing to pursue them? Every woman we met yearns for her daughter to find a "better life," but we wonder if there will be room in that better life for a village craft. Will a young woman with the education to qualify her for a better-paying job find time to sit down at a loom and weave a rug in her grandmother's tradition?

We are thankful for our opportunity to make friends in these few communities now, before further homogenization occurs, because they are surely changing and losing bits of their special color week by week. We are also intensely grateful that there exists a small universe of dedicated specialists collecting, documenting, and teaching the arts of the world's craftswomen. They are professionals, working in museums, universities, and galleries and in the field, and members of volunteer organizations; some are themselves indigenous artisans. Because of the work of these cultural conservationists, we dare to hope that, though the world continues to change, we will not be bereft of the traditional crafts we love.

ON THE PLANE

Guide to Women's Crafts

IN MANY CULTURES certain crafts are considered the province of women. Very young girls learn by mimicking their mothers' craft-making techniques; often, they are proficient before they are ten years old. Although a "women's craft" in one culture may be a "men's craft" in another (gender assignments are almost always as inexplicable as they are inviolable), all the crafts in this book are considered in their societies to be women's crafts.

KNITTED DOLLS

Quechua women in southern Bolivia used to knit neutral-colored doll-shaped purses, which they wore dangling from their belts. In 1968, a Peace Corps volunteer encouraged them to substitute bright yarn colors and market the doll purses. A female doll, whose dress is a money pouch, is always paired with a male doll; every doll couple is unique in pattern and color.

CUYUSCATE WEAVING

Cuyuscate, *colored cotton that is native to Guatemala, grows in tones of gray, pale green, and brown. It was used by ancient Mayan weavers but has not been grown commercially until now. In an effort to revitalize the weaving and embroidery markets, the Ixchel Museum in Guatemala City selected the most talented craftswomen in the country's highlands to use* cuyuscate *thread to create pillow covers, placemats, bookmarks, and other home accessories.*

BACKSTRAP WEAVING

In the Chimaltenango area of Guatemala, 450 widows of the thirty-six-year civil war that ended in 1996 now support their families. They weave traditional local patterns into tablecloths, placemats, and napkins, using subtly hued, colorfast yarns selected to appeal to a sophisticated consumer market. Mayans believe the Goddess Ixchel created weaving; illustrated native manuscripts show her using the same backstrap loom the weavers use today. Its continuous warp is anchored by bars at each end, with one attached to a belt that encircles her waist and the other attached to a wall or tree.

SHIPIBO POTTERY

Women in the indigenous Shipibo ethnic group, who live in the Pucallpa area of Peru's Amazon Basin, are known for their pottery, which is covered with webs of geometric lines. The pots are made by kneading tree ash into lake or river mud, coiling the clay into shape, scraping the surface smooth with pumpkin rind, painting and glazing, firing the pots on open bonfires, and burnishing the surface with smooth stones.

ARPILLERAS

Many Peruvian women who live in the squatter communities that surround Lima learned to make arpilleras, *three-dimensional appliquéd scenes, from an art teacher who brought the craft from Chile, where it originated. Although* arpilleras *are made of fine-weave cotton, the word itself means "hopsacking" or "burlap." When peasant refugees from Peru's recent Shining Path violence sought sanctuary in Lima, the women began creating for sale* arpilleras *showing the country villages they left behind.*

MOLAS

Molas—intricate, layered, appliquéd pictures showing contemporary life, recent history, and popular culture—form the front and back panels of the blouses that Kuna Indian women wear in the San Blas archipelago off the east coast of Panama. Molas *begin with reverse appliqué technique: stacked fabrics are slashed and colors in the lower layers are pulled to the surface; after they are sewn in place, more colors are stitched on top using traditional appliqué techniques. Kunas credit their ancestress, Kicadiray, with creating their women's colorful clothing, including* molas. Molas *are sold as pillow covers, placemats, and framed art.*

FLORAL PAINTING

In southeastern Poland, floral painting began in the 1800s when village women brightened the sooty walls of their two-room cottages with white lime dots that ultimately evolved into flowers. Today, women decorate their houses inside and out with floral designs. For the past fifty years, local flower artists have competed in annual juried competitions. In 1977, they opened the House of Painters in Zalipie where the artists work and sell vases, bells, and other blossom-bedecked ceramic gifts.

KRASLICE

Vnorovy, a town in the Czech Republic, is unique in the world: for the past hundred years, at least one woman in every house has created kraslice, *hand-painted Easter eggs. These women pioneered the batik technique for coloring eggs, using beeswax as the resist. Their signature designs—white, yellow, red, and black geometric and floral patterns—are each as unique as snowflakes.*

NDEBELE BEADWORK

During the Boer War in the late nineteenth century, South African Ndebele women in the eastern Transvaal reacted against efforts to decimate the group's distinctive character by resurrecting the beadwork that their foremothers began creating three hundred years earlier. Beadwork is now central to Ndebele personal, cultural, and political identity as well as history, rituals—and commerce. Today, the Ndebele bead women of Waterval make and market dolls, trivets, mats, and jewelry.

BOLIVIA *Knitted Dolls*

PERU *Shipibo Pottery*

POLAND *Floral Painting*

GUATEMALA *Cuyuscate Weaving*

PERU *Arpilleras*

CZECH REPUBLIC *Kraslice*

GUATEMALA *Backstrap Weaving*

PANAMA *Molas*

SOUTH AFRICA *Ndebele Beadwork*

ZULU BASKETS AND MATS

Forty-five botanical species of reeds, rushes, palms, and grasses grow in KwaZulu near Durban, South Africa. This proliferation provides easily available raw materials for products that range from museum-quality beer baskets (isichumo) woven from Ilala palm to simple mats made to sit on (isicephu) or sleep on (icansi) woven from Ncema grass.

WEYA ART

In the mid-1980s, Shona women from Weya, a communal area in eastern Zimbabwe, learned from Ilse Noy, a German art teacher, to create pictures of their villages, lives, and myths. Their work, rendered in oil paint, appliqué, and batik (for which readily affordable cornmeal porridge is the resist), has been shown at the National Gallery in the country's capital.

SOĞANLI DOLLS

The women make all the money in Soğanli, Turkey, where fifty women in fifty houses create dolls dressed in bright, silky costumes accented with sequins—much like the clothes they wear themselves. The doll industry began here in the 1960s when Hanife Ablak made a doll for her daughter, Döndü, to take to school for show-and-tell. The women's doll market, which fills the town plaza, is a convenient stop for tourists visiting Cappadocia.

DOBAG RUGS

When synthetic dyes caused the beautiful rugs created on the Aegean side of Turkey to run and fade, the market deteriorated dramatically. In 1981, the University of Marmara began DOBAG, a natural dye project that retrained weavers to use madder root, onionskin, oak gall, and chamomile dyes to create harmonious, stable colors. Today the cooperative includes four hundred families in nineteen villages; the quality of all rugs produced by member weavers is guaranteed for two hundred years.

FLORAL OFFERINGS

Every day on the Hindu island of Bali, Indonesia, women put offerings in high places to petition the heavenly gods and in low places to placate the demons. Materials for offerings come from the earth (flowers, leaves, fruit, grain, fowl) and are transformed by cooking, cutting, mixing, and assembling, which every Balinese woman used to do at home. Today, women with jobs have little time to make canang (daily offerings), so they buy them in the market from one of the Brahmin (priest caste) women whose spirit suffuses the offerings and becomes part of the gift to the gods.

ROYAL BATIK

In the nineteenth century, only women at the seven royal courts in central Java created the intricate, ceremonial, tulis (hand-drawn) batik patterns that sometimes required twenty-seven immersions in natural dyes. When the Javanese monarchies were dismantled in 1922, the kings' descendants began to sell their work. Now many of these talented courtesans have died, but some have launched the Pioneers, a foundation to teach, and hence perpetuate, the endangered classic art of royal batik.

HILL TRIBE NEEDLEWORK

Lisu and Hmong women in the rural Chiang Mai area of northern Thailand are experts at the embroidery and appliqué used to make placemats, purses, book covers, and household accessories. Some women learned these skills in their native countries, China and Laos, but others just mastered them. King Bhumibol Adulyadej's appliqué and silversmith skill classes help northern farm families replace opium revenue (growing has been outlawed); Queen Sirikit's SUPPORT program helps others supplement the income from crops that are harvested only annually.

BATIKED MULBERRY-PAPER GIFTS

Northern Thailand used to be the center of handmade paper making. Now that skill has been revived, and Women Against AIDS has taught AIDS patients, sex workers, and village women to create gift boxes, cards, folders, and picture frames covered with batik-patterned, handmade sa (mulberry) paper.

MIRROR EMBROIDERY

Gujarat, India, is one of the richest sources of folk embroidery in the world. When their daughters are born, mothers begin to create mirror embroidery for dowries that will include glittery wedding clothes for the bride and groom, household linen, and camel finery. The Self Employed Women's Association, a unique women's trade union, works with the Jat, Sodha, Ahir, and Rabari tribes in the Kachchh district and markets their mirror-embroidered fashion and home accessories.

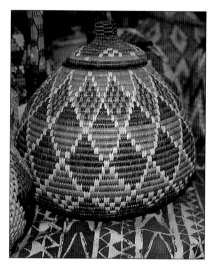

SOUTH AFRICA *Zulu Baskets and Mats*

TURKEY *DOBAG Rugs*

THAILAND *Hill Tribe Needlework*

ZIMBABWE *Weya Art*

INDONESIA *Floral Offerings*

THAILAND *Batiked Mulberry-Paper Gifts*

TURKEY *Soğanli Dolls*

INDONESIA *Royal Batik*

INDIA *Mirror Embroidery*

Resources for Action

HOW CAN YOU HELP enhance the craftswomen's efforts to improve their own lives? Here are some strategies:

○ *Locate and purchase handcrafted products like those in this book. Some sources of these products are marked ⊕.*

○ *Patronize retailers who post the Fair Trade Federation symbol—and ask other outlets how much of the retail price goes to the producer.*

○ *Contribute to institutions that help artisans buy raw materials and generate income—specifically micro-credit and craft-marketing organizations.*

○ *Learn how international development and trade policies affect indigent artisans and, if you do not feel they are fair and effective, lobby the policy makers.*

○ *Contact the people and organizations marked ⋏. It is they who helped make this book possible and are most knowledgeable about its craftswomen and crafts.*

○ *Read some of the books, articles, and reports that we found most helpful during our research.*

INDIGENOUS HANDICRAFT AND FOLKLIFE

CONTACTS

⋏ Aid to Artisans, 14 Brick Walk Lane, Farmington, CT 06032; TEL: 860-677-1649; FAX: 860-676-2170; EMAIL: atausa@aol.com; WEB: www.aid2artisans.org

⋏ Crafts Center, 1001 Connecticut Avenue NW, Ste. 525, Washington, DC 20036, ATTN: Leah Kaplan, Executive Director; TEL: 202-728-9603; FAX: 202-296-2452; EMAIL: info@craftscenter.org

Cultural Survival Quarterly, 221 Prospect Street, Cambridge, MA 02139; TEL: 617-441-5400; FAX: 617-441-5417; EMAIL: csinc@cs.org; WEB: www.cs.org

Fair Trade Federation, P.O. BOX 698, Kirksville, MO 63501, Cheryl Musch, Executive Director; TEL: 660-665-8962; WEB: www.fairtradefederation.com

⋏ The Folk Art Gallery, 1321 Fourth Street, San Rafael, CA 94901, ATTN: Sharon Christovich; TEL: 415-925-9096; EMAIL: folkart@wco.com; WEB: www.thefolkartgallery.com

⋏ Global Exchange, 2017 Mission Street, Room 303, San Francisco, CA 94110, ATTN: Deborah James; TEL: 415-255-7296; FAX: 415-255-7498; EMAIL: gx-info@globalexchange.org; WEB: www.globalexchange.org

Museum of Craft and Folk Art, Landmark Building A, Fort Mason Center, Laguna and Marina Boulevard, San Francisco, CA 94123; TEL: 415-775-0990

⋏ Museum of International Folk Art, Camino Lejo off Old Santa Fe Trail, Santa Fe, NM 87501; TEL: 505-476-1200; FAX: 505-476-1300 WEB: www.moifa.org

⋏ National Museum of African Art, 950 Independence Avenue SW, Washington, DC 20560; TEL: 202-357-2700

National Museum of Natural History, 10th and Constitution Avenue NW, Washington, DC 20560; TEL: 202-357-2700

National Museum of Women in the Arts, 1250 New York Avenue NW, Washington, DC 20005-3920; TEL: 202-783-5000

Oxfam America, 26 West Street, Boston, MA 02111-1206; TEL: 617-482-1211

PEOPLink, 11110 Midvale Road, Kensington, MD 20895; TEL: 301-949-6625; EMAIL: comments@peoplink.org; WEB: www.peoplink.org

Phoebe A. Hearst Museum of Anthropology, 103 Kroeber Hall, University of California, Berkeley, CA 94720-3712; TEL: 510-643-7648

Textile Arts Council, M.H. de Young Museum, Golden Gate Park, San Francisco, CA 94118; TEL: 415-750-3627; FAX: 415-750-7692; EMAIL: tac@famsf.org

The Textile Museum, 2320 S Street NW, Washington, DC 20008-4088; TEL: 202-667-0441

Womenshands, an Oxygen Media website, 75 Ninth Avenue, New York, NY 10011, Kathy Hammer, Executive Producer, Kristin Miller, Senior Editor; TEL: 212-651-5149; FAX: 212-651-5200; WEB: www.oxygen.com

World2Market.com, 100 West Harrison Street, Suite 430, Seattle, WA 98119; TEL: 206-374-3800; FAX: 206-374-3888; EMAIL: world2market.com

Opposite: Ndebele boys in Waterval, South Africa, enjoy the dragonfly viewers we took to thank them for sharing their mothers' time and attention.

FURTHER READING

Barber, Elizabeth Wayland. *Women's Work: The First 20,000 Years.* New York: W. W. Norton & Company, 1994.

Burenhult, Goran. *Traditional Peoples Today: The Illustrated History of Humankind, Continuity and Change in the Modern World.* New York: Harper Collins, 1994.

Crabtree, Caroline. *World Embroidery: 25 Original Projects from Traditional Designs.* Devon, England: David and Charles, 1993.

Etienne-Nugue, Jocelyne. *Talented Women.* Paris: UNESCO, 1995.

Glassie, Henry. *The Spirit of Folk Art: The Girard Collection at the Museum of International Folk Art.* New York: Harry N. Abrams, 1989.

Herold, Jacqueline. *World Crafts.* London: Lark Books for Oxfam, 1992.

Kahlenberg, Mary Hunt, ed. *The Extraordinary in the Ordinary: Textiles and Objects from the Collections of Lloyd Cotsen and the Neutrogena Corporation, Works in Cloth, Ceramic, Wood, Metal, Straw, and Paper from Cultures Throughout the World.* New York: Harry N. Abrams, 1998.

Kennett, Frances. *Ethnic Dress: A Comprehensive Guide to the Folk Costume of the World.* London: Reed Consumer Books, 1994.

Morris, Walter F., Jr. *Handmade Money: Latin American Artisans in the Marketplace.* Washington, DC: Organization of American States, 1996.

MICROENTERPRISE LOANS

CONTACTS

⋀ Freedom from Hunger, 1644 Da Vinci Court, Davis, CA 95617, ATTN: Claire Thomas, Vice President/Development and Public Affairs; TEL: 530-758-6200, 1-800-708-2555; FAX: 530-758-6241; EMAIL: info@freefromhunger.org; WEB: www.freefromhunger.org

Global Volunteers, 375 E. Little Canada Road, St. Paul, MN 55117; TEL: 800-487-1074

Office of Microenterprise Development, Economic Growth Center, Global Bureau, USAID, 1000 16th Street NW, Washington, DC 20036; TEL: 202-712-1140

World Bank, Consultative Group to Assist the Poorest, 1818 H Street NW, Washington, DC 20433; TEL: 202-477-1234; FAX: 202-522-3744; WEB: www.worldbank.org

FURTHER READING

"Closing the Gap." *The Economist,* September 2, 1995, 74.

Creevey, Lucy. *Changing Women's Lives and Work: An Analysis of the Impacts of Eight Microenterprise Projects.* London: Intermediate Technology Publications, 1996.

Danaher, Kevin, and Muhammad Yunus. *50 Years Is Enough: The Case Against the World Bank and the International Monetary Fund.* Boston: South End Press, 1994.

Jhabvala, Renana, and Jane Tate. "Out of the Shadows: Homebased Workers Organize for International Recognition." *Seeds* 18 (1996): 1–23.

Kodish, Marilyn, ed. *Pearls of Bangladesh: The Workers and Borrowers of Grameen Bank.* Washington, DC: RESULTS Educational Fund, 1993.

Sebstad, Jennefer, and Gregory Chen. *Overview of Studies on the Impact of Microenterprise Credit.* Management Systems International in cooperation with the Harvard Institute for International Development, the University of Missouri,

and the Small Enterprise Education and Promotion Network, April 25, 1997.

Stix, Gary. "Small (Lending) Is Beautiful." *Scientific American,* April 1997, 16.

Watkins, Kevin. *The Oxfam Poverty Report.* Oxford: Oxfam, 1995.

Wright, Robin. "Women as Engines out of Poverty." *Los Angeles Times,* May 27, 1997, 1.

WOMEN IN DEVELOPING COUNTRIES

CONTACTS

⋀ Association for Women in Development, 666 Eleventh Street NW, Suite 450, Washington, DC 20001, ATTN: Caryl Garcia, Executive Director; TEL: 202-628-0440; FAX: 202-628-0442; EMAIL: cgarcia@awid.org

⋀ Global Fund for Women, 425 Sherman Avenue, Palo Alto, CA 94306-1823, ATTN: Kavita Ramdas, President; TEL: 650-853-8305; FAX: 650-328-0384; EMAIL: gfw@igc.apc.org; WEB: globalfundforwomen.org

International Center for Research on Women, 1717 Massachusetts Avenue NW, Suite 302, Washington, DC 20036; TEL: 202-797-0007; FAX: 202-797-0020; EMAIL: icrw@igc.apc.org

⋀ Peace Corps, Women in Development, 1111 Twentieth Street NW, Washington, DC 20526, ATTN: Lyn Messner, Coordinator; TEL: 202-692-2654; FAX: 202-692-2651/2601; EMAIL: lmessner@peacecorps.gov

United Nations Development Fund for Women (UNIFEM), 304 East 45th Street, New York, NY 10017; TEL: 212-906-6400; FAX: 212-906-6705; EMAIL: unifem@undp.org

United States Agency for International Development (USAID), Office of Women in Development Global Bureau, 1300 Pennsylvania Avenue, RRB 3.8-042U, Washington, DC 20523; TEL: 202-712-0570; FAX: 202-216-3173

Women's Edge, 1825 Connecticut Avenue NW, Suite 800, Washington, DC 20009, ATTN: Ritu Sharma, Executive Director; TEL: 202-884-8394; EMAIL: rsharma@womensedge.org

Women's Ink, Women and Development Resources, 777 United Nations Plaza, New York, NY 10017; TEL: 212-687-8633; FAX: 212-661-2704; EMAIL: wink@igc.apc.org; WEB: www.womenink.org

World Bank Gender Unit, 1818 H Street NW, Washington, DC 20433; TEL: 202-477-1234; WEB: www.worldbank.org/gender/

FURTHER READING

Baird, Vanessa, et al. *Eye to Eye Women, Their Words and Worlds: Life in Africa, Asia, Latin America and the Caribbean as Seen in Photographs and in Fiction by the Region's Top Women Writers.* London/New York: Serpent's Tail, 1997.

Ballara, Marcela. *Women and Literacy.* London and Atlantic Highlands: Zed Books, 1992.

Buvinic, Mayra. "Women in Poverty: A New Global Underclass." *Foreign Policy,* fall 1997, 38–53.

D'Alusio, Faith, and Peter Menzel. *Women in the Material World.* San Francisco: Sierra Club Books, 1996.

Eisler, Riane, David Loye, and Kari Norgaard. *Women, Men, the Global Quality of Life: A Report on the Gender Equity and Quality of Life Project for the Center for Partnership Studies.* Pacific Grove, CA: Center for Partnership Studies, 1995.

Fiol-Matta, Liza. "Beijing and Beyond: Toward the Twenty-First Century of Women." *Women's Studies Quarterly* 24, nos. 1, 2 (spring/summer 1996).

Fontanel, Beatrice, and Claire d'Harcourt. *Babies Celebrated.* New York: Harry N. Abrams, 1998.

Joekes, Susan, and Ann Weston. *Women and the New Trade Agenda.* New York: United Nations Development Fund for Women (UNIFEM), 1994.

Karl, Marilee. *Women and Empowerment: Participation and Decision Making.* London and Atlantic Highlands: Zed Books, 1995.

———. *Children Just Like Me.* New York: Dorling Kindersley Publishing, 1995.

Kindersley, Barnabas, and Anabel Kindersley. *Celebrations! Festivals, Carnivals and Feast Days from around the World.* New York: Dorling Kindersley Publishing, 1997.

King, Elizabeth M., and M. Anne Hill. *Women's Education in Developing Countries: Barriers, Benefits, and Policies.* Baltimore: Johns Hopkins University Press, 1997.

Klein, Cecilia F., ed. *Mother, Worker, Ruler, Witch: Cross-Cultural Images of Women.* UCLA Museum of Cultural History Pamphlet Series, vol. 1, no. 9, 1980.

McCorduck, Pamela, and Nancy Ramsey. *The Futures of Women: Scenarios for the 21st Century.* New York: Warner Books, 1996.

Morris, Walter F., Jr. *Handmade Money: Latin American Artisans in the Marketplace.* Washington, DC: Organization of American States, 1996.

Neft, Naomi, and Ann Levine. *Where Women Stand: An International Report on the Status of Women in 140 Countries, 1997–1998.* New York: Random House, 1997.

Pietila, Hilkka, and Jeanne Vickers. *Making Women Matter: The Role of the United Nations.* London and Atlantic Highlands: Zed Books, 1994.

Rao, Aruna, Rieky Stuart and David Kelleher. *Gender at Work: Organizational Change for Equality.* West Hartford: Kumarian Press, 1999.

Seager, Joni. *The State of Women in the World Atlas.* London: Penguin, 1997.

Snyder, Margaret. *Transforming Development: Women, Poverty, and Politics.* London: Intermediate Technology Publications, 1995.

United Nations Development Program. *Human Development Report 1995, 1998, 1999.* New York: Oxford University Press, 1995, 1998, 1999.

Women: Looking Beyond 2000. New York: United Nations, 1995.

The World's Women, 1995: Trends and Statistics. Social Statistics and Indicators, series K, no. 12. New York: United Nations, 1995.

Zwingle, Erla. "Women and Population." *National Geographic* (Millennium Supplement no. 4: Population), October 1998, 36–55.

BOLIVIA

CONTACTS

⋀ Freedom from Hunger, 1644 Da Vinci Court, Davis, CA 95617, ATTN: Claire Thomas, Vice President/Development and Public Affairs; TEL: 530-758-6200, 1-800-708-2555; FAX: 530-758-6241; EMAIL: info@freefromhunger.org; WEB: www.freefromhunger.org

FURTHER READING

Healy, Kevin. "La Khochalita's Export Saga: Can Artisanal Craft Organizations Afford the Business of Development?" *Grassroots Development* 20, no. 2 (1996).

CZECH REPUBLIC

CONTACT

⊕ Cesky Narodni Podnik s.r.o., Retezova 10, 110 00 Prague 1, Czech Republic, ATTN: Michal Pavlas, Export Director; TEL: 420-2-242-10886, 420-2-242-48792; FAX: 420-2-242-48790; EMAIL: export@cnp.cz

GUATEMALA

CONTACTS

⊕ Colibri, 4 Calle Oriente, 3B, Antigua, Guatemala, ATTN: Vey Smithers; TEL: 502-832-0280 (widows' weaving)

⊕ Museo Ixchel del Traje Indigena, 6a Calle Final-Zona 10, Campus de la Universidad Francisco Marroquin, Guatemala Cuidad, Guatemala, ATTN: Thelma de Willemsen, President/ Pro-Teje Project; TEL/FAX: 502-331-3638, 331-3634, 331-3622 (*cuyuscate* weaving)

FURTHER READING

Altman, Patricia B., and Caroline D. West. *Threads of Identity: Maya Costume of the 1960s in Highland Guatemala.* Los Angeles: Fowler Museum of Cultural History, University of California, 1992.

Burgos-Debra, Elizabeth, ed. *I, Rigoberta Menchu: An Indian Woman in Guatemala.* London-New York: Verso, 1984.

De La Haba, Louis. "Guatemala, Mayan and Modern." *National Geographic,* November 1974, 660–89.

Deuss, Krystna. *Indian Costumes from Guatemala.* 2nd ed. Great Britain: CTD Printers, TWI Oeknjaus, 1990.

Maya Textiles of Guatemala. Austin: University of Texas Press, 1993.

Miller, Mary Richardson. *The Women of Candelaria.* San Francisco: Pomegranate, 1996.

Miller, Mary, and Karl Taube. "Ixchel." In *Ancient Mexico and the Maya: An Illustrated Dictionary of Mesoamerican Religion.* London: Thames and Hudson, 1993, 100–101.

Pettersen, Carmen L. *The Maya of Guatemala: Their Life and Dress.* Guatemala City: Ixchel Museum, 1976.

Popol Vuh: The Mayan Book of the Dawn of Life. Revised. trans. Dennis Tedlock. New York: Simon & Schuster, 1996.

Sayer, Chloe. *Mexican Textiles.* Hong Kong: British Museum Publications, 1985.

Scagliarini, Loris, and Brigit Sole-March. *Guatemala: Festivals, Markets and More.* Brochure, Sierra Leone. Editorial Evergraficas, March 1995.

Schevill, Margot Blum, Janet Catherine Berlo, and Edward B. Dwyer. *Textile Traditions of Mesoamerica and the Andes.* Austin: University of Texas Press, 1991.

Vecchiato, Gianni. *Guatemala Rainbow.* San Francisco: Pomegranate, 1989.

INDIA

CONTACT

⊕ Self Employed Women's Association, SEWA Reception Center, Opposite Lokmanya Tilak Baug, Bhadra, Ahmedabad 380 001, Gujarat, India, ATTN: Mona Dave, Kutchcraft Project Coordinator; TEL: 91-79-550-6477, 550-6444; FAX: 91-79-550-6446; EMAIL: sewa.mahila@axcess.net.in, bdmsa@ad1.vsl.net.in; WEB: banascraft.org

FURTHER READING

"The Artisans Are Their Own Designers." *The Economic Times, Ahmedabad,* November 25, 1993, 18.

Banascraft: Rich Craft Heritage of the Women Artisans. Ahmedabad, India: Self Employed Women's Association, n.d.

Bose, Anil Baran. *Women in India: A Country Profile.* New York: United Nations Economic and Social Commission for Asia and the Pacific, 1997.

Brown, Judith M. *Gandhi: Prisoner of Hope.* New Haven: Yale University Press, 1989.

Cooper, Ilay, John Gillow, and Barry Dawson. *Arts and Crafts of India.* London: Thames and Hudson, 1996.

Davidson, Robyn. *Desert Places.* New York: Viking, 1996.

———. "Wandering With India's Rabari." *National Geographic,* September 1993, 64–93.

Fisher, Nora. *Mud, Mirror and Thread: Folk Traditions of Rural India.* Ahmedabad: Mapin Publishing, 1993.

Frater, Judy. *Threads of Identity.* Seattle: University of Washington Press, 1995.

Green, Martin. *Gandhi in India in His Own Words.* Hanover: University Press of New England, 1987.

Hick, John, and Lamont C. Hempel. *Gandhi's Significance for Today: The Elusive Legacy.* New York: St. Martin's Press, 1989.

Huyler, Stephen P. *Painted Prayers: Women's Art in Village India.* New York: Rizzoli International Publications, 1994.

Jhabvala, Renana, and Jane Tate. "Out of the Shadows: Homebased Workers Organize for International Recognition." *Seeds* 18 (1996): n.p.

Minturn, Leigh. *Sita's Daughters: Coming Out of Purdah, The Rajput Women of Khalapur Revisited.* New York: Oxford University Press, 1993.

Murphy, Veronica, and Rosemary Crill. *Tie Dyed Textiles of India: Tradition and Trade.* New York: Rizzoli International Publications, 1991.

Rose, Kalima. *Where Women Are Leaders: The SEWA Movement in India.* New Delhi: Vistaar Publications, 1992.

"A Survey of India's Economy: Work in Progress." *The Economist,* February 22, 1997, 3–26.

Yeadon, David. "The Mirage of Life." In *The Back of Beyond: Travels to the Wild Places of the Earth.* San Francisco: Traveler's Tales, 1995.

INDONESIA

CONTACTS

⊕ Ibu R. Ay. Praptini Partaningrat, Kangjengan Batik Tulis Tradisional, Jl. Ronggowarsito No. 128, Solo, Java, Indonesia; TEL: 62-271-44165 (royal batiks)

⊕ Toko Sri Djaja, Pasar Klewer, Los E 58-59, Solo, Java, Indonesia, ATTN: Sri. Rahayu; TEL: 62-271-635-397 (batiks)

FURTHER READING

Ananta Toer, Pramoedya. *Child of All Nations.* New York: William Morrow, 1993.

Brinkgreve, Francine, and David Stuart-Fox. *Offerings: The Ritual Art of Bali.* Sanur, Bali: Image Network Indonesia, 1992.

Covarrubias, Miguel. *Island of Bali.* Singapore: Oxford University Press, 1987.

Eiseman, Fred B., Jr. *Bali Sekala and Niskala: Essays on Religion, Ritual, and Art.* Hong Kong: Periplus Editions, 1990.

Gavin, Traude. *The Women's Warpath: Iban Ritual Fabrics from Borneo.* Los Angeles: UCLA Fowler Museum of Cultural History, 1996.

Gillow, John, and Barry Dawson. *Traditional Indonesian Textiles.* London: Thames and Hudson, 1982.

Richter, Anne, and John Storey. *Arts and Crafts of Indonesia.* San Francisco: Chronicle Books, 1993.

Suleeman, Evelyn. *Women in Indonesia: A Country Profile.* New York: United Nations Economic and Social Commission for Asia and the Pacific, United Nations, 1998.

Suryani, Luhketut, and Gordon D. Jensen. *Trance and Possession in Bali: A Window on Western Multiple Personality, Posession Disorder and Suicide.* Kuala Lumpur: Oxford University Press, 1995.

PANAMA

CONTACTS

Congreso General Kuna, Comarca Kunayala, ATTN: Salomon A. Guerro, Secretario General, Edifice Domino, Office 18, second floor, P.O. BOX 6-8299 El Dorado, Republic of Panama; TEL: 507-263-3615; FAX: 507-263-3765

⊕ Dolphin Island Resort, ATTN: Yasmina Eloina De La Ossa Tejada, Isla de Uagidup, Comarca de San Blas, Republic of Panama (*molas*)

Kuna Cultural Center, ATTN: Kalu Ipakki "Colman" or Carlos Perez Bounaparte, President, Apartado Postal 6-8723 El Dorado, Republic of Panama, TEL: 507-262-5025; FAX: 507-262-3717 (accepts tax-deductible donations for the House of Culture/Hogar Cultural Kuna Yala school on Ailigandi Island)

FURTHER READING

Auld, Rhoda L. *Molas: What They Are, How to Make Them, Ideas They Suggest for Creative Appliqué.* New York: Van Nostrand Reinhold, 1977.

Parker, Ann, and Avon Neal. *Molas: Folk Art of the Cuna Indians.* New York: Clarkson Potter, 1977.

Patera, Charlotte. *Mola Techniques for Today's Quilters.* Paducah, KY: American Quilter's Society, 1995.

Puls, Herta. *Textiles of the Kuna Indians of Panama.* Great Britain: Shire Publications, 1988.

Salvador, Mari Lyn. *The Art of Being Kuna: Layers of Meaning among the Kuna of Panama.* Los Angeles: UCLA Fowler Museum of Cultural History, 1997.

Soltow, Willow Ann. "In the Land of Sun and Sea: Molas and their Makers." *Piecework,* November/December 1994, 50–55.

Tice, Karin E. *Kuna Crafts: Gender and the Global Economy.* Austin: University of Texas Press, 1995.

PERU

CONTACTS

⊕ Carolyn Heath, Calle 1 Oeste s/n, Edificio MITINCI, piso 13, Lima 27, Peru; TEL: 51-1-224-3347, 224-2660; FAX: 51-1-224-2660; EMAIL: alaexport@mitinci.gob.pe (Shipibo crafts)

⊕ Organización de Mujeres Indígenas de la Amazonia Peruana, Jr. Circunvalación No 313, Apdo 24, Yarinacocha-Pucallpa, Peru, ATTN: Segundina Cumapa, President, or Rosa Cumapa Rengifo, Mothers Club President/San Francisco; FAX: 51-6457-596488, 578442 (Shipibo crafts)

⊕ Oxfam Fair Trade Company, Ave. La Paz 1232, Miraflores, Lima 18, Peru, ATTN: Graciela Magan; TEL: 51-1-445-8198, 447-4338; FAX: 51-1-445-6768 (*arpilleras*)

FURTHER READING

Acevedo, Sara. "Regional Identities and Popular Art." *Peru El Dorado Magazine,* January–March 1999, 51–63.

Braun, Barbara. *Arts of the Amazon.* London: Thames and Hudson, 1995.

Davies, Lucy, and Mo Fini. *Arts and Crafts of South America.* San Francisco: Chronicle Books, 1994.

Eakin, Lucille, Erwin Laurfault, and Harry Boonstra. *People of the Ucayali: The Shipibo and Conibo of Peru.* Dallas: International Museum of Cultures, Publication 12, 1986.

Gebhard-Sayer, Angelika. *The Cosmos Encoiled: Indian Art of the Peruvian Amazon.* Americas Society, 1984.

Sirch, Willow Ann. "Arpilleras: Pictures from the Land of the Sun." *Piecework,* November/December 1995, 52–58.

Soltow, Willow Ann. "Chile: Arpilleras." In *Quilting the World Over.* Radnor, PA: Chilton Book Company, 1991.

Soustelle, Jacques, and Hans Silvester. *The Land of the Incas.* London: Thames and Hudson, 1977.

POLAND

CONTACTS

⊕ Dom Malerek, Zalipie, Poland, ATTN: Wanda Chlastawa (floral painted gifts)

♁ Muzeum Etnograficzne im. Seweryna Udzieli, ul. Krakowska 46, 31-066 Crakow, Poland, ATTN: Maria Zachorowska, Director; TEL: 48-12-56-56-01

♁ Regional Museum in Tarnow, ul. Rynek 20-21, 33-100 Tarnow, Poland, ATTN: Adam Bartosz, Director

FURTHER READING

Kozacka, Grazyna J. "In the Village That Always Blooms." *Piecework,* March/April 1994, 70–79.

SOUTH AFRICA

CONTACTS

⊕ Ilala Weavers, P.O. BOX 195, Hluhluwe 3960, KwaZulu Natal, South Africa, ATTN: Carol Sutton; TEL: 27-35-562-0630; FAX: 27-35-562-0361 (baskets)

⊕ National Multi-Skills Development Association, P.O. BOX 411, Shakaskraal, 4430 South Africa, ATTN: Daphney Zungu (mats)

⊕ Ndebele Bead Women, P.O. BOX 990, Siyabuswa, 0472 South Africa, ATTN: Dinah Mahlangu (beadwork)

⊕ Rural Crafts, 31 Tyrwhitt Avenue, Shop 42E, Mutual Gardens, Rosebank 2196, Johannesburg, South Africa, ATTN: Matilda Mashaba; TEL: 27-11-880-96512; FAX: 27-11-442-7691 (beadwork and baskets)

FURTHER READING

"An African Success Story." *The Economist,* June 14, 1997, 47.

amaNdebele: Signals of Color from South Africa. Tubingen: Ernst Wasmuth Verlag, 1991.

Asante, Molefi Kete. *The Book of African Names.* Trenton: Africa World Press, 1991.

Cameron, Elisabeth L. *Isn't S/He a Doll? Play and Ritual in African Sculpture.* Los Angeles: UCLA Fowler Museum of Cultural History, 1996.

Clinton, Hillary. "African Odyssey." *Vogue,* June 1997, 186.

Coob, Charles E., Jr., and James Nachtewey. "The Twilight of Apartheid: Life in Black South Africa." *National Geographic* 183, no. 2 (February 1993), 66–93.

Courtney-Clarke, Margaret. *Ndebele: The Art of an African Tribe.* New York: Rizzoli International Publications, 1986.

Eliade, Mircea. "Schembe." In *The Encyclopedia of Religion.* New York: Macmillan, 1993, VOL. 13, 239–40.

Fisher, Angela. *Africa Adorned.* New York: Harry N. Abrams, 1984.

Haskins, Jim, and Joann Biondi. *From Afar to Zulu: A Dictionary of African Cultures.* New York: Walker and Company, 1995.

Knight, Natalie, and Suzanne Priebatsch. *Art of the Ndebele: The Evolution of a Cultural Identity.* Atlanta: Atlanta International Museum, 1998.

Levinsohn, Rhoda. *Treasures in Transition: Art and Craft of Southern Africa.* Parklands: Delta Books, 1984.

Morris, Jean. *Speaking with Beads: Zulu Arts from Southern Africa.* London: Thames and Hudson, 1994.

Peoples of Southern Africa. New York: Facts on File, 1997.

Powell, Ivor, and Mark Lewis. *Ndebele: A People and Their Art.* New York: Cross River Press, 1995.

"Where Terror Reigns in South Africa: In KwaZulu Province, Free Speech Is Still a Contested Issue." *New York Times,* June 26, 1996, A8.

THAILAND

CONTACTS

⊕ EcoAccents, 2570 Superior Avenue, Fifth Floor, Cleveland, OH 44114, ATTN: Eric Ludwig, President; TEL: 1-888-295-9297; EMAIL: eric@ecoaccents.com; WEB: www.ecoaccents.com (exclusive distributor of mulberry-paper products in the United States and Canada)

⊕ Grassroots HQ Company, Limited, 3/31 Samlan Road, Tambon Phrasing, Amphur Muang, Chiang Mai, Thailand 50200, ATTN: Ben Svasti or Henry Quick, Co-Directors; TEL: 66-53-81-4717; FAX: 66-53-81-4719; EMAIL: ghq@loxinfo.co.th (batiked mulberry paper-covered gift items)

Hill Tribe Products Promotion Center, 21/17 Suthep Road (near Wat Suandok), Chiang Mai 50200, Thailand; TEL: 66-53-277743 (for Hmong and Lisu products; center is under the patronage of His Majesty The King; profits go to hill tribe welfare programs)

♁ NAPAC (Thai-Australian Northern AIDS Prevention and Care Program), Shinawatra Building, third floor, 14-10 Huai Kaeo Road, Chiang Mai, Thailand 50300, ATTN: Dr. Usa Duongsaa; TEL: 66-53-211454; FAX: 66-53-212743

⊕ Royal Folk Arts and Crafts Center, adjacent to Bang Pa-In Summer Palace, Bang Sai, Ayutthaya Province, Thailand, ATTN: Colonel Kasem Chatsathienpong, Deputy Director

FURTHER READING

Altman, Lawrence K. "AIDS Surge Seen in China, India and Eastern Europe." *New York Times,* November 4, 1997, A10.

Bevrdeley, Jean-Michel, and Hans Hinz. *Thai Forms.* New York: Weatherhill, 1980.

Campbell, Margaret, Nakorn Pongnoi, and Chusak Voraphitak. *From the Hands of the Hills.* Hong Kong: Media Transasia, 1981.

"Counting the Cost." *The Economist.* September 23, 1995, 26.

Hmong Art: Tradition and Change. Sheboygan, WI: John Michael Kohler Arts Center, 1986.

Lewis, Paul, and Elaine Lewis. *Peoples of the Golden Triangle: Six Tribes in Thailand.* London: Thames and Hudson, 1984.

Milinson, Jane, Nancy Donnelly, and Ly Hang. *Hmong Batik: A Textile Technique from Laos.* Seattle: University of Washington Press, 1997.

Newman, Thelma R. *Contemporary Southeast Asian Arts and Crafts.* New York: Crown, 1977.

Peterson, Sally N. "From the Heart and the Mind: Creating Paj Ntaub in the Context of Community." Ph.D. diss, University of Pennsylvania, 1990.

Report: AIDS Case in Thailand. CDC Region 10, Chiangmai: Department of Communicable Disease Control, Ministry of Public Health, 1996.

The Royal Project of Folk Arts and Crafts for Farmers. National Council of Women of Thailand under the Royal Patronage of Her Majesty the Queen, 1984.

Some Splendid Crafts of the SUPPORT Foundation of Her Majesty Queen Sirikit of Thailand. Bangkok: Siam Society under Royal Patronage, 1994.

"Translating Experience and the Reading of a Story Cloth." *Journal of American Folklore,* January–March 1981, 6–36.

Warren, William, and Luca Invernizzi Tettoni. *Arts and Crafts of Thailand.* San Francisco: Chronicle Books, 1996.

"Women and AIDS." *NAPAC Newsletter* (Thai-Australian Northern AIDS Prevention and Care Program) 3, no. 2 (April–September 1996).

TURKEY

CONTACTS

Return to Tradition, 3319 Sacramento Street, San Francisco, CA 94118, ATTN: Bill McDonald; TEL: 415-921-4180; FAX: 415-921-6024 (natural dyed rugs)

⊕ S.S. Soğanli Turizm Gelistirme Kooperatifi, c/o Sevim Karabiyik, P.K. 81, 50400 Urgup/Nevsemir, Turkiye; TEL: 90-384-341-4482; FAX: 90-384-341-5991 (dolls)

⊕ S.S. Süleyman Köy Tarismal Kalkinma Kooperatifi (DOBAG), Ayvacik-Çanakkale, Turkiye, ATTN: Şerife Atlihan; TEL: 90-3746-7121274; FAX: 90-3746-7121705

FURTHER READING

Anderson, June. *Return to Tradition: The Revitalization of Turkish Village Carpets.* San Francisco: California Academy of Sciences, 1998.

Ditmer, Joanne. "Magic Carpets: Brilliantly Hued Rugs Coveted on Two Continents." *Denver Post,* May 11, 1998, 10 F.

Glassie, Henry. *Turkish Traditional Art Today.* Bloomington: Indiana University Press, 1993.

Iten-Maritz, J. *Turkish Carpets.* Tokyo: Kodansha International, 1997.

Kinzer, Stephen. "Where Faith Infuses the Rock." *New York Times,* August 31, 1997, section 5, 6.

Thompson, Jon. "A Return to Tradition." *Hali* 30 (April 1986), 14–21.

Udesky, Laurie. "Innovative Co-Op Helps Weavers Earn Their Keep." *Turkish Daily News,* February 16, 1996, B1.

ZIMBABWE

CONTACTS

⊕ National Handicraft Centre, Corner Grant Street and Chinhoyi Street, P.O. BOX 66210, Kopje, Harare, Zimbabwe, ATTN: James Musiñacho, Manager; TEL: 263-4-721816; FAX: 263-4-721815 (Weya painting)

⊕ Smithsonian Institution Museum Shops, 600 Maryland Avenue SW, Washington, DC 20560, ATTN: Elysa Blacker, Buyer; TEL: 202-357-1300; FAX: 202-287-3080

FURTHER READING

Beach, David. *The Shona and Their Neighbours.* Oxford: Blackwell, 1994.

Eliade, Mircea. "Shona Religion." In *The Encyclopedia of Religion.* New York: Macmillan, 1993, vol. 13, 295–98.

Noy, Ilse. *The Art of the Weya Women.* Harare: Baobab Books, 1994.

Ponter, Anthony, and Laura Ponter. *Spirits in Stone: The New Face of African Art.* Glen Ellen: Ukama Press, 1997.

Winter-Irving, Celia. *Stone Sculpture in Zimbabwe: Context, Content and Form.* Harare: Roblaw, 1995.

Acknowledgments

WE ARE GRATEFUL to the ninety craftswomen who shared their stories so generously and welcomed us into their lives; to the interpreters who made understanding possible; to the six people who gave us continuous guidance and encouragement: Alev Lytle Croutier, Stephen Huyler, Nina Smith, Tim Tuttle, David Hill, and Judith R. Joseph, our publishing consultant; to Gianfranco Monacelli, our publisher, and Andrea Monfried, our editor; to our book designer, Joseph Guglietti—and to the experts and friends all over the world without whom this book would not exist:

Thomas Aageson, Christine Albertini, Krishna Amin-Patel, June Anderson, Miguel Arrutia, Şerife Atlihan, Adam Bartosz, Allen Bassing, David Beatty, Linda Beeman, Leah Ben-David Val, Constance Beutel, George Beylerian, Elysa Blacker, Barbara Blackwill, Bill Bonnell, Hedy Buzan, Ben Nighthorse Campbell, Kimberly Carter, Phisak Chakkaphak, Joan Chatfield-Taylor, Colonel Kasem Chatsathienpong, Mirai Chatterjee, Helen Chin, Freddy Flores Choque Jr., Sharon Christovich, Leslie Claxton, Linda Clever, Andrea Cohen, Diane Colasanto, Julio Benitez Colman, Ron Colnett, Father William Coy, Claudia Craig, Bonnie Dahan, Mona Dave, Betsy Davis, John Alfredo Davis, Juan Delgado, Ozlem DemiNoopan, Cennet Deneri, Emel Domagracci, Hlenge Dube,

Kenneth Duncan, Usa Duongsaa, Nancy Dutton, Janet Echelman, Clara Malcco Enriquez, Roger Valencia Espinoza, Georgia Evers, Dotty Ewing, Dianne Feinstein, Zenobia Ferrufino, Allison Field, Peggy Flynn, Anita and Miles Forsyth, Judy Frater, Estelle Freedman, Caryl Garcia, Valerie Gardner, Yaritza Gavidia, K. Gengenbach, Mike Gianturco, Henry Glassie, Peter Glusker, Kathy Hammer, Sally Havens, Haydar Haykir, Caroline Heath, Chris Hedge, Lucie Hempstead, Abby Hill, Suki Hill, Bonnie Himberg, Jerry Horovitz, Sinifisela Inhlanhla, David Inocencio, Khatri Alemohmad Isha, Ben Jacobsen, U. P. Jadia, Chris Jannes, Jack Jannes, Neil Jannes, Judith Jaslow, Pascale Jeambrun, Paula Jeppson, Tina Joemat, Margaret Kadoyama, I Wayan Kamar, Leah Kaplan, Sevim Karabiyik, Vincent Khuzunayo, Gary Kinley, Srisakul Kliks, Andy Kohut, Tuangthong Kreuatongsi, Susan Krieger, Tom Kruse, Ilhan Kucuk, Iris Litt, Sally Lovett, Kathy Lowry, Jing Lyman, Graciela Magan, Dinah Mahlangu, Florence Maposa, Katherine Martin, Matilda Mashaba, Norman Mauskopf, Father Thomas McBride, Bill McDonnell, Guinness McFadden, Stephanie McNair, Harriet McNamee, Lyn Messner, Kristin Miller, Linda Miller, Juan Carlos Montano, Mark Moran, Sharon Moran, Gunlaya "Tui" Muangmoon, Karen Mulvahill, James Musiwacho, Happy Bongiwe Mvuyane, Reema Nanavaty,

Grieta Ndala, Arlene and Clark Neher, Matgosia Oleszkiewicz, Bonnie Oliver, Luis Ovando, Michal Pavlas, Ann Peden, Linda Pei, Gail Perkins, Erroll Pires, Cynthia Pitt, Victor Policci, Janice Porter, Barbara Prag, Kavita Ramdas, Caroline Ramsay, Peter Randle, Nancy Reeder, Jana Kopelentova Rehak, Linda Rehor, Faye Richardson, Robert Ridgley, Songnam Ritwanna, Bill and Eliza Roberson, Julie Freund Roth, Karen Ruckman, Robin Ryan, Nina Sabnani, Jyotsana Sagara, Roxana Salinas, Joanne Sandler, Rob Sangster, Scott Sangster, Maria San Miguel, Leena Sarabhai, Ratna Sarkar, Margot Blum Schevill, Beth Schroppel, Kristin Seeman, Judy Sellars, M. Iman Setiadji, Zenneth Thembile Shabangu, Beena Shah, Marianne Shallenberger, Mohd. Bashir Shariff, Ritu Sharma, Minette Siegel, Jeed Skelton, Clare Brett Smith, J. Weldon Smith, Vey Smithers, Alicia Solomon, Liz Spander, Molly Sterling, Susan Sterling, Eva Stevetka, Graham Stewart, Marge Stewart, Paul Sutherland, Carol Sutton, Takeongsak Suvanadat, Ben Svasti, Paunja Taamsri, Angina Thacker, Claire Thomas, Mera Thomas, Amina Tirana, Mark Udall, Roger Valencia, Maria Elvira Velasquez, Maria Luz Villavicencio, Eleanor Vincent, Susan Walters, Cynthia Wardell, Nevada Weir, Thelma Willemsen, Nancy Williams, Lynn Woolsey, Ivy Young, Maria Luisa "Tiki" Yzaga, Daphney Zungu.

Opposite: In 1968, Trifonia Balderrama de Encinas of Tarata, Bolivia, shared her home with a Peace Corps volunteer who helped local women market traditional doll purses.

Index

Page numbers in italics refer to illustrations.

Following pages: **Dayu's daughter, age three, learns to create floral offerings by watching her mother at home in central Bali, Indonesia.**